Improving Literacy at Work

Modern societies demand high levels of literacy. The written word is pervasive; individuals with poor literacy skills are deeply disadvantaged; and governments are increasingly pre-occupied with the contribution that skills can make to economic growth. As a result, the basic skills of adult workers are of concern as never before, a focus for workplace and education policy and practice.

While *Improving Literacy at Work* builds on detailed research from the UK, the issue is a universal one and rising skill requirements mean the conclusions drawn will be of equal interest elsewhere in Europe, USA, Canada, Australia and New Zealand. The research findings have very direct implications and practical relevance for teaching and learning, as this valuable book demonstrates, providing clear advice on how to develop effective provision and how best to support learners at work.

Throughout the study, the authors address the following fundamental questions:

- How do adults' literacy skills impact on their working lives, and on the enterprises where they work?
- How can we develop these essential skills in the workforce?
- When and how can literacy instruction change individuals' employability and engagement with further learning?

Essential reading for trainers and managers in industry, teachers, researchers and lecturers in adult and further education and stakeholders implementing evidence-based policy, this book maps the fundamental changes taking place in workplace literacy.

Alison Wolf is Sir Roy Griffiths Professor of Public Sector Management at King's College London and Visiting Professorial Fellow at the Institute of Education, University of London, UK.

Karen Evans is Professor of Education in Lifelong Learning in the Department of Lifelong and Comparative Education at the Institute of Education, University of London, UK.

Improving Learning TLRP

Series Editor: Andrew Pollard, Director of the ESRC Teaching and Learning Programme

The Improving Learning series showcases findings from projects within ESRC's Teaching and Learning Research Programme (TLRP) – the UK's largest ever co-ordinated educational research initiative. Each book is explicitly designed to support 'evidence-informed' decisions in educational practice and policy-making. In particular, they combine rigorous social and educational science with high awareness of the significance of the issues being researched.

Improving Literacy by Teaching Morphemes
Terezinha Nunes & Peter Bryant

Improving Workplace Learning
Karen Evans, Phil Hodkinson, Helen Rainbird and Lorna Unwin

Improving Schools, Developing Inclusion
Mel Ainscow, Tony Booth and Alan Dyson

Improving Subject Teaching
Robin Millar, John Leach, Jonathan Osborne and Mary Ratcliffe

Improving Learning Cultures in Further Education
David James and Gert Biesta

Improving Learning How to Learn
Mary James, Robert McCormick, Paul Black , Patrick Carmichael, Mary-Jane Drummond, Alison Fox, John MacBeath, Bethan Marshall, David Pedder, Richard Procter, Sue Swaffield, Joanna Swann and Dylan Wiliam

Improving Learning through Consulting Pupils
Jean Rudduck and Donald McIntyre

Improving Learning, Skills and Inclusion
Frank Coffield, Sheila Edward, Ian Finlay, Ann Hodgson, Ken Spours and Richard Steer

Improving Classroom Learning with ICT
Rosamund Sutherland

Improving Learning in College
Roz Ivanic, Richard Edwards, David Barton, Marilyn Martin-Jones, Zoe Fowler, Buddug Hughes, Greg Mannion, Kate Miller, Candice Satchwell and June Smith

Improving Learning in Later Life
Alexandra Withnall

Improving Learning by Widening Participation in Higher Education
Edited by Miriam David

Improving Research Through User Engagement
Mark Rickinson, Anne Edwards and Judy Sebba

Improving What is Learned at University
John Brennan

Improving Inter-professional Collaborations
Anne Edwards, Harry Daniels, Tony Gallagher, Jane Leadbetter and Paul Warmington

Improving Mathematics at Work
Celia Hoyles, Richard Noss, Philip Kent and Arthur Bakker

Improving Literacy at Work

Alison Wolf and Karen Evans

with Katerina Ananiadou, Liam Aspin,
Andrew Jenkins, Sue Southwood and
Edmund Waite

Routledge
Taylor & Francis Group

LONDON AND NEW YORK

First published 2011
by Routledge
2 Park Square, Milton Park, Abingdon, Oxon OX14 4RN

Simultaneously published in the USA and Canada
by Routledge
270 Madison Avenue, New York, NY 10016, USA

Routledge is an imprint of the Taylor & Francis Group, an informa business

© 2011 Alison Wolf and Karen Evans for selection and editorial material.
Individual contributions, the contributors.

The right of Alison Wolf and Karen Evans to be identified as authors of
this work has been asserted by them in accordance with sections 77
and 78 of the Copyright, Designs and Patents Act 1988.

Typeset in Charter and Stone Sans by
HWA Text and Data Management, London
Printed and bound in Great Britain by
TJ International Ltd, Padstow, Cornwall

British Library Cataloguing in Publication Data
A catalogue record for this book is available from the British Library

Library of Congress Cataloging-in-Publication Data
Improving literacy at work / Alison Wolf ... [et al]. – 1st ed
        p. cm
    1. Workplace literacy. 2. Education–Economic aspects–Cross-cultural
    studies. 3. Education and globalization--Cross-cultural studies.
    4. Business and education. I. Wolf, Alison.
    LC149.7.I56 2011
    658.3'1244–dc22   2010021196

ISBN13: 978-0-415-54868-7 (hbk)
ISBN13: 978-0-415-54872-4 (pbk)
ISBN13: 978-0-203-83830-3 (ebk)

Contents

Illustrations

Figures

Tables

Boxes

Series Editor's preface

The Improving Learning series showcases findings from projects within ESRC's Teaching and Learning Research Programme (TLRP) – the UK's largest ever coordinated educational research initiative.

Books in the Improving Learning series are explicitly designed to support 'evidence-informed' decisions in educational practice and policy-making. In particular, they combine rigorous social and educational science with high awareness of the significance of the issue being researched.

Working closely with practitioners, organisations and agencies covering all educational sectors, the Programme has supported many of the UK's best researchers to work on the direct improvement of policy and practice to support learning. Over sixty projects have been supported, covering many issues across the lifecourse. We are proud to present the results of this work through books in the Improving Learning series.

Each book provides a concise, accessible and definitive overview of innovative findings from TLRP investment. If more advanced information is required, the books may be used as a gateway to academic journals, monographs, websites, etc. On the other hand, shorter summaries and research briefings on key findings are also available via the Programme's website at www.tlrp.org.

We hope that you will find the analysis and findings presented in this book are helpful to you in your work on improving outcomes for learners.

Andrew Pollard
Director, Teaching and Learning Research Programme
Institute of Education, University of London

Preface and acknowledgements

The research reported here formed part of the ESRC's Teaching and Learning Research Programme, Project reference RES-139-25-0120. Generous funding from the ESRC allowed us to conduct this project: but it would not have been possible to carry out the work described without substantial additional support from the National Research and Development Centre for adult literacy and numeracy (NRDC), funded by government as part of its Skills for Life programme to improve the basic skills of adults. NRDC funding made possible the development of the Go! test of literacy, without which we (and other basic skills researchers) would have been unable to carry out reliable tests of literacy skills and progress. NRDC also funded preliminary work on workplace basic skills (Ananiadou *et al.* 2004a) which formed the basis for our research design; and provided funding in part-support of our research team in the first three years of the study. In addition, they provided direct support for our additional study of collaborative learning (see Chapter 6), and for a number of international meetings and collaborations which have fed into our research findings. We are extremely grateful to NRDC (and the Department for Education and Skills – now BIS), and especially to Ursula Howard, Helen Casey and John Vorhaus for their consistent support. The conclusions reported here are, of course, entirely our own.

The ESRC LLAKES Centre (Learning and Life Chances in Knowledge Economies and Societies) at the Institute of Education has supported further analysis, research and publication beyond the life of the project, extending to 2011.

The research team was headed by Alison Wolf (Principal Investigator), with Karen Evans as Co-director. Alison Wolf took major responsibility for the quantitative aspects of the work; in this book, she is lead author on the Introduction and Chapters 1, 3, 5, 7 and 10. Karen Evans, who took major responsibility for the qualitative analyses, is lead author on Chapters 2, 4, 6, 8 and 9, and made substantial inputs into the Introduction and Chapter 10. Kat Ananiadou made major contributions to Chapter 3; Liam Aspin to Chapters 5 and 7; Andrew Jenkins to Chapter 5; Sue Southwood to Chapter 4, and Ed Waite to Chapters 4, 6 and 8. Chapter 3 draws on work carried out for an earlier publications for NRDC (Ananiadou *et al.* 2003); and a portion of Chapter 7 first appeared, in somewhat different form, in the *Oxford Review of Education* (Wolf *et al.* 2010). We are grateful to the editors and Routledge for permission to use this material.

Over the five years of research work, a number of individuals made major contributions; and we thank, in particular, Jay Derrick, Rachel Emslie-Henry, Lul Admasachew, Amanda Nicholas, Wendy Robins, Martin Race and Joyce Shaw. We are also very grateful for the contributions of our original co-applicants, Tom Jupp and John Bynner, both in formulating the research enquiry, and for their very valuable inputs in the early stages of the research. Comments from members of the core TLRP Director's team, and the opportunity to participate in regular TLRP events, and discuss our ongoing findings with related projects, were extremely valuable to us at all stages of the research.

The administrator throughout the project was Magdalen Meade. She was responsible for preparing all questionnaires, organizing data input and archiving, preparing tables, charts and figures for reports, organizing steering group meetings and the distribution of our regular newsletters, and for the preparation of this manuscript. She has been central to the conduct and completion of the research.

In addition to those named above, we would like to express sincere thanks to the members of our advisory group: Angela Armstrong, Neil Robertson, Judith Swift, Alan Brown, Les Perkins, Jo Pye, Clare Hannah; and to Chris James, the librarians of NIACE, John Comings, Stephen Reder, John Benseman, Catherine Kell, the New Zealand Department of Labour, and, in Canada, to Maurice Taylor of the University of Ottawa and the Valuing Literacy in Canada funding program through SSHRC/NLS; the Ottawa-Carleton Catholic School Board and Trudy Lothian; the Ottawa-Carleton District School Board and Christine Pinsent Johnson; the University of Ottawa research assistants; the learners and instructors who took time to participate in the study; John Collins from the University of British Columbia who conducted the TPI analyses.

We would also, and above all, like to thank all the learners, supervisors, managers, and tutors who collaborated with us and gave so much of their own time to help us. They must all remain anonymous but we extremely grateful to them, learnt an enormous amount from them all, and hope very much that they have found the experience, and our results, of interest.

Introduction

Adult learning has been a priority for recent governments, largely for economic reasons; seen in broader perspective, it can be transformative for those involved, in a multitude of ways. Research on how best to design and provide courses which are well-suited to *adults* as opposed to younger learners has, however, been relatively neglected, compared with studies of children's learning, and school-based teaching. Similarly, the workplace as a site of adult learning has been relatively neglected compared with college-based or community-based settings, and low-paid workers are typically given less attention than those in, or entering, occupations associated with intermediate or 'high skills'.

This book discusses the findings of a five-year longitudinal research study into this neglected area. The study, which examined the impact of workplace literacy courses for adults, formed part of the Teaching and Learning Research Programme's (TLRP) strategy to ensure that all age-groups and learning environments received serious attention. In supporting research projects on many ages and stages in education, training and lifelong learning, the Programme has been concerned with 'patterns of success and difference, inclusion and exclusion' throughout the life-course.

The study involved over 500 learners in 53 different workplaces across England and Scotland, along with managers, tutors and union officials. Its overarching concern was to discover when, and how, workplace courses for the low-paid 'work' and make a difference to people's lives. This involved, at the core, three quite specific research objectives:

1 To determine whether adult participants in workplace programmes demonstrate substantive, long-term changes in measured basic skills and other life-course variables.
2 To determine whether workplace basic skills programmes increase the potential productivity of sponsoring enterprises.
3 To develop an interdisciplinary understanding of the interrelationships between formal learning, workplace experience, and life-course trajectories (including career, family, leisure and learning activities).

While these objectives are quite specific and tightly phrased, they spring from, and feed into, much more general, learning-related issues. These are of relevance to anyone concerned with adult or 'lifelong' learning, and with patterns of inclusion and exclusion in adult lives.

Adults learning in and through the workplace

Lifelong Learning encompasses people of all ages learning in a variety of contexts – in educational institutions, at work, at home and through leisure activities. National and international debates[1] are now focusing on adults returning to learning rather than on the initial period of education, and giving much greater prominence to the view that workplaces are important sites through which adults can access learning.

Literacy learning at work is currently high on policy agendas, as part of a more general concern with adult basic skills. There are some major assumptions in this policy discourse: that workers' and employers' interests are always the same; that improving literacy through the workplace always contributes to economic success; that people with low literacy skills always struggle at work and have lower productivity. These assumptions, we argue, require critical examination if policy and practice are to be improved.

We do know that adults with low basic skill levels are at greater risk of unemployment and poor health. They are also less likely to undertake further learning – formal or informal – during adulthood. This limits not simply their future labour market opportunities, but also their access to social networks, and their ability to understand, cope with and access official services and benefits. At the start of our study the evidence available about what constitutes effective teaching in workplace contexts was very sparse. Only a few well-founded sources gave evidence of positive outcomes in terms of employment, wage gains, further education and impact on likelihood of unemployed adults re-entering the labour market. These lacunae in the evidence pointed to the issues and questions that it has been important for our research to address.

How can the teaching and learning of literacy be introduced into organizations whose purposes are, first and foremost, the production of goods and of services, and what are the challenges involved in organizing and sustaining provision over time? What does it take to get workplace literacy programmes off the ground? Needs and interests have to be identified, the role of public funding and relationships between external and internal providers established, and participants selected. Then there are the challenges of organizing teaching and learning support around day to day working practices and requirements such as shift work.

The book aims to establish how and in what ways engagement in workplace programmes can be effective in improving adults' basic skills, as well as having influence on employment stability, promotion, and enrolment in further educational programmes. Previous research has showed that what happens to adults in the labour market is largely predictable from their educational and socio-economic background. However, we examine how far workplace provision can be successful not merely in retaining adult learners but in affecting, and changing, their future learning activities and employment trajectories. We look at participating workers as individuals who are part of their workplace environment and culture but also separate from it, having lives outside it. Adults bring to their workplace their prior knowledge, understanding and skills; they contribute to and learn from workplace practices, with important spill-overs into their family and personal lives beyond work.

How important is adult literacy learning through work for potential improvements in productivity and changed attitudes or commitment to the organization? Government thinking typically focuses on the supply side of subsidised training and qualifications rather than on employers, work organization and organizational competence. Moreover there is in the UK a reliance on voluntary rather than compulsory measures to improve workplace learning.

However, with curriculum frameworks and requirements tied to public funding an audit culture has developed. This is also manifested in increased report-writing, the effect of delegating responsibility to lower level employees and a general trend towards 'textualization' of the workplace and formalization of health and safety procedures. In some contexts, technological change necessitates increased literacy and numeracy skills while in other contexts these changes can pre-empt the need for such skills. The implications of statutory introduction of standards and qualification structures, as well as the speed and turbulence of organizational change also impact on adult learning and on attempts to support or direct it in work contexts.

All of these trends and issues emerged during the research and are addressed below. In treating them, this book builds on the earlier TLRP publication *Improving Workplace Learning* (Evans *et al.* 2006) which showed that adult workplace learning is neither an inherent good, nor an automatic high priority but depends heavily on regulatory frameworks and the factors that govern the employer-employee relationship.

Research design

In order to address the key research questions, it was vital that the research be longitudinal. It therefore involved repeated collection of data from subjects over a two and a half year time period. It was also necessarily mixed-method, involving a combination of quantitative and qualitative techniques.

The research took place at a time of unprecedented increases in government funding for adult basic skills provision. This in turn led to a large increase in the number of courses made available in the workplace, and

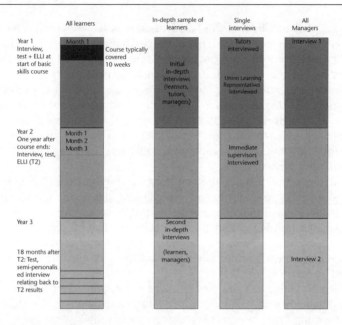

Figure 0.1 Data collection

targeted at adults who normally received little or no general training, and did not normally attend further and adult education classes. Learners were recruited from among this population (see Methodological Appendix). They, their places of employment, and all other interviewees were guaranteed anonymity, and pseudonyms are used throughout the pages that follow.

Sites were recruited across four occupational sectors. Within the sample, we identified a sub-set of ten sites, and within each of these, a sub-set of learners for additional in-depth interviews. The focus here was on understanding life-course trajectories. In addition, another small sample of four courses was studied in depth with reference to collaborative learning practices.

Figure 0.1 shows data collection activities in diagrammatic form; the instruments used are described in the Appendix.

Learners were tested formally on three occasions. Reading and writing were tested each time, learning dispositions twice. The first follow-up test was scheduled for a year after course completion, rather than at the end of the course, since it is well-established that gains made during an intensive learning experience are not necessarily permanent and secure (Cooper *et al.* 1996; Downey *et al.* 2004). The second and final follow-up, a year and a half further on, allowed for two and a half years in which changes in learning trajectories might become evident.[2] All tests used an instrument especially developed for adults, and suitable for detecting small changes in skill levels. Figure 0.2 displays a sample question.

Look at page 4 of *Go!* magazine. Answer these questions.

According to expert Josh Walker, what is the best proof of purchase?

_____

How does expert Dr Yokota make her advice personal?

_____

_____

_____

Figure 0.2 (1) Sample page from Go!, the basic skills test for adults developed in conjunction with NRDC, (2) Sample questions

Detailed structured questionnaires were used (see Appendix). Interviews were conducted with managers, tutors, Union Learning Representatives where present, and learners' immediate supervisors. In-depth interviews (learners, tutors, managers) were conducted at the sub-sample of sites.

The timing of data collection was determined by the initial basic skills courses in which learners were enrolled. These began during the period 2004–2006, with later interviews determined on a site-by-site basis accordingly. We are unable to identify any major changes in the labour market between 2004 and 2006 which might generate systematic differences between early and late-recruited learners (e.g. in perceived likelihood of lay-offs and need to seek new employment).

The sample All participants received regular newsletters from us, reporting findings as they emerged; this is received good practice in longitudinal studies and many learners expressed their appreciation during later-stage interviews. Nonetheless, sample attrition was somewhat greater than predicted. Five hundred and sixty-seven learners were recruited originally, in 53 workplaces; 532 provided substantive data, but full data including final (time 3) reading scores are available only for 201.[3] Having compared the characteristics of the original and final sample, we do not believe that differential attrition poses serious problems for the analysis.[4] Any research project must, by necessity, reflect the particular time and place within which it took place; but we believe that, overall, our findings have relevance well beyond this, to the world of adult learning in the coming decades.

The structure of the book

The book discusses our specific findings but also relates them to general issues in adult and workplace learning, and learning trajectories, and to the broader policy environment. Part I addresses the major issues which underlie the research questions posed, and the research design adopted. Chapter 1 explains the policies, and policy assumptions, which produced huge 'Skills for Life' expenditures on adult basic skills and support for workplace provision. Chapter 2 relates our research design to the wider research environment, and explains the theoretical underpinnings of the research. Chapter 3 summarizes what was already known, in advance of our work, about levels of literacy in the adult population, their consequences, and the likely results of interventions.

Part Two discusses our findings in detail, moving between the whole sample (and largely quantitative approaches) in Chapters 5 and 7, and in-depth, qualitative analysis of the smaller sub-samples in Chapters 4, 6 and 8. Chapters 4 and 7 focus on the organizations in which the learning took place, including (Chapter 4) the findings on collaborative learning and (Chapter 7) the evidence on whether the courses do indeed impact on the wider organization. Chapter 5 summarizes the findings with respect to skill gains; Chapters 6 and 8 deal with the interactions between learning, work environment, and life-course and relate our findings directly to developing research on informal learning.

Part Three places our study in international context (Chapter 9), and Chapter 10 summarizes the implications of the study for both adult education and training policy, and for our growing understanding of the dynamics of learning, and of development and change in individual life-chances.

Part I

What are the issues?

Chapter 1

Literacy learning at work

This chapter discusses the political and policy context within which workplace literacy provision was expanded in the early 2000s. The effectiveness of workplace learning depends on a host of factors, many specific to the workplace concerned. But whether such learning is subsidized depends on government policies, and the beliefs that underpin them; and subsidies drive the scale of provision. Policies influence not only what is subsidized but the way that money is spent, down to very detailed aspects of provision. In the case of workplace literacy provision, government beliefs about economic growth, its preoccupation with international rankings, and its general management philosophy had far-reaching effects.

The policy context

Literacy classes, or 'adult basic skills' provision, are a standard part of almost all developed countries' public education systems. They date back to the days when many adults had little formal schooling as children, and wanted to improve their skills later; and in many countries (though not the UK) an important part of adult provision remains, to this day, classes leading to the country's formal upper secondary leaving certificate.[1] In addition, many countries expanded provision as large-scale immigration became increasingly widespread, offering classes for non-native speakers. Although adult classes for non-native speakers pose different demands on teachers, and students, than classes for native speakers, in practice there has, across the world, been a great deal of overlap at delivery level (Carr-Hill et al. 1996, Wolf 1994).

Until the late 1990s, UK, and more specifically English provision, was both quite typical of international practice and quite low-profile. It was run by local authorities and adult education centres, making heavy use of volunteer tutors who provided small group or one-to-one tuition. From 1975 onwards, 'basic skills' had a national agency, funded by government to raise the profile of literacy and numeracy provision. From 1980 until 1995 it was known as the Adult Literacy and Basic Skills Unit, and was reasonably successful in raising the profile of basic skills provision and research; later it became the Basic Skills Agency. From time to time, efforts were made to develop workplace provision; but basic skills remained firmly rooted in traditional adult and community education, and general further education colleges.

Then, from the late 1990s, the policy environment and the organization of 'basic skills' changed out of all recognition. One major outcome was an unprecedented interest in literacy provision in the workplace – the subject of this book. More generally, adult basic skills classes became not just the beneficiaries of hundreds of millions of pounds in government spending, but also one of the most high-profile of educational activities, with targets set for the performance of central government departments, quangos and colleges and other 'providers'. This environment established parameters for workplace programmes which, as we will discuss below, were not always productive or appropriate. But why did this change occur?

The 'growth' agenda

The crucial pre-condition for transforming adult basic skills policy was the British government's espousal of an economic rationale for education policy and education spending, which over the last four decades has become ever more dominant.

During the last quarter of the twentieth century, the education policies of European and North American governments were increasingly directed towards immediate economic goals, especially in the post-compulsory, further and adult sectors. This development reflected concerns over increased global competition and countries' own economic performance, and was informed by a rather simplistic version of human capital theory. The development of the population's (and so the workforce's) skills came to be regarded as a critical, and a sure-fire, way of improving productivity (Green et al. 2000, OECD 2004a, 2004b, Grubb and Lazerson 2004).

In Britain, the policy rationale is similar to that of other developed nations: but there are, nonetheless, distinctive features especially in the English case. As a result, the country has embraced the idea of re-shaping education for economic ends with particular enthusiasm, under the Conservative governments of 1978–1997, and, even more, under their New Labour successors (see Coffield 2002, Wolf et al. 2006).

A preoccupation with the economic relevance of educational programmes, and a belief that 'skills' are an economic magic bullet, are rooted in debates over the whole structure of the UK economy in the post-war period. Its level of performance was, until the 1990s, markedly poorer than that of major neighbours and competitors. Influential analyses ascribed this, in large part, to previous failures of a non-vocational/non-technical education system; and argued that the economy remained caught in a 'low skill equilibrium' (see Barnett 1986,

Finegold and Soskice 1988, Prais 1995, Sanderson 1999, Keep 1999, Wolf 2002, Coffield 2004).

Successive governments (from Callaghan's onwards) set themselves to reform education, effectively nationalizing both academic and vocational examinations, creating a national curriculum, and creating 'key stage' tests for accountability purposes. The country's economic performance improved enormously in the 1990s and early 2000s, without any obvious accompanying change in educational attainment levels. However, this had no apparent effect on the senior civil servants and politicians responsible for education and skills policy. They remained, and remain, convinced that education has a direct and immediate impact on the economy: indeed, as Keep and his colleagues have pointed out (Keep et al. 2006), the only active policy for increasing productivity during the New Labour years has been to increase the supply of skills. Meanwhile, for adults, the economic rationale has become the only one which is felt to justify state subsidy to education (Wolf 2009).

The target culture

This preoccupation with growth, and impatience with any form of adult education that was not overtly 'economic' in its rationale, fed, and was fed by, ever greater central direction of spending and provision. Successive governments were determined to take control of spending and direct it to the 'best' ends, and duly created a system whereby the subjects and courses funded were subject to ever-greater degrees of central planning, delivered through a changing cast of quangos and ministries. This development has been discussed at length by a number of authors (Wolf 2009, 2010, Coffield et al. 2008, Schuller & Watson 2009, Keep 1999, Coffield et al. 2005). Here, we would highlight two consequences for basic skills.

First, at some periods, providing instruction in adult basic skills appeared an extremely attractive financial option for providers. English governments have created a detailed price list, paying providers different amounts for different courses, and manipulating these frequently in pursuit of their particular short-term priorities. At times, the adult basic skills 'tariff' appeared financially very lucrative.

Second, over time, quantitative 'targets' became increasingly important in driving the whole education sector. The idea of setting targets for educational outcomes, and especially qualifications, had become popular under the later Thatcher and the Major administrations; but became increasingly important under New Labour (see e.g. Hood 2007, Barber 2007). The use of qualification targets meant that governments had to have a way of categorizing and counting them. The result was the National Qualifications Framework, through which all qualifications are allocated an official 'level' and targets set in level terms (see Methodological Appendix).

The International Adult Literacy Survey

It was into this developing policy environment that in 1997 the results of the International Adult Literacy Survey burst like the proverbial bombshell (OECD 1997). Its findings gave an enormous boost to adult educators who championed literacy and numeracy education; but it was also used as an apparently powerful justification of the need for government-directed regulation of adult education. It remains so to this day.

This survey – conventionally shortened to IALS – was an entrepreneurial piece of educational research conceptualized by the OECD. It set out to measure the literacy of adults in developed countries, defined as the use of 'printed and written information to function in society, to achieve one's goals, and to develop one's knowledge and potential'. The survey used a range of 'applied' tasks, administered to adults in their own homes, and also collected a range of background data on education and employment, and the results received massive press coverage in participating countries.

The OECD has generally been influential in the field of education policy ever since it started to publish *Education at a Glance* in 1992, comparing every member country on a wide range of education indicators. The OECD indicators – arranged in league table form – are barely known outside government and some academic circles; but they are very widely read there, in almost all member states. Low rankings are seen as shameful and indicators of serious problems with one's education system (though see e.g. Thomas and Goldstein (2008) for a discussion of validity and reliability problems). Most of the data come from governments' internal data collection activities. But in addition, the OECD also carries out projects in which the attainment of young people, or adults, is measured directly.[2]

The IALS survey was administered in 13 countries, including the UK: the results shocked many.[3] Respondents' performance was grouped into one of five levels, with the lowest implying severe literacy problems: no fewer than 20% of British respondents fell into this group. This was translated, in press coverage and the perceptions of many, into 'illiteracy' – an actual inability to read or write. This is quite misleading; nonetheless, the survey indicated far lower levels of literacy than the government had ever anticipated.

David Blunkett, the then Secretary of State for Education responded by appointing a national inquiry chaired by Sir Claus (now Lord) Moser. It reported in 1999 and called for a major national effort to improve the basic skills of the adult population. Moser described 'a shocking situation and a sad reflection on past decades of schooling. (This) is one of the reasons for relatively low productivity in our economy and it restricts the lives of millions of people.'[4] The report called for wide-ranging entitlements for adults to attend basic skills classes; new qualifications and curricula; new teacher training; and better inspection.

Skills for Life and workplace provision

The Moser report was accepted in broad outline by the government, which two years later (2001) published the document which was to generate approximately £2 billion of expenditure on basic skills in the course of the next seven years. 'Skills for Life: the national strategy for improving adult literacy and numeracy skills' was, to an even greater degree than the Moser report, concerned with the economic costs of low skills. It claims that

> productivity per hour worked is 20% lower in Britain than in Germany and our poorer literacy and numeracy skills account for two thirds of that shortfall.
>
> (DfEE 2001: 47)

and that

> We must increase ...people's earning potential, and the country's wealth and productivity, by giving them the literacy and numeracy skills they need to participate in a global, knowledge-based economy.
>
> (DfEE 2001: 17)

In other words, 'Skills for Life' (SfL) expenditures were not just about increasing equality of opportunity in a job market where many jobs require literacy, and formal education is used as a screening device (Wolf 2004, Chevalier 2000). The strategy also rests on assumptions about the accelerating reach of the 'knowledge economy'. The formal rationale for the SfL programme, as presented to the National Audit Office, three years later, states that even low-skilled jobs have 'increasing literacy and numeracy requirements' (NAO 2004: 17). This is why SfL courses attracted favourable funding, and were the subject of top priority targets; in a 2008 keynote speech to the annual Skills for Life and Work Conference, David Lammy, the junior minister for Skills, argued that literacy and numeracy skills are

> essential in today's world . . . Britain has become a knowledge economy . . . For individual employers, the benefits of accessing Skills for Life are unambiguous . . . Skills for Life is . . . critical to the overall strength and competitiveness of our workforce.
>
> (Lammy 2008)

Funding basic skills courses in the workplace

The period immediately after 2001 saw an unprecedented level of funding for basic skills provision within the workplace. Much of this was funded under the Skills for Life rubric; providers were strongly encouraged by the Learning and Skills Council (the post-16 funding quango), and by the Department's own Adult Basic Skills Strategy Unit and regional teams, to approach employers and offer them on-site courses for their employees, at no direct cost. The funding for these was largely processed through mainstream revenue streams (and so funded at the same rates as college-based provision), but in negotiating contracts with and payments to providers, there was strong encouragement to prioritize SfL provision, and especially SfL provision in workplaces.

Other funds came through the Treasury's generously funded Employer Training Pilots which, in selected areas, provided both funds for training courses on-site and wage subsidies to allow employees to be released; and from European Social Fund grants (see Chapter 7). ('Train to Gain', the successor programme to ETPs. also encourages basic skills qualifications, but does not offer paid time off.) In Scotland, a separate programme was launched, called the Scottish Adult Literacy and Numeracy Strategy: this was less employer-oriented than in England, but did funnel some money to workplace-based schemes.

Other funding came through learndirect (run by UfI, originally the 'University for Industry'). This provides courses which are entirely IT-based, and can be accessed on a drop-in basis by registered learners. While most of these are in colleges, major efforts were made to encourage companies to house centres. Finally, a major impetus in establishing in-house provision often came from union officials, and field officers funded by the Union Learning Fund, established in 1998 in order to encourage the take up of learning in the workplace. Alongside it, the government introduced measures to encourage the appointment and training of Union Learning Representatives, who work with employees and facilitate workplace learning, and imposed obligations on unionized companies to assist ULRs. Grants to unions through the Fund pay for the training of Union Learning Representatives, and also support full-time field officers who can help set up and organize workplace learning. (Courses themselves can then be funded in the normal way.)

One consequence of this plethora of funding streams is that, while we know that funding for workplace basic skills reached an all-time high in the years after Skills for Life was launched, there are no precise figures available on the number of workplace learners who actually enrolled. Data were never collected on that basis, and subsequent parliamentary questions to ministers have confirmed that the numbers are not available.

It is equally impossible to provide national statistics on the length of courses offered, how many were face-to-face or on-line, or how many were taught by individuals with specialized adult literacy qualifications. However, we do know that the vast majority of workplace courses were quite short: 30 hours was usually the maximum, as a result of the funding tariff offered and the pressure to maximize throughput at a period of ever-more demanding 'targets' (Wolf *et al.* 2010). Currently, with almost all workplace SfL provision offered through Train to Gain, contact hours have shrunk further to less than 20.

Organizing assumptions: the rationale for programme design

Traditional 'basic skills' provision had been characterized by individuals seeking help with their literacy (and to a lesser extent numeracy), either because of events and pressures in their individual circumstances or, sometimes, in response to national campaigns to raise awareness of basic skills provision. Both the Moser report and the Skills for Life strategy, in comparison, were largely preoccupied with the links between employment, productivity and basic skills. Both assume that direct economic pay-offs are both the prime justification for public spending and the driving force for individuals. As the Moser report phrases it:

> Basic skills ... are a key to employability ... Conversely, poor basic skills affect the efficiency and competitiveness of the economy. . . One of the prime motivations for many adults to improve their skills can be their work.
>
> (Paragraphs 190–192 *passim*)

The Skills for Life strategy, as conceived and implemented, is also an exercise in top-down delivery. It involved the creation of a standard national curriculum for each of the key areas – literacy, numeracy and English as a Second Language – and compulsory and standardized teacher training. It led to the creation of new qualifications delivered through centrally set national tests at different levels; and national targets were set for the number of basic skills qualifications awarded. There was a perception – possibly quite justified – that much existing basic skills provision was undemanding of learners, and that heavy use of untrained volunteers, *ad hoc* materials, and the absence of dedicated teacher training courses, greatly reduced the effectiveness of teaching. But equally strong was the assumption that a single syllabus and approach were appropriate for all learners, and could be defined centrally and 'cascaded' downwards to them, across the country. The 'skill gaps' manifested by these essentially passive learners would thus be closed; and their skills adequately certified by a set of standardized assessment measures.

These more or less tacit assumptions determined much about the activities undertaken by the Adult Basic Skills Strategy Unit. For practitioners in an unfashionable and historically under-resourced area, the arrival of generous funding and a high profile was generally welcomed. But there were also, from the start, tensions between the centralizers' view and that of many practitioners and many of the leading academic analysts of basic skills learning. As discussed in detail in Chapter 2, there are important alternative perspectives which emphasize that the learning trajectories of adults are individual and complex, that 'basic skills problems' are far from uniform, and that both literacy problems and literacy gains need to be understood accordingly.

In its encouragement of and approach to workplace programmes, the Skills for Life strategy also made some additional, and in this case quite explicit, assumptions. These were that the 'skill gaps' associated with low literacy levels have a direct and major impact on productivity across the economy. The evidence base for this is discussed in Chapter 3; but it is central both to the earlier period of Skills for Life implementation, in which our research got underway, and, even more strongly, to current government priorities and funding, which increasingly direct money through employers, providing adults with learning 'entitlements' only when they are 'sponsored' by their employers.

On this view, the interests of employers and employees are both standard and coterminous. Skill gaps exist. They reduce productivity and thereby employees' wages and employers' profits. Literacy is one of the most important areas in which such gaps exist; and workplace programmes are therefore one of the most important priorities for basic skills activity, and adult education and training generally.

For our research project, this approach raised a number of major issues. First of all, was the delivery mechanism as developed effective in the most basic sense: did it improve the literacy skills of adults who undertook workplace learning? Second, was the underlying analysis correct with respect to the learners themselves? Were their motives overwhelmingly economic, and did it make sense to see literacy learning as essentially about uniform skills, which could be taught in a standardized way? Third, was the analysis of employer motives correct? Were there skill gaps that needed filling, and did provision of adult literacy classes in the workplace have an immediate, or longer-term, impact on the functioning of the workplaces where it occurred?

In the second part of this book we will examine the empirical evidence and relate it to the wider research context. First, however, we explain our underlying theoretical perspectives, and summarize the pre-existing literature on workplace basic skills.

Chapter 2

Perspectives and key concepts

Introduction

In our research on workplace literacy we adopted, from the start, multiple perspectives and a mixed method approach. This chapter explains this orientation and relates our approach to those adopted by other key research.

There are two analytic perspectives and two theoretical lenses that have particular relevance for the investigation of adult literacy learning organized in and through the workplace. The two analytic perspectives start with the social organization of learning and the learning individual respectively. The first theoretical lens focuses on literacy as sets of individual skills that are part of human capital, and on literacy development as human capital accumulation. The second theoretical lens sees pluralities of literacies, shaped in and through context and reflected in social practices; literacy development is thus closely intertwined with literacy usage in context. Both of these lenses can be trained on the ways in which adult learning and adults' access to learning is organized in different social contexts, including those of workplaces. Equally, both can be trained on the part played by literacy in and through the life-course, and the ways in which literacy development is linked with personal and work situations in adult life.

In advocating a 'pragmatist' approach to mixed research methods we have viewed these differing research perspectives on literacy, that tend to coalesce around either quantitative or qualitative research methodologies, as potentially useful avenues for exploring varying facets of literacy rather than as being the intrinsic components of sharply divided and irreconcilable epistemological traditions. The employment of mixed methods in this research has allowed us to explore both literacy 'gains' in their human capital sense, and how literacy is actually employed in differing contexts. In doing so we are in a position to take issue with assumptions underpinning Skills for Life discourse about the existence of large-skill deficiencies in literacy and numeracy that inevitably impact negatively on performance at work. We pursue a more nuanced approach that illustrates the diverse range of techniques that are employed in literacy practices whilst highlighting those cases where skills deficiencies do exist.

Analytical perspectives and theoretical lenses

These key perspectives and lenses can be combined with each other to provide four distinct but highly complementary ways of approaching literacy learning. These are summarized in Table 2.1.

Literacy as human capital that focuses on the learning individual (quadrant 1)

The concept of 'human capital' as analogous to fixed capital (machinery, land) has been one of the most influential ideas in applied economics and policy-making of the last half-century. It was coined by Becker (1993) and emphasizes the way in which an individual's skills and abilities can be applied again and again over time, to produce things – as can fixed capital. Although Becker was not only interested in economic outcomes, the research literature is dominated by studies of how higher levels of skill (and higher levels of education) are associated with higher incomes and more favourable economic opportunities for the individuals who possess them.

In the context of literacy studies, this perspective translates into policy arguments which assume that improving adult individuals' literacy will bring them higher salaries or a better job. Research studies which adopt this approach are necessarily longitudinal, since they need to track individuals'

Table 2.1 Perspectives and lenses

	Literacy as human capital	Literacy as social practice
Focus on the learning individual	1. Literacy is perceived as a clearly defined set of technical skills, the absence of which can impact negatively on an individual's economic and social opportunities.	3. Emphasizes the social context of literacy usage, often framed by relativist and hermeneutical perspectives.
Focus on social organisation of learning	2. Emphasises shaping and organising education and adult learning 'provision' for socio–economic ends such as increased productivity, social mobility.	4. Emphasises contexts and environments for learning; communities of practice; informal and 'everyday' learning

Source: Evans 2009.

trajectories over time, and are consequently rather few in number. They also underscore the complexity of the relationship between adult learning and adult experiences: for example, Reder's (2009) and Comings' (2009) work in the US shows that significant gains require long periods of instruction, and translate into different literacy practices in advance of any evident changes in other life-circumstances. The data from the major UK cohort studies, which indicate the usual close relationships between attainment as a young person and later economic success, also allow one to examine the links between increased 'human capital' acquisition as an adult and later trajectories, and also show that the relationship is far from simple (Machin and Vignoles 2005, Machin et al. 2001).

Literacy as human capital that focuses on the social organization learning (quadrant 2)

Although most of the literature on human capital examines the relationship between individual human capital and individual earnings and life-experiences, human capital is also seen as having a broader social dimension. It is argued that higher levels of human capital have spill-over effects. In other words, a society with large numbers of educated and skilled people is believed to benefit as a whole, in ways which go beyond the higher incomes and better life-chances of the skilled individuals themselves. And in organizations, it is hypothesized that the organization as a whole, or teams within it, will be more productive by virtue of containing highly skilled people: the people who work alongside them will also be more productive, and there will be organization-wide changes which would not occur without the presence of skilled individuals.

Although this sounds plausible, it is extremely difficult to study, or demonstrate; the few studies that do exist tend to examine geographic areas with clusters of very highly-skilled people (see e.g. Koepp 2002). They find some evidence for the phenomenon, but it is also possible that highly productive companies come to these areas because they are a good place to hire highly skilled people. In the adult literacy, and more general adult skills context, there is a severe paucity of evidence. Although policy-makers and public agencies argue that upgrading individuals' skills will benefit the organization as a whole, well beyond the individuals concerned (ALBSU 1993; DfEE 2001; DfES 2003b), our own work was one of the first to attempt an empirical study at this level.

Literacy as social practice that focuses on the learning individual (quadrant 3)

In this perspective learning trajectories in adult life are defined in terms of biography and socially embedded learning. Chisholm has argued adult learning takes on a genuinely active, unpredictable quality when it takes the form of a critically reflexive engagement with personal and social life, drawing on these resources in varied, autonomous and 'borderless' ways (Chisholm 2008; see also Evans 2009).

In this process new forms of learning are superimposed on old forms which retain much of their original power. Social institutions, old and new, continue to interlock to shape life courses which may still be typified according to social position. There is a need to understand better the reflexive ways in which people's lives are shaped, bounded or change direction as they interact with the social institutions which structure aspects of the social landscape in which they move.

Furthermore, people's beliefs in their ability to change their situation by their own efforts, individually or collectively, are significant for the development of skills at work and beyond (Evans 2002). These beliefs change and develop over time and according to experiences in the labour market and beyond. The ability to translate these beliefs into action is achieved rather than possessed (Biesta and Tedder 2007) and capabilities are limited by bounds that can be loosened (Evans 2002, 2009). Positive versions of 'borderlessness' view learning as becoming more extensive (lifelong), more specialized (life-near), more differentiated (life-wide), more flexible, more individualized and more contingent (Chisholm 2008: 142). Literacy researchers such as Appleby and Barton (2008) who focus on the social practices of literacy learning in individual lives thus focus on complexities and contingencies in the adult life course.

Although the workplace provision examined in our research aims to boost skills relating to economic productivity and is focused quite narrowly on one spatial environment – the workplace – this perspective examines whether, and how, learners' actual motivations relate to a wider range of differing environments. Apart from using newly developed skills in the workplace how do adults recontextualize and use their learning in and through their domestic situations, community involvements and family environments?

Literacy as social practice that focuses on the social organization of learning (quadrant 4)

Those who advocate the importance of researching literacy as a 'social practice'– emphasizing the social context of literacy usage – tend to employ qualitative methods framed by more relativist, hermeneutical perspectives. The concept of literacy itself is dissolved into a plurality of literacies shaped by differing contexts (see for example Street 1995 and Papen 2005).

Thus, the workplace becomes an important arena for skills development and immersion in work cultures as well as place proving employment and income for the workers (Rismark and Sitter 2003). The new spaces themselves are characterized by being both work and learning spaces where the boundary between the two is considerably blurred (Solomon *et al.* 2006: 6). Situated learning theory further enriches the concept of learning space; emphasizing socialization into a wider community of practice that involves membership, identity formation and expertise development through participation in the activities of the particular work practice (Lave and Wenger 1991, Evans *et al.* 2002, Unwin and Fuller 2003 and Hughes *et al.* 2007). In this view the group is seen as important rather than the individual, and people learn through shared practices of the community (Billett 2004) which shows how individuals actively influence one another's learning and enculturation through a process of 'co-participation'. Workplace literacy learning thus becomes an expanded concept which locates learning in the social relations of work.

Pushing the boundaries of analytic and theoretical positions

Researching literacy at work takes each of these analytic and theoretical positions to the limits of their explanatory and exploratory power. For example, life-course research that models literacy gains statistically and through a human capital lens eventually concludes, tentatively, that literacy proficiency is likely to be linked to skills use in practices at work and beyond and in a social context. However, statistical modelling lacks a way of capturing and modelling the qualities of social practice that are involved. By the same token, situated learning theories, that are well able to capture the significance for learning of workplace environments, activities and tools in workplace learning, have difficulty in summarizing or explaining *what* is learnt, and struggle to untangle the interplay between practice-based learning, prior learning and that provided through courses.

In researching literacy development in and through workplace courses and work practices, the necessity of working across existing boundaries, 'exploring through different avenues', quickly becomes apparent. The idea of 'borderlessness' can help to forge new conceptual and practical connections between learning subjects (who), learning sites (where) and learning pathways (when and how).

Connecting the logic of the learning individual with the social organization of learning: life-course approaches

A commitment to *longitudinal* data collection and analysis was central to our research, in recognition of how much it offers across a range of analytical perspectives. For example, longitudinal research highlights the dynamics of individuals' learning, and the benefits of relating them fully to the social organization of learning (both human capital and social processes versions). Pallas (2002), an important source for the theoretical framing of adult participation in learning from a life-course perspective, showed how sociological theory had been slow to catch up with expanding opportunities for education and learning that are not 'highly age graded' and that take place outside formal systems. In particular, Pallas analysed the probability of participation in three forms of adult education in 1994[1] – those leading to a college credential of some kind, work-related programmes not embedded in a credit bearing programme, and 'other structured activities or courses referred to as 'personal development' courses, including ESOL and adult basic education. Lifecourse perspectives have more recently developed in ways that ensure that educational trajectories are studied in ways that recognize their 'complex intertwining' with social institutions and social roles as experienced at different stages of the life-course (Bynner and Parsons 2009). Life-course perspectives that explore the ways in which individuals' ages, work and family roles influence learning trajectories have much to offer to an understanding of the literacy learning that can and does take place in and through work.

Life-course approaches are also present in some aspects of the work of Gorard and Rees (2002) whose work on adult learning trajectories provides typologies that can be explored in other contexts. The employees in our sample are distributed across Gorard and Rees's categories. They are 'non-participants' in lifetime learning (prior to engagement in the workplace literacy courses), follow 'transitional trajectories', involving periods of further education and training end on to schooling but not beyond and fall into the 'lifetime trajectory'. (This accounted for almost one third of the respondents in Gorard and Rees's study, and is defined as comprising those whose experiences of education/work-based training extend beyond initial schooling and includes at least one substantive episode of education/ training in adult life.)

Significantly for our study, Gorard and Rees's modelling of the determinants of lifetime learning (based on logistic regression) showed that those with no qualifications are more likely to return to learning later in life than those who do not achieve the benchmark of five GCSEs or equivalent. Furthermore, determinants of later participation differ according to the circumstances of adult life and the access people have to learning, including through their work. According to Gorard and Rees, these findings provided 'important correctives to the conventional view of participation in lifetime learning'.

The diversity of individuals' accounts is striking. There are no simple patterns (consistent with our own qualitative evidence, as discussed in Chapters 6 and 8) and Gorard and Rees argue that such complexity lends weight to theoretical perspectives that foreground choices made by individuals – with the important caveat that any choices made were also heavily constrained by external circumstances.

Gender differences in social roles and expectations over time are highlighted in life-course approaches, as are the ways in which learner identities are rooted in prior experiences of education, particularly in schooling. These studies thus focus on differences in participation rather than on what is gained through participation, and are very broad in their delineation of categories. They provide some useful sketches but few insights into the relationships between literacy learning and adults' participation in workplace and educational practices over time.

Exploring the relationships between learning 'gains', changing attitudes and work practice

As explained in the Introduction, our research employed a wide range of instruments and approaches, reflecting the complex set of perspectives outlined in Table 2.1. The rationale for employing in-depth interviews, in addition to repeat application of measures of literacy skills and structured questionnaire surveys, included such factors as the need to collect more detailed, narrative-based biographical data. These could shed light on the more subjective aspects of the learning experience (e.g. the effect of previous learning experiences, motivation/confidence, stigma surrounding poor basic skills, social capital). They also allowed us to pursue the broader organizational context through organizational case-studies. The in-depth interviews added to the longitudinal dimension of our research in that they asked the participants to think, at different stages of their 'trajectories', about past, present and future in their experiences of using literacy and learning at work and how these have changed over time.

In-depth interviews allow for a more detailed exploration of how literacy is actually employed in differing contexts. The respondent-led features of in-depth interviews also allow for the exploration of attitudinal changes that cannot be so easily explored within the confines of a structured questionnaire. Finally, in-depth interviews with learners, managers and tutors at selected sites allow for the exploration of key organizational processes that impact on the usages of literacy, including the impact of an 'audit culture' manifested in increasing report-writing, the effects of delegating responsibility to lower level employees and a general trend towards textualization of the workplace (Scheeres 2004).

These qualitative aspects of the project benefited from the quantitative data in a very direct way: we are able to consider the findings from the in-depth sample against the broader sample of structured interviews. For example, we were able to benchmark learners against the wider data set. Table 2.2 provides an example of how this complementary analysis operates, and how learner biographies are enriched by the ability to benchmark individual data against a larger sample.

Table 2.2 Employee data benchmarked against the full sample

	Kathleen Croft	Victoria Appiah	Tracy Beaumont	Bill Williams	Trevor Woodford	Faiza Anwar	Melanie Taylor	Abdull Nazif	Bob Murphey	Fareena Ahmed	Laila Rahman	Overall sample
Gender	F	F	F	M	M	F	F	M	M	M	F	65% Male 35% Female
Age	50	54	38	45	24	29	38	35	44	51	52	Mean age: 42*
Age at leaving school	16	16	16	15	16	16	16	16	16	15	16	Mean: 17.2 Mode: 16 Median: 16
Qualifications on leaving school	CSEs including English and Maths	None	None	5 CSEs (not Grade 1)	None	D/K	GCSEs	none	none	Indian A level	none	None: 55% Some qualification: 44%
Literacy level	Level 2 or above	Level 1	Level 1	L2 or above	Level 1	L2 or above	L2 or above	Level 1	E3	L1	E3	Below E2: 5.5% E2: 3.4% E3: 19.65 L1: 45.65 L2 or above: 25.75
Likes/dislikes job (on a scale of 1–7 with 1=dislike, 7=like a lot)	7	7	7	6	6	5	6	7	7	5	7	5.8

	Kathleen Croft	Victoria Appiah	Tracy Beaumont	Bill Williams	Trevor Woodford	Faiza Anwar	Melanie Taylor	Abdull Nazif	Bob Murphey	Fareena Ahmed	Laila Rahman	Overall sample
Likes/dislikes the course (on a scale of 1–7 with 1=dislike, 7=like a lot)	5	7	7	7	6	Missing	7	6	7	5	7	6.7
ELLI growth orientation/challenge	3.5	3.8	3.1	3.1	2.6	3.1	3.2	3.4	3.5	2.6	3.6	Mean: 3.0
ELLI dependence/fragility	1.9	2.2	1.7	2.0	2.4	2.2	2.2	2.67	2.8	2.2	2.5	Mean: 2.3
ELLI imagination/creativity	3.3	3.4	2.7	1.5	2.0	2.9	3.5	3.3	3.0	1.9	3.1	Mean: 2.6

*Mean age is 42 (18–24 3.5%; 25–34 23%; 35–44 32%; 45–54 24%; 55–64 15%; 65 + 1.5%).

An appropriate literacy measure

The employment of the specially designed literacy test (*Go!*) provided us with an independent measure of literacy which can track small changes of literacy level over time (see introduction). This was also directly relevant to the conduct of in-depth interviews. It allowed us to explore the individuals' own perceptions of their literacy skills, including the question of whether they are coping/struggling in the workplace, against an external source of evidence.

The importance of these various research instruments in allowing for a more complete understanding of literacy practices in the workplace can be illustrated by the case of Love who is a deputy manager of a care home, though recently 'acting up' as the head of the care home. According to the *Go!* assessment she has literacy level of Entry 3 and she reveals that she has failed her Literacy Level 1 exam. Yet she explains, through the in-depth interviews, that she employs a variety of techniques to 'get by', including relying heavily on administrative staff within the care-home to help her with her written English. An understanding of her case would be much diminished if we were dependent on one research method alone. If we solely employed in-depth interviews, we would be aware of Love's experience of literacy practices and her methods for coping in the workplace but we would have no independent assessment of her literacy skills. In other words, we would not appreciate the degree to which these strategies are important for her survival in the workplace. Conversely, if we merely employed the *Go!* assessment along with structured questionnaire we would be aware of her literacy needs but would have no clear idea of how this individual managed to carry out her job.

The evidence yielded by mixed methods approaches points beyond polarized conceptualizations of literacy and numeracy learning as either technical skills development or the expansion of social practices, towards a more ecological understanding of the phenomena observed. A 'social ecology' of learning in the field of adult basic skills leads us to consider the relationships between the affordances of the workplace (or those features of the workplace environment that invite us to engage and learn), the types of knowledge afforded by literacy and numeracy learning (including knowing how and 'knowing that you can') and the agency or intention to act of the individual employee, reflected in their diverse motivations. These are reflexive relationships and point the way forward to developing better understanding through a wider social ecology of adult learning in workplace environments.

Exploring interdependencies in the wider social contexts of work and learning: towards a social ecology

As will be clear in Part 2 of this volume, our analysis and understanding of what actually happens in the workplace draws on recent related work. The research perspectives employed for this research have benefited in particular from the previous Teaching and Learning Research reported in another volume of the TLRP Gateway Series. Evans, Hodkinson, Rainbird and Unwin's research on 'Improving Workplace Learning' (2006) examined many forms in which learning takes place in and through the workplace and engages different groups of workers. The conclusion of that study was, in some ways, a springboard for the present, in its finding that:

> Most workplace learning takes place informally through everyday working practices, and measures need to focus on enhancing the qualities of this broader environment. Second, even the best individualized approaches to learning improvements are only partially successful. These two facts represent realities that have to be dealt with, not ignored. Doing so offers more realistic opportunities to improve workplace learning. They are a source for hope, not despair.
>
> (page 175)

The usefulness of a social ecology metaphor is that it provides a way into understanding the complexity of factors that impact directly or indirectly on education and lifelong learning without losing sight of the dynamics of the whole. Every contextual factor and every person contributing or influenced is part of a complex ecology, or system of social relations and relationships that sustains the system through a set of interdependencies. Applications of ecological conceptualizations are found in studies ranging from macro-level analyses of organizations to ecologies of the inner workings of families.

Recent applications of this approach are found in the field of policy studies in education. These start with education policies and attempt to make visible the complexities of policy processes as interdependent and political, to incorporate 'the messy workings of widely varying power relations, along with the forces of history, culture, economics and social change' (Weaver-Hightower 2008: 154). According to Weaver-Hightower's overview, the four categories of *actors, relationships, environments and structures, and processes* lie at the heart of social ecological analyses. These differ in the degree of significance that is accorded to personal agency, through which actors 'depending on their resources and power, are able to change ecological systems for their own benefit' (ibid. p. 156). Because ecologies are self-sustaining through interdependencies that operate without centralized controls, individuals and groups have spaces in which to exercise their 'agency' in ways that can influence the whole dynamic. While applications in policy studies sometimes focus on the ways in which resistance is exercised through the collective agency of (for example) teachers' unions or pressure groups, more often than not the account shows how agency is eventually 'squeezed out' through the power relations that operate over time in favour of those most powerfully placed.

As previously argued, the family of approaches that starts with the 'learning individual' as the unit of analysis, argues that people do not act *in* structures and environments – they act through them. In research that starts with the workplace, Hodkinson *et al.* (2004) have argued that these processes are best understood when individual worker/learner perspectives are built into the dominant social–organizational view of learning at work. This perspective is integral to *Improving Workplace Learning* (Evans *et al.* 2006) which has revealed through an integrated pro*gramme of research that three scales of activity have to be kept in view*. At the 'macro' level, wider social structures and social institutions can be fundamental in enabling or preventing effective learning from taking place. This includes the legal frameworks that govern employees' entitlements, industrial relations and the role of trades unions as well as the social structuring of business systems.[2]

At the *intermediate* scale of activity, the nature of the learning environment in the organization can expand or restrict learning (see Fuller and Unwin 2004, 2006). Establishing cultures that support 'expansive' learning environments and so promote learning, is problematic. For most employers, workers' learning is not a priority and whether or not to support it actively is a lower-order decision. First-order decisions concern markets and competitive strategy. These in turn affect second-order strategies concerning work organization and job design. In this context, workplace learning is likely to be a third-order strategy (see also Keep and Mayhew 1999).

In other words, improvements to workers' learning always have to be balanced against other priorities. The interdependencies of interests play out as senior managers exert influence over the culture of an organization and its approach to supporting workplace learning. Moreover, corporate expectations are rarely transmitted into practice in large and complex organizations, as workforce development policies 'as espoused' at the top of the organization often depart substantially from workforce development as enacted, and so may be far removed from what is experienced, particularly at the lower end of the earnings distribution.

Third, for the *individual* worker, past experiences, dispositions and present situation will all affect the extent to which they take advantage of the opportunities afforded by their immediate work environment. These factors change over time. Professionals and other highly qualified workers are more likely to have access to continuing training and professional development than less-qualified workers (Sargant 2000) and are more likely to experience work environments that are rich in opportunities for learning, than workers in lower-level jobs. The challenge is to create the conditions in which all workers can take advantage of all of these kinds of opportunities. One mechanism may be through entitlements to learning, established in law, through collective bargaining, or through the interventions of enlightened managers, trade unionists, trainers and coworkers. Another mechanism is to build worker confidence through the recognition of tacit skills, discussed in more details by Evans and Kersh (2006).

Although all three levels or scales of activity are important, they should not be treated as fixed and separate levels of analysis. Instead it is more appropriate to keep the three scales in view in the same way that one might when 'zooming in and out' in internet maps, in ways that keep the interdependencies in view. Hence work on communities of practice can be understood in the context of the social relations of the workplace and the contradictory and antagonistic aspects of the employment relationship.

The ways in which employees can themselves, individually or collectively, influence their employment and life chances in and through the workplace environment have been documented through previous and current research . These have to be understood as part of a wider dynamic, keeping in view the macro organizational and policy environments and the interdependencies set up within and beyond the workplace. Workers are both part of the work system and have lives outside it; they are engaged in multiple overlapping structures and 'communities of social practice' that can themselves be analysed in terms of social-ecological interdependencies.

A social ecological analysis has also to extend to factors beyond the workplace. For workplace ecologies the interdependencies already mapped by Evans *et al.* (2006) in *Improving Workplace Learning* highlight the dynamic activity in the political, regulatory and cultural spheres. The research in this volume will reveal major disjunctions between policy assumptions about large scale literacy and foundational work skills deficiencies in the UK and employees' capacity to cope with their existing skills and competencies. Such a disjunction has emerged as a result of the adoption of a narrowly defined skills agenda together with vague assumptions about the increased significance of literacy and numeracy skills in a post-industrial, 'knowledge economy' era.

The adoption of a 'deficiency model' of adult skills for those at the lower end of the earnings distribution often fails to take account of individuals' capacity to make do with their existing skills and competencies and tailor them to the actual demands of the workplace (Livingstone 1999). Do companies that aim to expand and enrich job content in jobs at all levels find employees working to expand their capacities accordingly? Do those who send employees on 'basic skills' courses return them to a job and work environment that utilizes or underutilizes their capabilities? How realistic are policy-makers about the motivations and benefits involved? When employees attend literacy courses while continuing to engage in day-to-day tasks which have little or no literacy content, what are the motivations and incentives to sustain, let alone increase, any gains in literacy skills?

Summary and conclusion

This chapter has introduced two analytic perspectives and two theoretical lenses that are used in exploring different facets of adult literacy learning. The two analytic frameworks start with the social organization of learning and the learning individual respectively. The first theoretical lens focuses on literacy as sets of individual skills that are part of human capital, and on literacy development as human capital accumulation. The second theoretical lens sees pluralities of literacies as shaped in and through context and reflected in social practices.

The experiences of employees engaged in workplace literacy learning have to be understood as part of a wider social dynamic, keeping in view the macro-organizational and policy environments and the interdependencies set up within and beyond the workplace. This includes the recognition that workers are both part of the work system and have lives outside it; they are engaged in multiple overlapping structures and 'communities of social practice' that can themselves be analysed in terms of social-ecological interdependencies.

While learning needs to be seen as an integral part of practice, attention has be paid to the environment as a whole and the lives of people outside and beyond work. The work environment also fundamentally impacts on how far formal learning can be a positive trigger for the learning through day-to-day work and other social practices.

Each workplace brings to mind Steel's (2001) observations on the contingencies of knowledge acquisition in the workplace: 'each has its own culture influencing the nature and dynamics of the program; each has its own vocabulary or jargon that the practitioner must learn and use correctly; each has its own set of economic imperatives influencing the need for a sustainable program; each has its own code of labour practice affecting why, how and when the program will be offered' (p. 151). Each chapter that follows sheds light on a different aspect of the complex interdependencies involved in learning at work.

Chapter 3

The effects of literacy development in the workplace
The dearth of evidence

Introduction

In this chapter, we examine the existing research literature on workplace basic skills in so far as it sheds light on the key tenets of current policy: namely that many adults are seriously lacking in essential skills, that improving their literacy and numeracy will benefit them and their employers, and that this can be achieved through formal instruction in workplace settings.

The first thing to note is that very little good research exists. There is a growing body of work on basic skill instruction for adults (see e.g. Comings 2009, Torgerson et al. 2004, Brooks et al. 2001) and on the types of workplace which most encourage informal learning (including basic skills: see Chapter 8).[1] But there is very little on workplace basic skills instruction. We discuss first the evidence on the individual effects of poor basic skills and the probable effects of improvements in basic skills and then, because of the limited data, discuss the returns to individuals of general training in the workplace. We then look at evidence related directly to employers and enterprises. Finally, we summarize the few studies which shed light on the likely effects of formal workplace provision.

Basic skills and individual benefits

Before looking at the potential gains to individuals from improving their basic skills, it is important to recognize the substantial body of research linking basic skills to individuals' earnings and employment. This body of evidence has been the main foundation not only for basic skills initiatives generally, but also for specific predictions of the benefits to the economy of raising adults' basic skills (see especially Dearden et al. 2000, Bynner et al. 2001, De Coulon et al. 2007).

The most detailed UK estimates come from the major longitudinal studies which track individuals born in Great Britain in 1946, 1958, 1970 and 2000. The 1958 and 1970 studies have been able, uniquely, to measure adults' literacy and numeracy directly, as well as using formal qualification data and test data from when people were at school.

The National Child Development Study (NCDS) tracks people living in Great Britain who were born there in March 1958. (For more details on the NCDS see, for example, Bynner and Parsons 1997, Ferri *et al.* 2003). They are now adults in their fifties, many with extensive labour market experience. Of particular importance for present purposes are the results of work carried out when respondents were 37 years old (1995). A random and representative 10 per cent of the cohort (with 1,714 respondents) were assessed directly using a specially developed literacy and numeracy test.

Using these data Bynner and Parsons (1997) discuss the impact of basic skills on various aspects of an individual's life. For the analysis, participants' scores were converted into four ability categories: 'very low', 'low', 'average' and 'good' (for literacy and numeracy separately). For the cohort as a whole, only 6 per cent were assessed as having very low and a further 13 per cent as having low literacy skills; and 23 per cent and 25 per cent respectively as having low numeracy ones. Women scored better than men on the literacy items, and the reverse was true for numeracy. The overwhelming majority of workplace basic skills schemes (and indeed of Skills for Life classes more generally) have concerned themselves with literacy. This is also true of the schemes in our sample, and we therefore concentrate on the findings for literacy, However, it should be emphasized that the relationship between numeracy attainment and life-course variables is also very strong.

The results of the survey fully support the general belief that low basic skills are associated with labour market disadvantages; key findings are summarized in Box 3.1.

Dearden and colleagues (Dearden *et al.* 2000, 2002) examined earnings effects using data from both the NCDS 10 per cent sub-sample discussed above and from the International Adult Literacy Survey (see Chapter 1). They examined whether the skill levels displayed by adults exert an independent influence on earnings over and above the impact that is captured by measuring qualifications and early school achievement measures.

They found that individuals with average or above average numeracy skills[2] can expect, on average, to earn between 15 per cent and 19 per cent (according to the NCDS and IALS respectively) more than individuals below this level, *when not controlling for any other factors that may influence earnings*, such as family background (e.g. mother and father's education) or education level. The premium for literacy at this level is only slightly smaller, at about 15 per cent for both datasets.[3] This impact is partly explained by the association of skill levels with qualifications and with other background variables. However, effects on earnings remain, even when controls are introduced for factors such as family background, ability at age 7 and 16 and education level achieved, though far more

Box 3.1   The impact of poor basic skills for 1958-born individuals

Qualifications achieved at age 37: half of the respondents with very low literacy skills had no formal qualifications.

Employment and unemployment: 23 per cent of men in the very low literacy group reported being unemployed or sick at the time of the survey. The above percentages compare with 4 per cent and 3 per cent respectively in the high literacy and numeracy groups. The case of women is more complex as home-care and part-time employment are more common. For the very low literacy group, 31 per cent were in full-time employment and 34 per cent were in part-time employment. These percentages are 43 per cent and 39 per cent respectively for women in the high literacy group.

Employment history: Men with very low or low literacy skills were more likely to be in full-time employment at an earlier age compared with their better-skilled peers. However, this reversed itself with time. At age 31, 75 per cent of men with very low literacy skills were in full-time employment, compared with over 90 per cent of men with good literacy skills. A similar picture is found for women.

Promotion at work: Between the ages of 23 and 37 almost two thirds of men and three quarters of women with very low literacy skills had never been promoted, compared with under one third of men and two fifths of women with good literacy skills.

clearly for numeracy than for literacy. Results are presented in more detail in Table 3.1.[4]

Recent confirmatory evidence is available from 2004, when members of the 1970-born cohort (the British Cohort Study 1970 or 'BCS70' sample) were both interviewed and had their literacy and numeracy assessed. They were 34 years old at the time, and had for the most part completed formal education well over a decade earlier. 9,965 individuals were involved on this occasion, and they had also been included in all or most of the cohort's previous sweeps (at birth, 5, 10, 16, 26 and 30). In addition, a 10 per cent sample of the entire cohort (1,185 people) had been interviewed and tested for both literacy and numeracy at age 21, in 1991.

On this occasion, the researchers used official government categories to classify performance. Overall, about 8 per cent of the sample performed at 'below Level 1' on the literacy tests: that is, below the level of a GCSE pass at Grade D or E. (A pass at Grade A–C is a Level 2). Another 30 per cent scored at Level 1 and the remainder at Level 2 or above. The relationship between basic skills and other life-course variables was very similar, for

Table 3.1 Wage effects associated with level 1 numeracy and literacy skills

	Raw effects	With some controls	With full controls
Numeracy level 1			
IALS estimates	0.187	0.066	
NCDS estimates	0.147	0.069	0.057
Literacy level 1			
IALS estimates	0.152	0.114	
NCDS estimates	0.148	0.026	0.013
Controls (X=control introduced)			
Family background		X	X
Age 7 ability			X
Age 16 ability			X
Education level		X	X

Source: Dearden *et al.* 2000.

these young adults in 2004, as it had been for their predecessors in 1995 (Bynner and Parsons 2006 *passim*). See Box 3.2.

The sub-group who were also tested at age 21 is of particular interest. They provide information on what happens as individuals spend time in the labour market; although it is difficult to compare average performance at 21 and 34 with any fine degree of discrimination. This is because while the tests 'in essence ... remained the same' (Bynner and Parsons 2006: 48), individual items were changed and updated. (The two versions were not – and probably could not be – formally equated. They were designed to reflect contemporary everyday life at the time they were administered).

Overall, it appears that the literacy levels of these individuals remained much the same but numeracy levels improved somewhat in the intervening 13 years (Bynner and Parsons 2006: 56–58). Performance was also much more stable for those who had high scores at age 21: the large majority of this group remained high scorers. Many of those who scored badly at age 21 had, in contrast, much higher scores at age 34: in fact, far more of the 'poor' group improved their performance than did not. (Conversely, the stability of overall means implies that many 'middle-level' scorers must have performed worse at age 34 than age 21).

Less reliable and consistent performance by the less skilled might simply be making their scores fluctuate more. Equally, the skills of the lower performing group may have been more directly influenced by home and work life and practices; there was room for improvement if people used their skills, and the likelihood of substantial decline if they did not. It is clear, however, that any changes reflect the impact of people's 'normal'

Box 3.2   The impact of poor basic skills for 1970-born individuals

Those with very low literacy skills were far more likely to have left school with no qualifications than the population as a whole; and both the men and the women were less likely to be in work. The group with 'below Level 1' literacy scores could be further subdivided into 4 per cent with very low scores ('Entry 2 level or below') and 4 per cent with low ('Entry Level 3') scores. Less than 20 per cent of 'Entry Level 2' men used a computer at work compared with over 80 per cent of those scoring at Level 2 or above; 24 per cent of women with Entry Level 2 literacy had a full-time job compared with 48 per cent of those with Level 2 literacy; 14 per cent of men with Entry Level 2 literacy were on income support and 23 per cent were in non-working households. Overall, the relationship between literacy (and numeracy) skills and labour market success was clear.

lives between ages 21 and 34 rather than the effects of later, formal instruction; only 3 per cent of the (entire) sample reported attending a course to improve their literacy or numeracy.

De Coulon *et al.* (2007) used these BCS70 data to look in more detail at the relationship between basic skills and labour market experiences for this group. They found, as had previous researchers, that there is a very strong relationship between both literacy and numeracy skills and earnings. Controlling for formal qualifications and for performance at age 10 reduces the size of the effect, but it remains significant.

Unlike the data analysed by Dearden *et al.*, these more recent data do not suggest that literacy may be significantly less important than numeracy. The researchers note that, even after including early test scores and family background variables, 'an additional standard deviation in literacy results in approximately 14 per cent higher earnings, whilst an additional standard deviation in numeracy results in 11 per cent higher earnings' (de Coulon *et al.* 2007: 13).

One might think that including highest educational level in the analysis would wipe out any impact of 'basic skills' on earnings, since educational attainment presumably incorporates the substantive skill level the individual reached. In fact, this is not the case: the measured effect of performance on earnings is reduced only slightly and remains highly significant (see Table 3.2). Note that what is actually being measured, once one controls for education, is the impact of basic skills within a given educational group). In this study, the wage premia associated with higher measured skill levels are similar for men and for women.

As noted above, because a sub-sample of the BCS70 cohort had taken basic skill tests at the age of 21, it was also possible to look at

Table 3.2 Earnings effects of age 34 basic skills (men and women)

	(1)	(2)	(3)	(4)
Standardized age 34 literacy score	0.164	0.134	0.114	0.091
Standardized age 34 numeracy score	0.138	0.094	0.084	0.064
Controls				
Age 10 scores		X	X	X
Family background variables			X	X
Highest educational level achieved				X
Labour market variables				X

Results all significant, p<0.01

Source: adapted from De Coulon et al. 2007.

whether performance at 21 and at 34 had independent effects. Measured performance at 21 had a strong effect on earnings at 34 when earlier attainment was included and attainment at 34 was not. When attainment at 21 *and* at 34 were included, the magnitude of the effect on earnings of performance at 34 was considerably reduced. Nonetheless, it remained significant and substantial for both literacy and numeracy.

Overall, it is clear that the importance of substantive skills – including literacy – has been and remains great. Employers consistently reward them, and not only because they are responding to the 'signal' of a formal qualification. However, the skill levels being measured in these studies were, overwhelmingly, acquired during formal education at a young age. Can one reasonably infer from them that, if adults improved their skills, they would then gain commensurate increases in earnings? Here the evidence is much less clear.

The impact of basic skills improvements

The most sophisticated attempt to model the results of improving adults' basic skills again uses NCDS data from the UK. Machin *et al.* (2001) set out to examine whether *improvement* in literacy and numeracy since age 16 has any significant impact on earnings. Four measures were used: (1) asking respondents if they had followed a literacy or numeracy course between survey dates; (2) comparing scores of literacy and numeracy tests at ages 16 and 37 for the ten per cent who took tests at age 37; (3) the acquisition of any qualifications between the ages of 22 and 33 by low-qualified individuals (below Level 1); and 4) self-reported changes in numeracy and literacy skills over the last decade.

Of all these measures, the clearest effects were found for self reports. Individuals who reported that their skills had improved in the period of time since the last sweep of the survey (between a quarter and a third of the sample) earned more than those who did not believe that their skills had improved.

For other measures, however, the results were largely insignificant. Less than 1 per cent had actually taken a literacy or numeracy course. Taking a numeracy course was, for men, negatively associated with earnings, perhaps because of self-selection into such courses: other coefficients for course-taking were insignificant. Direct measures of skill improvement using scores at 16 and 37 showed no significant effects for women: for men, there were some positive effects from improved numeracy but *only* for those who were not very low achievers at age 16. Finally, and surprisingly, there did not appear to be any positive outcomes in earnings or employment for poorly qualified men and women who gained additional qualifications in their twenties.

Similar results are available for Sweden (Ekström 2003). Here there has been strong support for adult education (including but going well beyond basic skills), and many older adults and immigrants have completed extensive adult education programmes. The expectation has been that labour market effects will be clear and positive: but analysis of the Swedish Longitudinal Individual Data (LINDA) for 1983–2000 indicates no positive earnings effects for Swedish-born males or females, although there are significant and positive effects for female immigrants

The most recent (2004) BCS70 cohort data have not, to date, been used to explore systematically whether improved basic skills impact on employment and earnings. They do, however, provide some suggestive insights into the processes associated with skill improvement in adult life. Bynner and Parsons (2006: 58–62) looked in some detail at those individuals who scored poorly at age 21 but well at age 34, and compared them to cohort members whose literacy skills remained poor. Very few of these improvers had been on any sort of formal literacy course in the interim.

People whose skills improved were much more likely than non-improvers to be in full-time employment, using a computer at work, or have received recent work-based training. They were more likely to be co-habiting and have children; more likely to have voted and be interested in politics; and more likely to have a computer at home. All of these factors are also likely to increase the extent to which people use their literacy skills, and have opportunities to improve them. Of course, it is also possible that the 'improving' group was already significantly different from the 'non-improvers' when they were tested at age 21, even though their scores were similar (see Box 3.3). However, as discussed in Chapters 4 and 6, their improvement between 21 and 34 is entirely consistent with what we know about how adults improve their skills via informal learning in the workplace and the home.

Box 3.3   Identifying causality: the problem of endogeneity

When looking at any variable that appears to have a positive effect on earning, it is important to be cautious. A major reason for this is the problem of *endogeneity*, i.e. the fact that the estimates may be only partly (in this case) of returns to basic skills themselves, and partly reflect unobserved characteristics of the individuals studied. In other words, rewards – such as higher wages, or lower chances of unemployment – may appear to be linked to the skills or qualifications an individual possesses, when they are actually, in whole or in part, the result of other unobserved characteristics, such as innate ability. If differences between high- and low-skilled individuals are only partly the result of the skills, then, equally, improving skills in the less proficient group will not eradicate the differences. The same is true for formal qualifications.

This endogeneity problem is very well recognized in the social sciences in general, and the use of panel or longitudinal studies – i.e. studies collecting data at two or more points in time – and a focus on the results of *changes* in skill levels is for that reason highly desirable. Such panel studies are preferable to cross-sectional estimates of links between skills levels and wages or employment status; and their findings should be given commensurate weight.

In summary, it appears that low levels of basic skills had a negative impact on both earnings and employment even after other factors have been taken into account. These data are, by necessity, historical. However, it also seems likely that they will be replicated as, if not more, strongly for young people now entering the workforce.

As emphasized above, it is results such as these that have persuaded politicians and policy-makers of the importance of raising adults' basic skill levels, and so improving their earnings (and, by extension, the productivity and wealth of the economy).

The impact of qualifications

As we saw above, much – though by no means all – of the apparent effect of measured skills on earnings and employment vanishes when qualifications are included in the analysis. However, that does not mean that the skills were not really as important as they first appeared. On the contrary: it is quite possible that people can only gain the qualifications if they have the skills.

In the labour market, qualifications may signal to employers that someone is a skilled employee; gaining a qualification as an adult should involve skill acquisition, and should signal this to employers.

Unfortunately, it does not follow that all and any qualifications will automatically have value; or that adults who obtain qualifications will derive the same labour market benefits from them as young people. Indeed, in the current UK labour market, this is clearly not the case.

Governments have, in recent years, placed enormous emphasis on 'accrediting' adults, notably through ambitious qualification targets (including for Skills for Life), and have commissioned repeated evaluations of the impact on earnings, using NCDS, BCS70 data, but also large national surveys, notably the LFS. Jenkins *et al.* (2003) studied whether qualifications obtained by adults between the ages of 33 and 42 had an effect on their wages at the end of this period, controlling for a wide range of other factors. In general there were no effects on wages. The exception was men who left school with only low-level qualifications (for example, lower grade CSEs) and who acquired *degrees* in their 30s or early 40s. They earned more than their peers who had not engaged with lifelong learning. The research also uncovered employment effects. Gaining a qualification between 1991 and 2000 was associated with a significantly higher probability of being in employment in 2000 among women who were out of the labour market in 1991. These very weak wage effects found here are also consistent with weak effects previously found for qualifications acquired in people's twenties (Machin *et al.* 2001).

A succession of studies has borne out this general conclusion (see e.g. Dearden *et al.* 2002, Dearden *et al.* 2004, Jenkins *et al.* 2007). Lower level (sub-degree) qualifications obtained in adulthood (which would include any basic skills awards) have, on average, no discernible positive impact on earnings. These findings may appear puzzling given the strong effect of measured skills on wages, and the importance of qualifications obtained in youth as predictors of later life-chances: but they underline the danger of extrapolating to adults from young people. More generally, estimates of effects based on the current earnings of the more highly skilled offer *upper* bounds to the likely impact.

Individual gains from workplace training

Because so little direct evidence is available on the results of basic skills instruction for adults, in this section we summarize the major findings on financial gains from workplace training for individuals. In general – though not universally – the literature finds strong evidence of wage effects of training for individuals; in some cases, these gains can also be seen as indicative of likely productivity gains for employers. Good overviews of this literature include Blundell *et al.* 1999, Greenhalgh 2002 and Asplund 2004.

Studies with direct relevance to contemporary English policy include Blundell *et al.* 1996. They used NCDS data from 1991 which asked about courses in the previous ten years which led to qualifications, and about other training courses during this time designed to develop work skills. The research suggested that training in the current job boosted the real wage of men by, on average, some 3.6 per cent (for on-the-job training) and 6.6 per cent (for off-the-job training). For women the effects of training in the current job were 4.8 per cent (on-the-job training) and 9.6 per cent (off-the-job training). Training in previous jobs also had a positive effect on wages. The average effects for men of training in a previous job were 5.7 per cent (on-the-job training) and 5.4 per cent (off-the job training), while for women they were 4.6 per cent (on-the-job training) and 6.2 per cent (off-the-job training). These estimates refer to training which did not lead to a qualification.

Returns were higher if a qualification was obtained at the end, but only higher vocational qualifications (such as professional qualifications, nursing qualifications, HNDs, etc.) had statistically significant effects. Moreover, obtaining such a higher vocational qualification on an employer-provided course provided a higher return than obtaining a qualification on a non-employer provided course. Overall, the research also suggests that training transfers readily across employers.

Arulampalam *et al.* (1997) also used data from NCDS and looked at the effects of both training and educational courses on wage growth, for males only, over the period 1981 to 1991. Compared to Blundell *et al.*, these results confirm the value of *employer-provided* (as opposed to self-funded or government-funded) training but indicate lower transferability: employer provision was found to have a large positive effect on earnings growth (12 per cent on average), while non-employer provision had no such effect.

Groot (1995) provides evidence from the Netherlands that the wage returns to training for individuals vary according to the type of training provided. The training data covered three different types of training: technical training, economic/administrative training (defined as covering 'economic, administrative and commercial') and other training.[5] OLS wage equations, including controls, suggested that technical training increased wages by about 4 per cent, economic/administration training by some 14 per cent, and other training by about 12 per cent.

Lillard and Tan (1992) studied male wages and employment in the United States using five different data sources – the Current Population Survey (CPS), three cohorts of the National Longitudinal Survey (young men, old men, women), and the Employers Opportunity Pilot Project (EOPP). They found that the earnings effects of training varied both by the type of training, and who was providing it. Once again, as suggested by the UK data, company training had the largest effects on earnings, and this persisted over a 13 year period.

Bartel (1995) used data from the personnel records of a large US manufacturing company over the time span 1986 to 1990. She found that number of days of training had positive wage effects. Distinguishing between three different types of training – core training (managerial and leadership programmes), employee development, and technical programmes (such as quality control, computer programming) she found that that largest wage effects were for core training.

Training and job mobility

Studies on the benefits of training to employers have generally found a strong association between company-provided training and lower workforce turnover (Green 1997). Individual-level data generally confirm this association: those who are trained are less likely to leave. For example, Booth and Satchell (1994) investigated the effects of apprenticeship training on job tenure in Britain, again using data from the NCDS. Completing an apprenticeship substantially reduced the exit rate from the first job into each of the three possible destinations, while failing to complete an apprenticeship increased each exit rate compared with the base of no apprenticeship training.

Elias (1994) found that, controlling for a range of factors, training had a negative effect on the probability of a job ending. The effect was weak for males and not statistically significant, but for women training had a statistically significant effect on mobility, reducing the propensity to leave an employer. Dearden *et al.* (1997) used the NCDS and the Quarterly Labour Force Survey, both with multiple controls. For men in NCDS, receipt of employer-provided training reduced job mobility by some three percentage points, while other work-related training increased job mobility by about 2.5 percentage points. In QLFS, for men employer-provided training leading to a qualification reduced job mobility by some four percentage points; whereas 'outside' work-related training raised it. For women employer-funded training lowered mobility by 1.6 percentage points.

It seems clear that employer-provided training can have a major direct impact on recipients' wages. It seems reasonable to conclude that these wage gains reflect, at least in part, substantive changes in the productivity and value of the employee to the employer. But it is difficult to extrapolate this to the likely effects of increasing training volumes (e.g. through subsidies or legislation), let alone to something as specific as government-funded basic skills training.

Basic skills training in the workplace: the benefits for employers

The literature discussed relates to training which has been paid for and provided by the employer. However, current UK government policy on workplace basic skills, and on training policy generally, assumes that such training should be subsidized, and organized, by the public sector. Why?

The argument for subsidizing training *in the workplace*, derives from a classic analysis by Becker (1964, 1993). Becker argues that workplace, and 'on-the-job', training is very important for economic productivity. It can be divided conceptually into 'specific' and 'general' components. Specific training is defined as training which is only relevant to a particular company or employer. It makes economic sense for employers to pay for this, in exactly the same way as they pay for new machinery, rent on premises, etc, because they (and only they) can expect to reap the benefit when they sell the resulting output.

General training is different. Becker notes that 'general training is useful in many firms besides those providing it' (Becker 1993: 33). Such general skills are actually the more common: skills which are valuable to just a single employer are rare. But the more general the skills, the less incentive there is for the employer to pay. If he does, his trained workers may well be 'poached' by competitors, who can offer higher wages – in part because they have not paid for the training.

The major possible outcomes of basic skills training in which employers have a direct interest are (higher) productivity, (lower) staff turnover and (greater) safety. In spite of the sizeable number of workplace schemes now available, very little evidence bears directly on how basic skills training impacts on any of these outcomes. We have located one plant-level study (Krueger and Rouse 1994, 1998) carried out in the US which compares outcomes for recipients/non-recipients of basic skills training, and because of its quality and uniqueness, summarize it in some detail. Nothing comparable is available for the UK.

Direct evidence on returns to basic skills training

The Krueger and Rouse study of the impact of workplace basic skills tuition (1994, 1998) examined the impact of workplace literacy programmes on a variety of outcomes, and was able to collect comparative data for trainees and non-trainees. Moreover the structure of financing was similar to that currently being offered to employers in England.

A basic skills tuition programme was delivered to 480 low-skilled, hourly-paid workers at two mid-sized New Jersey (US) companies (one service, one manufacturing). It ran for approximately 16 months and classes were taught on-site in five 8–12 week blocks. The programme was subsidized by the federal government, so employers only had to meet the indirect costs that it incurred, i.e. mainly the forgone costs of production due to staff release, rental of training rooms and wages of employees who organized (but did not deliver) the training. The content of training included subjects like basic reading, writing and maths and English as a Second Language and was in part tailored to specific company needs.

The authors found small effects of the programme on all outcomes investigated (although the follow-up period was quite short). In the service company, there was no significant effect on wage growth of programme participants compared with non-participants. Conversely, there was a larger growth in earnings for trainees at the manufacturing company compared with non-trainees. This was especially marked for those who took the education classes with a strong company-specific focus (e.g. blueprint reading); and remained even when controls were introduced.

There was evidence that trainees at the manufacturing company were 7 per cent more likely to apply for and gain (internal) promotion ('upgrade'). There was also some evidence that trainees at the service company were more frequently nominated for or won a performance award[6] compared with non-trainees. These awards were used by the researchers as a proxy for increases in productivity, although the differences might also be largely accounted for by other personal characteristics of the nominees. Workers who had participated in the programme had a lower absenteeism rate during the weeks in which they had classes and this effect continued for the next two months, although it was quite small. Finally, there was no evidence that participation in training made workers either more or less likely to leave the company after training.

The authors were not able to measure changes in productivity directly, but did ask participants about their own self-perceived productivity. In the service company, self-reported productivity was higher among trainees: this may reflect performance or may reflect higher self-esteem. Participants at both companies were significantly more likely to report that they planned to take additional classes in the future compared with non-participants.

This study is also highly unusual in providing some estimates of the rate-of-return to the employer of the training expenditure. On the basis of the actual costs incurred – namely, that the federal subsidy covered approximately half the costs of the training – the authors conclude that, at least in the manufacturing company, the training paid for itself: but that 'it is not clear that other (manufacturing) firms would find it worthwhile to undertake such training in the absence of a subsidy'.

As already noted, we have not identified any other well structured and documented empirical studies of the impact of basic skills training in the workplace, whether on productivity or other outcomes of direct concern to employers. Examples of workplace 'successes' have been collected by UK government departments, and generally allude to Skills for Life 'helping' to increase staff satisfaction, or reduce absenteeism, or to productivity having risen 'after' the introduction of Skills for Life-funded courses (see e.g. National Audit Office 2008, Appendix Five, 'Engaging Employers'). Some individual examples, provided in promotional literature by sector skill councils, cite changes which are very large, such as drops of 35 per cent in reportable accidents, and productivity increases of over 10 per cent.[1] However, it is unclear how these figures have been obtained, and whether there are any controls for changes in other variables, or for selective enrolment in the courses.

Indirect evidence: employers' views on the value of basic skills training

Other than the studies referred to in the previous section, the remaining published evidence relates to qualitative or subjective estimates of the impact of basic skills provision in the workplace. These are generally global judgments, and not based on collection and analysis of 'hard' data, but they are consistently positive. Bassi (1994) asked management representatives to assess the outcomes on their firm of such training by indicating whether it had had 'no impact', 'moderate impact', or 'significant impact'. The results show that about half the respondents report that training had had either moderate or significant impact on quality of output and ability to use new technology, whereas between 30 per cent and 40 per cent of respondents found that it had had moderate or significant impact on error rates, customer satisfaction, time savings and safety.

Bloom *et al.* (1997) report the findings of a survey of 41 Canadian companies to explore the benefits of improving literacy skills in the workplace. Twenty-one of the surveyed companies provided qualitative feedback on the benefits of literacy training to their organization, and all nominated one or more positive outcomes. Pearson (1996) reports similar results for a survey of 30 different Australian workplaces representing 13 industries across five states.

Another way of estimating potential gains from basic skills improvements in the workplace is by looking at the costs of poor basic skills at present. Gallup was commissioned by the (then) Adult Literacy and Basic Skills Unit (ALBSU) in late 1992 to conduct a survey of employers for that purpose. Employers were asked a series of questions relating to specific aspects of their company's business. Specifically, they were first asked to indicate how many customer orders were cancelled per year because of errors/ problems, how many orders were despatched/produced incorrectly and the number of customers lost per year through problems or misunderstandings. Subsequently, employers were asked to estimate what percentage of the above problems could have been avoided by better basic skills among staff. Further questions were asked addressing the issue of cost of supervisory staff that could be dispensed with if basic skills were better and the cost of recruiting staff externally because poor basic skills limit their own employees' potential for internal promotion.

The results are presented in Table 3.3. It is important to point out here that on average only 15 per cent of respondents (i.e. only 15 per cent of the 400 companies sampled) were able to provide an estimate of costs; percentages reported below are based on this 15 per cent's replies. Moreover, most companies did not hold the view that poor basic skills contribute to financial losses. On the contrary, 71 per cent of those surveyed responded that their company had never experienced a financial loss that might be largely attributed to poor basic skills and a further 16 per cent responded that this only happens rarely.

Table 3.3 Average cost of poor basic skills per company employing 51 or more

Approximate number of:	(a) Number	(b) % which could have been avoided if basic skills were better	(c) Typical cost in £ of one cancelled order/lost customer/ rectifying a problem order (1992 prices)	(d) Total cost per company in £ due to basic skills difficulties among staff* (1992 prices)
Customer orders cancelled per year because of errors, problems or misunderstandings	30	38.7	2,397	27,600
Customer orders despatched or produced incorrectly each year	161	41.4	1,123	74,600
Customers lost per year because of errors, problems or misunderstandings	12.5	35.3	5,957	26,200
Members of staff employed whose main task is to check and approve the work of others	30.1	2.3	12,473	28,330
Employees needing to be recruited externally each year for posts which could be filled internally if basic skills were better	35.9	11.2	2,183	8,800
			Total	165,530

Source: taken from ALBSU 1993.

* Overall costs are calculated by taking the percentage of (a) indicated at (b) and multiplying this by (c). Figures at (d) were calculated by computer using the raw data.

Table 3.3 shows that on average the estimated overall cost of poor basic skills for a company employing 51 employees or more is £166,000 per year in 1993 figures (£252,000 in 2009 prices). The cost for smaller companies (51–100 staff) was estimated to be approximately £86,000 (£108,000) per year and for larger companies employing more than 1,000 employees around £500,000 (£626,000) per company per year.

The data were subsequently grossed up in order to provide an estimate of the total cost of basic skills problems to industry as a whole, i.e. all 40,000 companies estimated as employing 51 staff or more. The estimates are presented below in Table 3.4 and arrive at a total of £4.8 billion annually (equivalent to £7.3 billion in 2009).

The study and its findings have a number of important limitations and have been criticized (e.g. by Robinson 1997). It remains, nonetheless, the only one in the UK that has attempted to provide an estimate of the costs to industry of problems with basic skills. Ernst & Young use it in their report of the same year on the impact on the UK economy of literacy, education and training (Ernst & Young 1993). The figure they cite is £8.4 billion, which is a 'grossed-up estimate to take account of companies of all sizes' of the one produced by ALBSU (1993). No information is given on how they arrived at this estimate. The Moser Report's figure of £10 billion is, we assume, also based on this figure, adjusted for inflation up to 1999. So, too, are the figures frequently cited in promotional literature for Skills for Life (see e.g. Basic Skills Agency 2000, DfES nd).

More recent evidence comes from the National Employers' Skill Surveys: annual surveys carried out by the Learning and Skills Council, the main funding quango for the sector. For the period 2001–2005 – overlapping with our study and years of economic boom and high

Table 3.4 Summary of total costs to industry of poor basic skills for companies employing more than 51 persons

	Grossed–up estimates (million pounds)
Cost of customer orders cancelled through poor basic skills	911
Cost of rectifying customer orders despatched incorrectly through poor basic skills	2,500
Cost of customers lost through errors, etc., due to poor basic skills	886
Cost of staff who could be dispensed with if basic skills were better	197
Cost of recruiting employees externally because poor basic skills limits internal promotion	334
Total	4,828

Source: taken from ALBSU 1993.

employment – an average of 8 per cent of employers reported hard-to-fill vacancies, but only 4 per cent said this was wholly or partly because of an absence of suitably skilled applicants. In 2005, 28 per cent of that four per cent – i.e. *one per cent of the sample* – give literacy skills as one of the skills lacking in connection with skill-shortage vacancies (Learning and Skills Council 2006: 37).

Answers to the vacancies question were unprompted and open-ended. In addition, Skill Survey respondents were given a long list of skills and asked to rate levels of skill in each for each main occupational group of employees. This list included both literacy and numeracy.

Every occupational group was judged to be seriously deficient in several areas. Overall, literacy skills ranked as the ninth most important out of 13 options, but were eleventh out of 13 for professionals, and seventh for 'personal services' and 'elementary' occupations (ibid.: 72).[7]

The effect of basic skills programmes

As discussed above, there is almost no good quality research evidence on the impact of workplace basic skills instruction. There is also very little research relating to direct measures of skill; although a recently published New Zealand study (Benseman *et al.* 2010), discussed in detail in Chapter 9, complements our own research in this respect. However, there are some large-scale evaluations of basic skills programmes for adults outside the workplace.

In the UK, the most relevant study is the longitudinal 'Evaluation of the Impact of Skills for Life Learning' (Metcalf and Meadows 2004, Meadows and Metcalf 2005, Metcalf *et al.* 2009, and also Metcalf and Meadows 2009). This five-year study, commissioned by the then-Department for Education and Skills, followed a sample of 2,000 Skills for Life learners, all enrolled in colleges on qualification-bearing courses. Outcomes for these learners were compared with those for a matched comparison sample of over 2,000 non-learners. Seventy-nine per cent of participants had gained a qualification by the end of the study: 22 per cent had obtained a GCSE, and the others had obtained another literacy or numeracy qualification, and/or an NVQ.

The evaluation considered a number of labour market outcomes. Skills for Life participation had no apparent impact on any of them. The proportion of learners in paid employment grew between the start and end of the study; but no more than for the matched, non-participant sample. Increases in earnings appeared slightly larger for the learners' group, over the period covered; but in most cases, differences were not statistically significant. The researchers conclude that 'the evidence from this study does not provide support for the hypothesis that taking a literacy or numeracy course leads to an increase in earnings' (Metcalf *et al.* 2009: 46). Participation did not improve perceived promotion prospects; nor were there significant differences between learners and non-learners with respect to changes in job satisfaction over the course of the study.

Most learners believed that their literacy and numeracy skills improved during the course of the study: so did many non-learners, though significantly fewer. However, the study itself found no evidence of this. The results showed no significant improvements in literacy for the learners overall, and this may explain the apparent absence of labour market effects. The authors were at pains to emphasize that the actual tests they administered were short, and consequently prone to unreliability; they were, nonetheless, the instrument used to classify learners for study purposes, and they were administered before and after course participation (see Meadows and Metcalf 2005: 12–13).

A number of UK government programmes for the young and longer-term unemployed have also, in the last decade, included basic skills courses of various types, with attendance more or less voluntary according to programme details. Overall, the results generally indicate that courses either make no significant difference, or that this approach is less effective, in terms of employment outcomes, than some others (notably those involving direct work placements). However, the results are difficult to interpret because the groups being compared often differ on important dimensions (see e.g. Lessof *et al.* 2003, National Centre for Social Research 2003).

One major evaluation of work-based learning for adults (Speckesser and Bewley 2006) used extensive controls to adjust for differences between participants and comparison populations, and found that Basic Employability Training, which offered up to 26 weeks of basic literacy and numeracy instruction, had no impact on levels of benefit receipt (and indeed was associated with an *increase*), but did seem to increase numbers in employment 40 months later compared with a matched population. Short, occupational training ('Job-Focused Training') was more effective in reducing benefit claimant rates and slightly more effective in increasing later employment.

These somewhat discouraging findings are consistent with many of the evaluations conducted of vocational training programmes for the low-skilled and unemployed (see Wolf 2009). It is important, however, to realize that many, indeed most, of these programmes lack key attributes conducive to effective learning (see Chapters 4 and 8). We can usefully contrast them with the outcomes of programmes which are intensive, comprehensive and voluntary. Effective learning is unlikely when people are obliged to participate (as with many government programmes – though not those in our study); moreover, we know that significant improvements in literacy skills require considerable amounts of contact and study time, whereas many government-financed programmes have been, and remain, intentionally brief and supposedly 'efficient'.

The single most exhaustive and relevant evaluation of a training programme to be carried out in recent years was for the Job Corps programme in the United States (McConnell and Glazerman 2001). This is a highly intensive, often residential programme for young people – typically in their 20s – who dropped out of high school and are socially disadvantaged, and it provides both academic and vocational training over a complete year. It is very expensive. It is also, as the evaluations have established, extremely cost-effective, with net benefits to society in the first few years of over $17,000 per participant (2000 prices), measured by their increased earnings and employment levels compared with matched non-participant groups. Job Corps indicates, in other words, that just as employer-based and employer-provided training can often yield significant earnings benefits, so too can government programmes *if they are structured correctly* and involve volunteer learners. At the end of this book we return to these considerations.

Conclusion

The evidence on the work-related effects of individuals' basic skills relates almost entirely to learning and skills acquisition which itself took place outside the workplace. It is nonetheless, as we have seen, quite detailed in respect of both wages and employment. How far does it justify governments' expectations that such programmes will greatly improve individuals' life-chances, productivity and earnings?

Much less than is generally supposed. Improved skills will certainly improve people's lives in many ways but it is not obvious that they will be direct economic ones. Policy-makers rely, in their predictions, on academic models which use the wage and employment advantages associated, in the current labour market, with individuals of a given skill level, and then assume that, if others reach that same level, they will enjoy the same benefits. So, for example, extrapolating from existing skills-related differences in employment rates and earnings, one arrives at figures which suggest that raising the population's literacy levels will increase aggregate employment by 70,000 (and numeracy by 130,000); and at increases in the wages bill (i.e. employed adults' earnings) of up to £7.27 billion at 2000 prices (Dearden *et al.* 2005, Bynner *et al.* 2001).

But it is not at all evident that this will actually occur. In fact, there is evidence which suggests the opposite. As we saw above, Machin's analysis of the results of basic skills changes in the NCDS cohort found that, while those who reported improvements in their own skill levels also showed gains, those who had measured improvements (in terms of scores at 37 compared with 16) did not. Other data, including evaluations of government programmes, indicate that a labour market impact is the exception rather than the rule for basic skills interventions. The next section of this book examines how far the workplace programmes we studied were such an exception.

Part 2

The findings

Chapter 4

The challenges of implementing literacy learning in the workplace

Introduction

Arguments for providing literacy programmes in and through the workplace are well rehearsed. They potentially provide better access to learning opportunities for adults and programmes situated in the workplace can, it is argued, more easily be linked to organizational as well as employee needs (see Introduction). This chapter explores what actually happened in mounting workplace literacy programmes in the 53 organizations that participated in the research.

Many different approaches and models are used in designing and providing literacy learning in and through the workplace. Employers may work with providers such as colleges or private training organizations to deliver training or they may provide the training themselves. How are programmes initiated and by whom? What are the barriers, and how are they resolved? How are they experienced by tutors and the managers who are at the sharp end of implementation? While many examples are found of effective practice, overall our evidence points to the longer-term sustainability of workplace literacy provision as the key challenge.

Setting up courses

In keeping with the heavily 'supply-side' nature of the Skills for Life national strategy the provider played the primary role in initiating courses in the vast majority of sites. Some colleges had marketing departments which undertook the task of promoting workplace SfL courses. In one college, funding from the local development agency (SEEDA) had been vital, allowing the college training coordinator to play an active role in approaching organizations and brokering the establishment of courses. This funding has allowed the programme manager to establish contacts with companies, undertake rudimentary Occupational Needs Analysis and then tailor courses to the specific circumstances of each organization. By contrast, in the majority of cases, the provider had to carry the costs of setting up the provision out of direct payments for enrolled courses, including the 'deadweight' costs where the negotiations did not result in a course starting up at all.

Courses were promoted in the workplace through promotional shows (e.g. 'roadshows'), flyers, posters, as well as through managers, supervisors and Union Learning Representatives. Several tutors and managers commented that 'word of mouth' was frequently the most effective means of enlisting learners on the courses. As Lucy O'Farrell, a tutor who worked in a variety of sites in south east England commented,

> we have fliers and we have leaflets, we do road shows, and we talk to people, because very often at the level at which we're trying to make contact with people they're not big readers of fliers. But they very rarely think 'oh this course is for me', word of mouth is incredibly important.

Similarly, Chris Turner, training manager at Thorpton Local Authority emphasized the importance of talking directly to a variety of individuals at different levels of the organization:

> They're promoted that way with local emails, with the staff magazine and the departmental newsletters, and they're promoted by going round sticking flyers on the walls ... If you spoke to a workforce development officer ... She'd say the most successful way is by speaking to people, in the order of, senior people first and then getting their authorization to speak to the people in ... positions below that and then getting to supervisor level and doing a TNA with them.

In all the sites we visited, considerable thought had been devoted to employing appropriate titles for the courses in order to overcome potential stigma associated with attending a literacy course.

Chris Turner, Thorpton Local Authority described this process as follows:

> the programme is called 'Get on at work' ... it's made very clear that a large element of that is ... er ... developing skills such as presenting yourself, customer service, speaking and listening and writing so it's ... its masked if you like. It's not like 'come to this to improve your literacy'.

June Williams, a tutor at STS Systems (transport company) mentioned that: 'We've always found the titles extraordinarily difficult and so we've always been incredibly straight forward ... and called it things like "improve your English" or "brush up your maths" or something like that'. Sally Jones encountered some negative feedback at initial course promotion,

> and it was at that point that I introduced the name of the Learning Zone and started calling them 'Improve your English', 'Improve your

Maths', and also introducing things like report writing and IT and outlook – things that sound a bit more upmarket if you like … because yeah, definitely there is … a stigma for people.

The combination of literacy with such subjects as ICT was regarded as a useful means of circumventing potential stigma and reinforcing the practical relevance of the courses and partly accounts for the prevalence of such courses in our overall sample.

George Lerman at Coopers, with a Learndirect centre, described the advantages of this approach in the following terms:

> I've been here since August 2003 and I knew that I couldn't just go out on to the factory floor and say 'do you want to come in and learn how to read and write?' I mean no one would ever dream of doing that so I had to be quite clever and put on activities that weren't related at all to reading and writing just to build relationships to get people into the centre.

Computer courses are an important means of overcoming learner barriers to developing their literacy and numeracy:

> A lot of the IT courses are based around literacy and numeracy but the learner doesn't realize till the end, they think they're learning spreadsheets or they think they're learning word processing but actually there's a lot of grammar, there's a lot of literacy and numeracy going through that.

Similarly, the programme manager at Cloville college described ICT as a useful 'hook' for engaging learners in literacy. More pragmatic considerations also lie behind the process of embedding literacy in ICT: 'Combining English courses with computers is … very useful from a college point of view in allowing the college to meet its targets. If we were not combining ICT with English, we would not be meeting our targets.'

In-depth interviews with learners confirmed that such strategies were sometimes effective. Gary Thompson, a learner at WDE –Weapons Defence Establishment, mentioned that the concealed literacy component had various advantages: 'I think it was probably good, the fact that I didn't know before, because I probably wouldn't have gone otherwise.' He explains his reluctance to go on a more explicitly literacy course in terms of 'Basically because I'm not very good at spelling. So sort of a fear in that area would have put me off'.

But equally, an ethical issue is raised as to whether learners are being misled over the nature of the course. As Roger Taylor from Weapons Defence Establishment (WDE) mentioned: 'I think we were slightly misled from the initial literature that came up, because it turned out to be more of a literacy thing. We said "well we haven't got a problem with it" but it wasn't something we expected when we initially went forward for it'. The tutor at Transpo bus company in Kent related an incident in which a learner, on discovering that the course included a literacy component, stormed out of the room and declared 'I don't want to go on a … literacy course!'

In those sites that had a strong union presence, the Union Learning Representatives usually played an important role in promoting the course, with 19 ULRs in the 53 sites researched. Jennifer Oates, ULR at Brightland Bakeries drew on her credibility as a fellow employee and union representative in order to convince learners of the merits of undertaking a course:

> I think it just helps, you know, when they see a familiar face, if they all recognize me. I've been out on the shop floor and I'm like branch chairperson of the bakers' union on site … so I've got high profile if you like … I've said to them I'm doing courses meself, you know if I can do it anybody can.

In Milton Bus Company the unions also played a particularly important role in promoting the course. The union put a note into the employees' wage slips promoting the course as a benefit which had been 'negotiated' by the unions on behalf of the membership. In the words of the training manager at this company:

> We looked at the union learning rep scheme and it's the perfect opportunity to make it happen. I think as a company if we stood on us own it would be hard to sell this. Because I think drivers would see it as a threat, I think if you weren't working with unions on this agenda it would be very hard, it would be pushing water up hill.

Intention and promotion do not, of course, always translate into a viable course 'up and running'. At 40 additional sites, courses that seemed 'firm' enough to be entered on our database (with, in some cases, manager interviews completed) in fact never started, or collapsed after the first one or two sessions.

Organizational needs analysis

The perceived advantage of workplace courses is that they can be linked to the organizational situation and embedded in organizational needs. 'Good practice', as recommended by, for example, the Network for Workplace Language, Literacy and Numeracy (originally DfES-funded), emphasizes the need to tailor content to the workplace and the individual learners.

This means carrying out both an 'Occupational Needs Analysis' (clarifying the literacy and numeracy requirements associated with the company's jobs) and a 'Training Needs Analysis', clarifying how many post-holders are likely to need training.

In practice, only 14 of the 53 sites in our sample reported carrying out some sort of ONA or TNA. None of our respondents was clear about the difference between the two, but we inferred from interview responses that, in most cases, what took place was a TNA related to general literacy needs rather than occupation-specific ones.

Tailoring the courses to the learners

As Table 4.1 shows, workplace courses were successful in recruiting from the groups most distanced from conventional courses provision:

Two thirds of the participants in our sample were male, compared with only 41 per cent and 23 per cent in contemporary publicly funded courses available through colleges and community-based adult learning centres. Older learners were also more in evidence in our sample than in other forms of adult education provision.

How is the literacy level of the employees targeted by the workplace programmes identified? A sample of 46 tutors were asked how they undertook initial assessments of the literacy levels of the learners. Just

Table 4.1 Characteristics of learner sample compared with overall adult learner population: 2005–2006 (%)

	Study learners	FE learners in publicly supported further education institutions 2005–6	Adult and community learners in publicly supported provision 2005–6	All forms of adult learning (self-reported and including workplace training) 2006
Male	67	41	23	48
Female	33	59	77	52
Under 25	6	51	35	15
25–34	22	17		16
35–44	32	15	58*	20
45–54	23	9		20
54+	17	8	7 (60+)	29

* Ages 25–59.

Sources: Learning and Skills Council Learner 2007, DfES First Statistical Estimates 2007, Aldridge and Tuckett 2008.

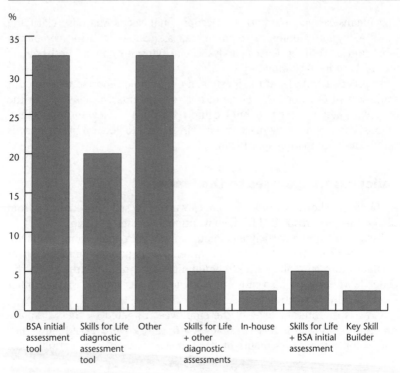

Figure 4.1 Diagnostic assessment tools used by workplace programmes

over one half of tutors employed the BSA initial diagnostic assessment tool or Skills for Life diagnostic assessment tool

The BSA initial assessment was most used in single focus literacy or numeracy programmes, with other approaches used in hybrid or other types of programme. The Skills for Life assessment tool was primarily used in ESOL programmes.

Tutors were most likely to report that their courses were designed to provide a mix of job-specific and general literacy learning.

Of the programmes that they were involved in running, only two programmes – ones that comprised a range of essential skills – were described by tutors as entirely job-specific. Approximately half of the tutors reported that they used the national Skills for Life core curricula (literacy, numeracy or ESOL as appropriate) in planning their teaching. SfL core curriculum was most used in literacy programmes.

In three sites, the courses were Learndirect (see Chapter 1), so were pre-programmed. In 26 cases the content of the learning was entirely decided by the provider. In the remaining 23, content was determined by combinations of the provider with management and/or unions; but the large majority reported that it was 'mostly' the provider who decided.

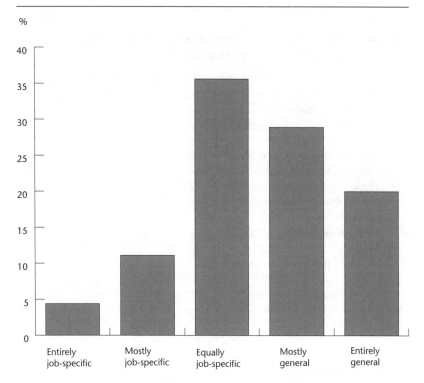

Figure 4.2 The balance between general and job-specific content: proportion of courses by content category

Connecting learning to work practices

Further insights into the ways in which tutors aimed to connect teaching to work practices came from a subset of six tutors working in different occupational fields. These tutors talked about the ways in which they have aimed to support learners to connect, or to recontextualize their literacy learning as they move between sites of practice.[1] Box 4.1 describes activities before the course.

Most tutors aimed to obtain inputs from workplace supervisors and learners after Initial Assessments 'so we knew what level we were teaching and had a realistic idea of what could be achieved'. Box 4.2 describes the process of bringing contextualized content into the course.

Tutors used a combination of formal and informal feedback methods. They reported changes in knowledge, skills and scanning) and in attitudes, but most emphasis was placed on attitudes:

We create a learner.

> ### Box 4.1　How tutors connect literacy learning to practices before the course
>
> The tutors generally used workplace practices, procedures and situations for language/writing/speaking development in the course. These were often translated into 'contextualized materials'.
>
> One tutor explained the process:
>
>> Use workplace forms, be aware of all literature employees are required to read. Speak to key people about particular difficulties regarding numeracy and literacy and work on these skills. Attend training courses and talk to training staff.
>
> Examples provided by this tutor from the transport company (STS) are 'Maths for the Booking Office' in response to staff making mistakes, courses to support staff through the internal selection process for promotion, e.g. writing competencies and compiling CVs, using email, writing customer information boards, report writing, also oral language practice classes for people who felt their language skills were holding them back at work.

> I think students who are initially Entry level develop self esteem and confidence following successful completion of a literacy qualification and want to continue.

> The biggest change you see is the impact on self-esteem and confidence – getting people to believe they can tackle things instead of avoiding them. Often learners get a huge appetite for lifelong learning after a positive experience.

Such observations are certainly consistent with the learner accounts in Chapter 6. The barriers or inhibitors to using and 'applying', or recontexualizing learning are also often perceived by tutors as rooted in learner confidence.

> Confidence … very often students think they are impossible to teach
> …

Pressures of personal and work commitments also featured strongly. Tutors referred to time constraints at work, long hours, shift work and demanding home lives impacting on the completion of homework.

> Lack of time to do work on their own (homework) due to family and work commitments. They may be tired if they are shift workers and

---

Box 4.2   How tutors incorporate 'contextualized' content

As you get to know your learners, how do you incorporate content into your programme that is relevant to the learners' working life?

Tutor 1: Ask them to bring in real 'problems' e.g. reports they have to write.

Tutor 2: I always start my course by asking each student to give a short presentation. In the presentation they are asked to talk about their family, education, country of origin, what their job entails and what they would like to do in the future. Based on what they say I understand what they require now and for future development.

Tutor 3: Initial interview, reviews and discussions. Personal goal setting.

How, if at all, are you connecting the general content of the programme to real examples in the learners' personal lives?

Tutor 4: We have not often used instances from their personal life unless the student really asked for it as on the whole we are teaching in employers' time. We had one student who needed to do a presentation at his son's ATC unit and we did some work around that as an example because he was so stressed about it.

What kinds of materials do you use to help make the connection from the classroom to the workplace?

Tutor 5: Holiday and absence forms, salary slips, newsletters, work magazines, graphs and charts, copies of reports.

---

have been up all night before their lesson. The pattern of learning can also be interrupted if they can't be released from their jobs due to staff shortages or they go on prolonged holiday back to their country of origin. After the course they may well slip back into bad habits and forget quite quickly much of what they have learnt.

Asked for evidence of literacy learning impacting on activities in 'real-life' situations in work or beyond it, typical responses from care sector tutors are encapsulated in the words of this tutor:

Following success in Literacy examinations I know of students who have paid considerable amounts of their own money to study for Level 3 qualifications in Care, on the expectation that in the future they will be able to move into management positions in Care or go on to higher education. They have become confident in their ability to study and achieve and this confidence has also become apparent at work and noticed by their managers.

A counter example comes from cleaning services, in which the tutor admits to finding it 'hard to see' why learners in cleaning jobs with an hourly rate at minimum wage should learn 'for no more reward':

> Where supervisors are recruited from among the cleaners, and the organization wants to encourage cleaners towards promotion, the barrier is less ... 'I'm just a cleaner' is an effective barrier. The tutor has to look for ways round the barrier.

In cases where tutors sought to relate the course to the workplace context, this was generally on the basis of tutor's initiative. The embedded materials developed by the DfES were not utilized in any of the sites selected for in-depth qualitative research and were rarely found in use. However, the tutor at Milton Bus Company adapted embedded materials on catering for the customer service and literacy course: 'It actually enabled me to compare how they'd embedded literacy into catering with how we were embedding it into customer care.'

In addition, this tutor encouraged the learners to practise filling in incident report forms.

> The first week someone gave me an incident and we wrote it up and it had some good points and some bad points, and subsequent weeks it was then used as a model to look at what was good about it and where it was lacking, where it could be improved, what phraseology was good, what would improve it and that sort of thing.

Similarly, at Manning Social Services, the tutor encouraged the learners to fill in care plans on a computer.

Lucy O'Farrell at Cloville college:

> At the initial interview we will talk to them about the sort of work that they do, what they write, what they read and where they're having specific problems. That is then written up and passed on to the tutor ... who will develop it.

Sally Jones at STS Systems, encouraged learners to bring in samples of their work:

> Whenever I started with a new student I would always say ... bring your own examples of things that you need to fill in and people did do that. So it was, it was done as part of class work.

However, she regretted that she was not able to undertake a more detailed analysis of their uses of literacy in the workplace:

> train drivers need to write, there's certain forms they need to fill in, there's incident report forms, station supervisors, lots of form filling ... little books in the office and things, there's lots of examples but, such an interesting question, there are times where I thought I should really look at this, at one point I was going to go out with a train driver and try and look at all the literacy that they needed but there just never seemed the time to be able to do it really. You know when you look back and think yeah I should have done that.

In many cases, tutors were merely assigned to a workplace course by their manager. Several tutors (particularly those paid on an hourly basis) complained about the time and inconvenience involved in undertaking workplace provision, felt insufficiently recompensed and were therefore ill-equipped to develop courses that were effectively tailored to the workplace environment.

As discussed further in Chapters 5 and 7, a good many learners wished to pursue interests that were not tailored to the work environment. The courses provided a valuable antidote to the routine and pressures of work. At STS Systems, the tutors embraced the principle of learning for its own sake and developed a course that entailed the learners studying Shakespeare as part of a GCSE in English. Although the tutors in this organization made some attempts to tailor the courses to the workplace (as mentioned above),

> We didn't go down the route of the work based curriculum, because people come in their own time, let's face it you have enough of work while you're there, you don't want to do it. But that's quite a big issue in work based basic skills; there are a lot of people who feel that it should be just about filling in forms and learning how to spell fire extinguisher and all those sort of things, where as we weren't in favour of that, we were very much more geared towards the general approach.

After the course

Several sites organized award ceremonies. Chris Turner, training manager at Thorpton, mentioned

> Some people thought it's a bit patronizing giving certificates just for going on a course, but ... I've got photographs to prove the effect on those learners because some people have got something they've never had in their lives and er ... and we've given them a real start.

Robert Day received a certificate from his area manager at the end of the course at Milton Bus Company:

It was a little bit of apprehension, everybody was a little nervous, ... and yet we were all thrilled to bits to come out the other side, I mean they might as well have put an Olympic medal round our necks. The feeling you get at the end of, well a lot of us older ones had never done anything like that for such a long time.

Tutors played an important role in encouraging learners to undertake further learning and could signpost them towards opportunities that were provided by the college. For example, June Williams at STS Systems mentioned

I was actually saying to people, because the lovely thing about most of our classes is that the majority of people come to improve their English, and then you see them looking at the computers and so I'm trying to give them a push, sign up? Fancy going on the computer? And so there's been a fantastic feed in that way.

However, as discussed further in Chapter 7, national funding arrangements often created barriers to additional learning rather than facilitating it. Several learners expressed frustration that they were not provided with opportunities to undertake further SfL workplace provision. Shenila Rahman at Brightland Bakeries:

I wanted to do level 1, then level 2 ... but they said they do not do that, because the government only fund you for the first one and don't fund you for the rest, you have to do it yourself at college or whatever. Which I was a bit disappointed. Because now I'm in a limbo, I'm just doing my own things.

Insights into effective practices: collaborative learning

Often referred to as cognitive apprenticeships, collaborative learning involves learning with peers (Rogoff, 1995). It is used in groups where a more practised worker helps a less experienced learner by modelling, mentoring, scaffolding or coaching. This is particularly relevant to workplace literacy, where the complexity of scheduling classes around work patterns, different sites and personal lives, means that there are rarely enough students to further break classes down into levels of ability. Collaborative workplace learning can also be important in helping adults to 'recontextualize' what they have learnt through sharing, mutual support and challenge (Evans *et al.* 2010). A focused inquiry into collaborative leaning was undertaken as a spin-off from the larger project, to follow up indicators of effective practice and to engage practitioner researchers who had much to offer the research. The final section of this chapter discusses its findings.

How do adult learners learn collaboratively with other peers in workplace Language Literacy and Numeracy (LLN) programmes?

Sociocultural theories are best fitted to the search for better understandings of the processes involved in work-based learning. As discussed in Chapter 2, they recognize skill and knowledge as embodied in the learning individual, and they acknowledge the significance of power relations. They consider the tacit as well as the explicit dimensions of skills and knowledge, and the ways old knowledge and new can be linked in processes of knowledge construction.

Observations, interviews with tutors and learners, focus groups and a Teaching Perspectives Inventory provided in-depth insights into three contrasting forms of provision:[2] a short, focused course in a transport organization (Site A), a drop-in course for dyslexic employees (Site C) and a short general improvement course for a team of street wardens (Site B). Learners in sites A and C chose to attend the course from a menu of options whereas the learners in site B attended a bespoke course for their team. The initial findings were compared with those generated by a Canadian team (see Taylor *et al.* 2007a) and are discussed further in Chapter 9. Table 4.2 summarizes the course and tutor data.

The study showed how the make-up of the group can be critical to some learners. They need to feel part of the group and the quality of the teaching alone will not be enough for them to stay.

> We have examples of (employees) giving up after one class but then returning six months to two years later and sustaining their attendance. Furthermore, one of our long-established, successful and high-achieving classes is at a station where all the employees are friends as well as workmates. They have good relationships inside and outside of the classroom and have worked together for many years.
>
> (Tutor Site A)

Peers can play an important role in helping those who are unconfident, negative, worried or have low self-esteem (see Box 4.3). For many people, the idea of returning to learn is not attractive because their initial experiences of education were negative, unrewarding or even damaging.

Table 4.2 Literacy provision in the collaborative learning study

	Gender	Age	Qualification
Site A			
Six-week course (two hours per week) in report writing. Employees attend in their own time and a process of initial assessment ensures the course fits their needs.	Female	45–50	Qualified primary school teacher. Retrained to teach adults in 1998 – City and Guilds 9285 Teaching, Literacy to Adults.
Site B			
The course is designed to help employees be more effective in their role. Includes completing paperwork and giving short talks to community groups. There is no selection process and the teacher estimates the range of skills within the group.	Female	40–45	Qualified to teach literacy and ESOL (City and Guilds). All experience with adults including TEFL.
Site C			
The course is an ongoing 2-hour weekly class for learners with dyslexia. Each student has had a full diagnostic assessment where dyslexia has been identified. The students range in ability and come from different parts of the organization.	Female	35–40	Dyslexia specialist. Qualified with LLU+ to diagnose and teach dyslexic adults

For example, Pat collaborates well as she is always ready to share her viewpoint. She thinks that collaborative learning is about being cooperative, working with others, and being open-minded to their suggestions. Pat said she liked it because she got to know the other members of the class. She felt it built trust and she got other people's ideas and views.The supportive environment of the class enabled Pat to build her confidence, reflect on her contributions and work towards becoming an independent learner.

Learners can adapt their behaviour to work collaboratively

In Site A, Jenny is the most capable learner in the group. She is a train driver who has lost her job due to health problems and has 12 weeks to

---

Box 4.3   Peer support in groups

The tutor asks the group to work in pairs and organize jumbled up paragraphs into the correct order; she gives them 15 minutes to do this. Pat works with Lyn, a more capable and confident student. At the start of the task, the women move closer together and begin by reading the worksheet separately, making marks on their papers. This takes five minutes. The women have got the same answers and because the pair next to them (Jenny and Daryl) also finish quickly they start to share their answers. Daryl and Jenny have a different answer. Daryl asks Pat and Lyn why they have chosen that order. First, Pat laughs, 'Good question, how did we get that!' Lyn says 'Women's logic!' The tutor interjects, 'There is no right answer, you may both be right'. Pat then explains, 'If you link the paragraphs about youths and litter it seems accusatory'. She has thought about her decision and later tells me that reflecting on her answers is one of the reasons she enjoys working in small groups.

---

be re-deployed within the company. During this time, she is applying for jobs and taking courses in IT and report writing. She has an obvious sense of humour which she uses to break the ice, get her point across and to hide her concerns about her work. When asked her reasons for joining the course she says, 'It's a good thing to do, you can never learn too much.'

When the group breaks into pairs and are asked to brainstorm their ideas for a report, the tutor asks Manny and Jenny to work together. Jenny is lively, talkative and more confident orally than Manny although their written ability level is similar. Jenny moves to sit closer to Manny and takes the lead in the task. Manny is reticent and Jenny appears to notice this immediately and stops directing and starts to assist Manny to cooperate with the task. She leans in towards him and tries to build on his comments instead of making her own points. She appears to make a conscious attempt to work at Manny's slower pace. Immediately they disagree but are able to discuss their points and reach a compromise.

When asked about the strengths of having students work together in pairs or in small groups, the tutor says, 'Working with others helps you see another viewpoint and stops a student being locked into their own paradigm. It builds confidence in their own ability to communicate.'

Approaches and environments for learning

All the tutors observed worked in similar surroundings – learners sat around a large, conference-style table with the teacher combining working with them as one group, dividing them into small groups or pairs, or working individually. The tutors knew the varying levels of ability and skilfully used this knowledge to facilitate collaboration:

> I try to put them at similar levels otherwise weak ones end up doing less and feeling uncomfortable. However personal characteristics are also important, for instance I wouldn't pair Roger and Bill because Roger is very dominant and Bill would just follow him.

Tutor C says she tries to promote independent learning beyond the classroom:

> For instance, David is more capable so I give him homework to bring back next week, I encouraged him to borrow a book from the class library – I am trying to get him to do work at home and be an independent learner. He reads a tabloid newspaper everyday, I'll bring him in an article from a broadsheet and encourage him to see the difference. I am encouraging him to do the pre GCSE course.

The Teaching Perspective Inventories is an instrument which measures teachers' dominant values. All the tutors in this part of the research shared a dominant 'nurturing' profile. At the same time clear goals and a structured path to achieving them were important.

> I think that the tutor should be clear about the purpose of both the lesson and the tasks. I try to build up positive experiences in reading, writing and oral skills and create a safe environment to ask questions. I take them through an ordered structured path.
>
> (Tutor Site A)

Guided learning to independent learning

In a collaborative learning environment, learners move from guided learning to greater independence; however, their progress towards independent learning is through interdependencies with other group members. In a Site C class, Paul's learning is guided by the tutor but when he works with Carol in a later class, he takes the lead – inviting Carol to participate in the class and displaying the confidence of an independent learner.

> Paul is clearly more confident when David and Roger aren't in the class. When he works in a pair with Carol, he talks more, interacts more and takes on the role of capable peer even though Carol's skills match his. When doing a creative writing exercise about picture

postcards, he uses inviting behaviour 'Shall we pick one we like first?'

(Observation note)

Paul thinks that collaborative learning is bouncing ideas off each other. He says it makes him feel confident as everyone in the class finds the activities challenging. He says the more his confidence grows in the classroom, the more he feels he can contribute. Carol is a new student and respects the fact that Paul is older, has been attending the classes longer and has been in the job for longer. Perhaps these factors lead to her allowing Paul to lead the learning. These cases highlight the ways in which issues such as job role, seniority and gender appear to influence peer learning in ways that could be problematic for participants.

Relationships outside the classroom impact on how adults learn collaboratively

When teaching in the workplace, tutors need to be sensitive to the roles that learners have outside the class and appreciate the impact this has within the group. For example, at Site B, Peter, the supervisor tells Janet he got 36 spellings correct in the test when in fact he scored 30. It is difficult when a person has a supervisory or managerial role outside the classroom to have their level of literacy exposed in front of their team and this may be compounded by asking learners to work collaboratively. Another tutor observed that 'if pairing doesn't work, it can be destructive in work-based projects, people with insecurities but good jobs can feel exposed'.

All the learners at Site B appeared to be defined by their work role, the class talk revolved around their work outside and, as they were in working hours, the classroom seemed to be an extension of the workplace even though it was off site. Contrastingly, at Sites A and C, classes were held on-site but made up of learners from all areas of the business. This seemed to enable people to be less affected by their work role.

Collaborative learning can influence the work-based curriculum. The Site C tutor noticed problems with planning their writing which were common to all learners in a literacy group. She opened up planning styles and found that her input helped guide them. When her manager asked her to run a 'business related' course, together they came up with a course in 'good practice in report writing' that incorporated this planning element.

Overall, the intensive study of collaborative learning provided further evidence of ways to overcome some of the barriers that adult literacy learners face (see Chapter 9). Reder (1994) has suggested that collaborative activities are seen to be 'critical contexts' for literacy development in which 'individuals share their literacy-related knowledge and skills, just as they share other kinds of knowledge and skills, often on a reciprocal basis' (p. 43). Reder (2009) postulates that individuals acquire literacy through participation in various literacy practices and they participate in these practices in different ways. Incorporating peer learning, in which learners learn with and from each other, within a broadly collaborative teaching approach creates an environment in which literacy learners can come to a different view of themselves.

Summary and conclusion

This chapter has explored what actually happened in mounting and carrying through workplace literacy programmes in the 53 organizations that participated in the research. Providers have to negotiate not only varied interests and learning dispositions of the participants, but also the demands, pressures, expectations and variable environments afforded by the workplace itself. In Chapter 7 we return to the longer-term prospects for such programmes; which are clearly related to the challenges described here.

Indicators of good and problematic practice can always be found. Workplace provision is inherently patchy in both quality and take up, with most of the sources of variation embedded in the working environment (Evans *et al.* 2006). Barriers to learning in the workplace can include shift patterns, lack of suitable facilities and time for supervision and support, perceived stigma in attending literacy, language and numeracy classes and the risks to employees in admitting problems or weaknesses. Issues include the complexity of many organizations, how the programmes are promoted, whether screening is voluntary or mandatory, whether employees attend in their own time or company time, and how participation in initial short course programmes is supported and followed up in the workplace and beyond it. While programmes modelled on collaborative learning offer particular benefits in building engagement and confidence, they also have potential drawbacks in reinforcing workplace inequalities.

Chapter 5

Literacy learning at work
The benefits to individuals

Introduction

As we have seen in earlier chapters, there is extensive evidence that possessing adequate or better literacy skills is associated with higher wages and better prospects of being in employment. People who lack basic literacy skills are likely to be disadvantaged in the labour market. In promoting and paying for workplace literacy programmes, the governments of the UK have hoped and expected that individuals will indeed improve their skills; and that this will translate into higher incomes and higher productivity for individuals and their employers alike.

This chapter looks at how far the workplace programmes which we studied have indeed had an impact on participants' skills, in the ways that government policy intended and expected. We measured literacy attainment directly, and also looked at whether participation in formal workplace learning shifted people's behaviour in ways that, over time, are likely to affect their literacy levels. This chapter discusses our findings for the sample of learners as a whole. Before turning to the evidence, however, it is worth asking how likely it was that policy-makers would achieve their ends.

As we saw in Chapter 3, the evidence base for government policy is very thin. There is some indication that adult literacy programmes can improve literacy skills – but only sometimes, and only on the basis of considerably greater amounts of contact time than were funded on this occasion. Very little evidence is available at all on possible links between improving your literacy as an adult, and making significant economic gains – and the results from the few studies that exist are very unclear either way.

However, the courses that we studied did have a number of important positive features. Learners were mostly very motivated; and motivation plays a critical role in effective learning (Ross 2006). Courses were largely 'general' in orientation (see Chapter 4): and some of the most positive findings on learner progress are for work-specific courses (Sticht and Mikulecky 1984; Benseman *et al.* 2010). However, given that, as we shall see, most learners were actually interested in *general* skills, this was likely to be a positive feature, increasing motivation.

Moreover, the courses were genuinely supplementary, meaning that they did not simply replace something employers were already paying for with equivalent training paid for by the taxpayer. Studies of contemporaneous government-funded workplace programmes have indicated that, for the most part, the volume of training undertaken has increased little or not at all: government funding has simply displaced employer payments (Abramovsky *et al.* 2005). In our sample, however, we were confident that every one of the programmes was indeed separate from and additional to mainstream workplace training. These programme features made positive outcomes appear considerably more likely.

Data and method

Research design and data collection were discussed in the Introduction; but to recapitulate, participating learners were tested formally on three occasions. Reading and writing were tested each time. The first test took place at the start of the workplace course; and the first follow-up test was scheduled for a year after course completion, rather than at the end of the course, since it is well-established that gains made during an intensive learning experience are not necessarily permanent and secure (Cooper *et al.* 1996; Downey *et al.* 2004). The second follow-up occurred a year and a half after the first.

The literacy assessment instrument was the *Go!* test developed by NFER for NRDC in 2003 (Rhys Warner *et al.* 2008). The test is built around a glossy magazine; is explicitly designed for adults; and allows quite small changes in skill to be measured accurately (see the Methodological Appendix). The reading scores on the *Go!* tests can be translated into percentage scores (out of 100) and into national level equivalents (using a conversion table developed by NFER, who developed and validated the test). In addition to collecting direct measures of literacy skills, we also collected and analysed information about further learning activities, about the benefits that learners felt they had obtained, and about their work and life experiences in the two and half year period following course participation (see Methodological Appendix for further details).

The vast majority of courses were entirely voluntary for learners. However, in three enterprises, the courses were organized with the collaboration of the union, but were effectively compulsory. Although unintended, this did provide a small-scale natural experiment, and allowed us to distinguish between voluntary and involuntary learners in our data analysis. It was not feasible to create a properly matched control group, but for some parts of the analysis baseline data from the LFS (Labour Force Survey), which provides panel data covering an 18 month period was used for comparison.

This is satisfactory for native English speakers; but the LFS unfortunately under-recruits mobile and recent immigrant populations, and no robust comparator data for these learners could be identified. This was unfortunate, since there was a high and unexpected number of ESOL (English for Speakers of Other Languages) learners in the sample. Some 41 per cent of learners did not have English as first language. The ESOL learners on average had higher levels of qualifications than other participants but, unsurprisingly, their proficiency in English was markedly lower at the start of the courses (see Appendix Table A.3 and Table 5.1 below). Given these substantial differences we undertook analyses separately for ESOL/non-ESOL learners as well as for the sample overall.

The courses typically offered 30 hours of tuition. After this, no further free instruction was available to participants. Previous research among college-based adults, much of it from the US suggests that substantial progress requires much longer than this. A recent review of evidence in Comings (2009) reported that 100 hours of instruction was the minimum needed in order for adults to make a one grade level equivalent gain on a standardized reading test. Thirty hours is a very small amount of time, bearing in mind that a single term for school pupils offers well over 200 hours of direct instruction.

As in any longitudinal study sample attrition was an issue. Originally, 532 provided substantive data; but full data including final (Time 3) reading scores are available only for 201. There was, fortunately, no relationship between initial reading level and likelihood of dropping out. Learners were much more likely to drop out if they had not provided initial data on qualifications, and somewhat more likely to drop out if they were male; and working in cleaning or transport rather than health or food processing. English language status was not significant. Work sector was not significant in the regression analyses relating to literacy gains, and gender routinely controlled for; so we do not believe that differential attrition poses serious problems for the analysis.

Literacy skills

As we saw in Chapter 1, there is a widespread belief in the media and among policy-makers that a significant proportion of the UK workforce is 'illiterate' in the sense of being effectively unable to read or write. This in fact misrepresents the evidence (especially for the British-born population). In our sample, as Table 5.1 indicates, learners enrolled in order to improve their literacy skills, but did not do so in order to learn to read.

Two-thirds of the total sample could read at above entry level at the time they started the course, which is to say that they were operating at a level above that expected of an 11 year old leaving primary school. Among native English speakers, only 2 per cent had reading problems severe enough to place them below the expected level for 11 year olds (whereas just over half the ESOL learners started off at or below the level of an 11

Table 5.1 Reading levels at the start of basic skills course (%)

	Whole sample	Non-ESOL	ESOL
Below Entry 2	6	1	12
Entry 2	5	1	8
Entry 3	22	14	32
Level 1	43	47	38
Level 2 or above	24	37	10

year old); and over a third were already operating at Level 2 which is officially defined as equivalent to GCSE Grade A–C.

The *Go!* test was normed using the government's descriptors for its adult literacy tests, and items used for the on-line tests employed for government-developed adult literacy tests. It is questionable whether these are precisely equivalent to the Key Stage 2 tests used for 11 year olds, let alone GCSE English. Figures 5.1, 5.2 and 5.3 provide a concrete illustration of what different basic skill levels mean in practice. As shown in Appendix table D1, government qualifications policy at the time of our study provided for 'Entry Level' plus five higher levels of qualification; and in the basic skills area, Entry Level was subdivided into Entry 1, 2 and 3.

Figure 5.1 provides an example of writing attainment, from one of our learners, at Entry Level 2; Figure 5.2 an example at Level 1, and Figure 5.3 illustrates performance at Level 2 (which is formally equivalent to GCSE A–C).

Many learners already possessed formal qualifications, although often only at quite low levels; and among older UK-born learners, fewer held formal certificates of any sort. They had typically left school at a time when fewer formal qualifications were awarded. Among the ESOL population a sizeable number of learners held qualifications at quite a high level – Level 3 (A-level or equivalent) or higher (see Appendix Table A.3). Overall, learners were interested in improving their literacy rather than becoming literate; while, in the case of the ESOL learners, they were highly interested in improving their English language skills.

Although only a few learners had very acute literacy problems, most were doing jobs which made few demands on their literacy skills, and gave them little opportunity to develop them. The courses enrolled overwhelmingly – as was intended – from people doing routine and often repetitive jobs (although these might demand high levels of responsibility, and interpersonal skills): people working in food processing companies, as cleaners, care assistants, bus-drivers, or in local government jobs such as caretaking. A few held managerial or sales positions.

Attainment levels at the first test were highly varied, ranging from zero to 100 out of 100. Ten per cent of learners scored less than 10 per cent; 10 per cent scored 77 per cent or higher (see also Table 5.3) Translated

Write down your thoughts about football violence. Write at least two paragraphs.

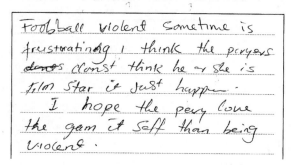

Figure 5.1 Entry Level 2, non-ESOL learner

What do you think of *Go!* magazine?

Write one or two sentences.

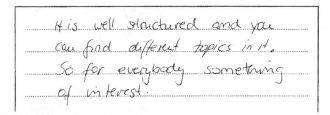

Figure 5.2 Entry Level 1, ESOL learner

Write down your thoughts about football violence. Write at least two paragraphs.

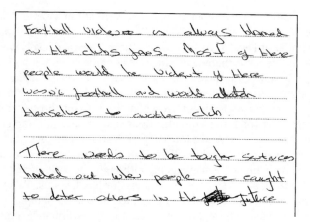

Figure 5.3 Level 2, non-ESOL learner

Table 5.2 Regression analysis of factors affecting initial reading score

	Coef.	Std. Err.	t	P>|t|
Female	8.46	2.01	4.21	0.000
Age	–0.07	0.08	–0.94	0.348
ESOL	–24.75	2.09	–11.84	0.000
Qualifications (base=none)				
Level 1 or 2	6.10	2.09	2.92	0.004
Level 3 or above	7.29	2.54	2.87	0.004
Quals missing	3.05	3.58	0.85	0.394
Sector (base = transport)				
Cleaning	–18.80	3.99	–4.71	0.000
Food	–15.78	2.80	–5.64	0.000
Health	–6.63	4.86	–1.36	0.173
Mixed	–7.66	3.06	–2.50	0.013
Occupation (base = routine manual)				
Managerial	9.87	3.99	2.47	0.014
Skilled	7.09	5.48	1.30	0.196
Personal service	–0.79	4.46	–0.18	0.859
Sales	15.64	4.31	3.63	0.000
Elementary occupation	3.67	3.34	1.10	0.273
Constant	60.57	4.33	13.98	0.000

Number of observations = 457

R-squared = 0.4007

into qualification levels, about 10 per cent were at Entry Level 2 or below; just over 30 per cent at Entry Level 3; 25 per cent at Level 2 or above, and the remainder at Level 1. As one would expect, average levels were lower for ESOL learners but there was a high level of dispersion in both groups.

Table 5.2 shows the factors associated with lower or higher reading scores before starting a literacy course. Predictably, a managerial or sales job was associated with higher scores at the time of the first test, even after controlling for formal qualifications; as we saw in Chapter 3, skill levels 'matter' over and above formal qualifications, and jobs that demand literacy use also reinforce skills. Formal qualifications were also, as usual, associated with higher achievement, although the size of the effect is actually quite small, even after controlling for ESOL status. This probably reflects the considerable number of ESOL learners in the sample: for them, qualifications were not a significant predictor of performance, presumably because time spent in the country was the critical factor. (Tables A.7 and

A.8 in the Appendix present the same analysis for ESOL and non-ESOL learners separately).

The impact of workplace learning on literacy skills

Overall, the results of the literacy tests indicate that there was a very modest improvement over time in the average level of literacy, as measured on *Go!* However, positive changes in performance were consistently significant *only among learners for whom English is a second language*. This was the case for all measurement points in the study. We did not find any significant improvements in the performance of native English speakers: changes in mean test scores, though positive, were never statistically significant. This held whether we were looking at the period between two adjacent testing occasions or the full period between initial and final test.

Table 5.3 shows mean test scores on each occasion, both for the sample as a whole and separately for ESOL and non-ESOL learners. While individual learners may have benefited, the conclusion must be that, for these learners as a whole, the courses, and the workplace initiative overall, were unsuccessful in increasing literacy skills.

What of the second language learners? Here, we did find some significant improvements – not enormous, but evidence of genuinely improved performance between first and second, and second and third testing occasions. The average score rose by six percentage points (which might be the difference between incorrect, and correct, answers to two comprehension questions relating to a short piece of prose. It is also well under a quarter of the 'band' of marks covering a given literacy level such as Entry 3, or Level 1. In other words, the increase, though real, was also quite modest).

The difference between first and second language learners may mean that the latter progress differently and faster. However, it is also possible that their greater improvement (from a lower average base) may simply reflect more time spent in an English-speaking country. For that reason, gains cannot be confidently attributed to the effects of the course for this group.

Reading levels

As well as looking at changes in mean point scores, we also looked at performance in terms of the government's reading levels. We were particularly interested to know whether individuals with different starting levels of skill were more or less likely to move across thresholds, and into a higher reading 'level'.

The relevant analysis group was those learners for whom we had full data on all three testing occasions. Sixty-nine per cent of this sub-sample were at Level 1 or above when they started their course, 8 per cent at

Table 5.3 Average reading scores (standardized) at start of course, first and second follow–ups
(a) All available data

	No. of cases	Mean	Std Dev
Time 1	532	47.1	22.9
Time 2	277	49.2	23.0
Time 3	200	52.3	23.9

Difference between T1 and T2: (means) non-significant

Difference between T2 and T3: (means) non-significant

(b) Individuals with full reading score data at T1, T2 and T3

	No. of cases	Mean	Std Dev
Time 1	181	48.3	22.2
Time 2	181	49.0	22.7
Time 3	181	51.3	24.0

Difference between T1 and T2: non-significant

Difference between T2 and T3: significant @ 10% level (paired sample t-test)

(c) All ESOL cases

	No. of cases	Mean	Std Dev
Time 1	225	35.4	21.2
Time 2	111	36.7	19.9
Time 3	75	41.4	21.5

Differences between overall means: non-significant

For paired sample (using cases with full data):
 difference between T1 and T2 significant at 5% level
 difference between T2 and T3 significant at 5% level

(d) All non–ESOL cases

	No. of cases	Mean	Std Dev
Time 1	307	55.7	20.1
Time 2	166	57.5	21.1
Time 3	125	58.9	23.0

No significant differences, either for comparison of overall means or using paired sample t-test (for cases with full data)

Table 5.4 Changes in levels, time 1 to time 3
Sample: those with reading data on all three occasions

Reading level at T1	Reading level at T3					
	Below E2	E2	E3	L1	L2 or above	All
Below E2	4	1	2	0	0	7
E2	2	1	3	0	0	6
E3	2	3	19	19	0	43
L1	0	0	13	48	24	85
L2 or above	0	1	1	8	31	41
All	8	6	38	75	55	182

Entry 1 or 2, and the remainder at Entry Level 3. Over time there was little change in the proportions at Entry Level 2 or below Entry Level 2, but some modest improvement in those in the highest levels. Movement across thresholds was sufficient for an increase in the proportion at Level 1 or higher from 69 per cent at Time 1 to 71 per cent by Time 3.

Changes between Time 1 and Time 3 are summarized in the cross-tabulations of the data in Table 5.4, and the data are further simplified in Table 5.5 which just reports on whether learners improved their level, fell back into lower levels or remained at the same level. Most learners remained at the same level, just over a quarter moved up to a higher level while one in six dropped to a lower level.

As noted above, the small gains in mean performance for English speakers were non-significant, and changes were also non-significant for the total sample. This, plus the numbers of people dropping a reading level led us to question whether we were faced with substantial unreliability in individual performance, and scores. Initial reading score was a strong predictor of *absolute* proficiency on the first and second re-tests (with a correlation of 0.75 between tests 1 and 2, and between 1 and 3). However, we found that there was also a high level of regression to the mean: poor performers tended to make the most progress, from one occasion to the next, and vice versa. This suggests that multiple 'within-learner' (rather

Table 5.5 Summary of change in reading level, from time 1 to time 3
Sample: those with reading data on all three occasions

	N	%
Increased level	49	26.9
Stayed in same level	103	56.6
Decreased level	30	16.5
All	182	100

than test-related) factors may indeed be creating unreliability in individual scores (as opposed to sample averages).

Since learners were tested on three occasions, for participants with full data it was possible to check whether they made consistent progress from occasion to occasion or whether scores fluctuated. Here the following definitions were adopted:

- *Consistently improved:* standardized scores increased from Time 1 to Time 2, and increased again from Time 2 to Time 3.
- *Consistently worse:* standardized scores fell from Time 1 to Time 2, and fell again from Time 2 to Time 3.
- *Stable:* standardized scores increased from Time 1 to Time 2, and fell from Time 2 to Time 3, or *vice versa*, and the (absolute) change in score was less than 10 points on each occasion.
- *Inconsistent:* standardized scores increased from Time 1 to Time 2, and fell from Time 2 to Time 3, or *vice versa*, and the (absolute) change in score was greater than 10 points but less than 20 points on one or both occasions.
- *Unstable:* standardized scores increased from Time 1 to Time 2, and fell from Time 2 to Time 3, or *vice versa*, and the (absolute) change in score was greater than 20 points on one or both occasions.

Figures 5.4 and 5.5 summarize the results and convey the differences between the various categories. Note that, in pilot testing by NFER, 10 points was one standard deviation of the test score so, on that basis, a shift of up to 10 points equates to up to one standard deviation.

With these definitions it was apparent that some 19 per cent of learners made consistent improvements i.e. that their score was higher one year after the course than it had been at the start of the course, and that they went on improving in the subsequent 18 months (see Table 5.6). Approximately 11.5 per cent of learners got consistently worse. Nearly 70 per cent of learners saw their scores fluctuate – either an increase followed by a decrease or vice versa – and in half of all cases with data, 91 cases from 182, the changes were large enough for them to be categorized as inconsistent or unstable. Overall, therefore, few learners were making steady and continuing progress.

Correlates of progress

While, overall, progress was not great, there were, as we have seen, a number of learners who improved considerably; more generally, just as the sample started off with very diverse patterns of attainment, so, too, there was great diversity in their literacy attainment patterns over the following two years. We therefore looked for explanatory factors which might also provide pointers to future policy.

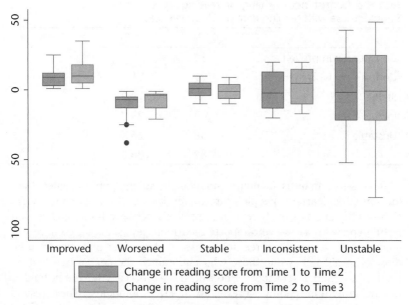

Figure 5.4 Box plot of change in reading score, by group

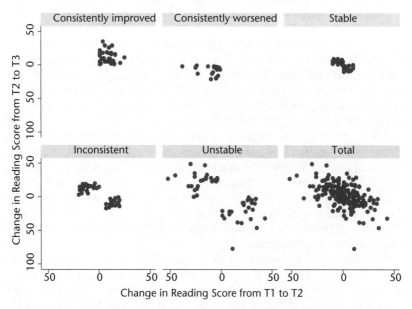

Figure 5.5 Scatter plot of change in reading score, by group

Table 5.6 Consistency of change in reading score over time
Sample: those with reading data on all three occasions

	N	%
Consistently improved	35	19.2
Consistently worsened	21	11.5
Stable	35	19.2
Inconsistent	43	23.7
Unstable	48	26.4
	182	100.0

Regression analysis (Jenkins and Wolf in submission) revealed that, for non-ESOL learners, people's direct experiences with their course were significantly and positively related to progress between initial and second testing ($p < 0.1$). Those who reported learning new skills on their course tended to have growth in reading scores of about four points more than those who did not; while those who maintained the course had had no particular benefits, and those who said it was too easy for them, tended to have growth in reading scores of six or seven points less. These results were only significant at the 10 per cent level but the size of the effects appear quite substantial.

The results suggest that there may have been large variations between learners in whether provision was appropriate to their needs. Although (see Chapter 4) courses were highly similar in length and general orientation, these differences may reflect differences in content or tuition quality; we have not identified any effects associated with site, but most had very few learners. Finally, and again only for non-ESOL learners, the data indicate that learners improved significantly more in programmes which led to a qualification (Jenkins and Wolf in submission).

These findings lend support to our more general hypothesis, that the very limited gains registered by learners reflect, above all, the short length of the courses, and the frequent mismatch with learners' skills and concerns that derived from the top-down, one-size-fits-all approach which funding and delivery patterns created in many cases. As discussed earlier, we know that adults need many hours of tuition if they are to improve their skills substantially – as, indeed, one might expect given the length of time children spend in school.

It is important to emphasize that *none of the relationships described above hold for the sub-group of ESOL learners*. This suggests that their much larger average gains are indeed largely attributable to experiences after and outside formal tuition, which mask any effects of quality and appropriateness of provision.

The findings for both ESOL and non-ESOL groups also highlight the importance, for adult learning, of opportunities to use, reinforce and improve on literacy skills at work; something which has been underscored by a growing body of recent work on informal workplace learning (see Chapter 8 and Evans *et al.* 2006) It seems very likely that formal literacy tuition will be effective to the degree that it is reinforced and extended by on-job experiences. We were unable to look directly at this relationship for whole sample as a whole. However, we did look at it indirectly, by examining the impact of job change.

In the period between the first and last test, just under a quarter of the sample changed the nature of their jobs (as opposed to simply changing employer). Of course, such changes could involve a reduction in the degree to which the workplace demanded and reinforced literacy skills, possibly leading over time to an erosion of skills: so any effects we found were likely to be underestimates of the relationship's strength. But we know from the in-depth sub-sample, and from open-ended questions to the sample as a whole, that for a good number of people, change involved additional tasks and new responsibilities.

The results are shown in Table 5.7. The relationship between this variable and change in reading score was positive: learners whose jobs changed showed a five or six point larger improvement in reading scores between first and second tests. This is consistent with learners utilizing and improving their literacy skills at work.

This finding was strongly supported by the qualitative research, as discussed in more detail in the following chapter. Among learners interviewed in depth, those who had made the greatest literacy gains between the first and second assessment had generally continued to develop their literacy skills in the workplace and beyond. Other learners who had neither been promoted, nor benefited from structural changes in the organization, and whose working routines still entailed minimal uses of literacy made either no progress or negligible gains (Evans and Waite 2008).

Modest progress in the overall sample is consistent with generally light use of literacy skills in the workplace. While course participation could and did affect learning trajectories, it is workplace experiences, not limited classroom exposure, which appeared to embed and boost literacy skills most powerfully. Whether or not the courses also contributed to total skill growth among 'job changers' is impossible to determine from our data.

Course participation, learning trajectories and life-course impact

Although course participation had little effect on most participants' reading skills, they were not, themselves, dissatisfied with their experiences. On the contrary, on a scale from 1 to 7, the average and modal ratings for the course were 6; only 1 in 10 gave theirs a rating below 5 (see Methodological Appendix Table A.13).

Table 5.7 Relationship between growth in reading score (between first and second interview) and job change

(a) All cases	Coef.	Std. Err.	t	P>|t|
Time 2 reading score	−0.38	0.05	−6.98	0.000
Version A	−12.34	2.66	−4.64	0.000
Job change	5.31	2.57	2.07	0.040
Constant	24.12	3.30	7.31	0.000

Number of observations = 182, R-squared = 0.2292

(b) non-ESOL cases	Coef.	Std. Err.	t	P>|t|
Time 2 reading score	−0.39	0.07	−5.86	0.000
Version A	−17.04	3.93	−4.33	0.000
Job change	6.08	3.08	1.98	0.050
Constant	26.16	4.34	6.03	0.000

Number of observations = 115, R-squared = 0.2654

(c) ESOL cases	Coef.	Std. Err.	t	P>|t|
Time 2 reading score	−0.41	0.10	−3.89	0.000
Version A	−7.79	3.92	−1.99	0.051
Job change	4.97	4.69	1.06	0.293
Constant	22.32	5.27	4.23	0.000

Number of observations = 67, R-squared = 0.2060

The *Go!* Reading tests have two overlapping question papers, one intended for very weak readers and one for stronger readers. Receiving version A of the test means that a learner is a very weak reader. (Readers were allocated tests on the basis of tutors' own pre-testing. In the event that this had not occurred, a short screening test was used.)

This is not as strange as it might appear, and underscores a major disjunction between policy-makers' expectations and those of learners themselves (or indeed employers: see Chapter 7). Policy-makers, as we have seen, were convinced that basic skill 'gaps' were having a major negative impact on firms' productivity and individuals' earnings, and that employees could improve their skills rapidly and expect significant economic gains in consequence. The evidence for this position was always slight (see Chapter 3): it was also not a view shared by learners themselves. They wanted to learn new skills – but had little expectation that this would have a major impact on their work circumstances.

At first interview, learners were presented with a list of possible benefits from their course, and asked to rank them. They ranked increased earnings last; promotion-related outcomes were only slightly more highly rated. At second interview, they were asked to identify important outcomes from the course – only 2 per cent cited increased earnings (see Appendix Table A.17). But with respect to 'learning new skills', which had been the most important desired outcome at first interview, the number stating they had indeed secured this was actually higher than had been the case beforehand. Figure 5.6 displays the outcomes which were more or less highly rated, before and after course participation, and underscores the relative unimportance of direct job benefits.

This does not, however, mean that the course had no impact at all. Participation, in a significant number of cases, appears to have changed their personal learning trajectories – which is consistent with what people told us about wanting to 'use their brains' and learn something new (see Chapters 6 and 8). The majority of participants had not recently been

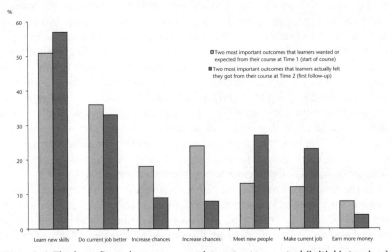

Figure 5.6 The benefits to learners: most important expected (initial interview) and actual (first follow-up) benefits from the course

involved in formal learning outside the workplace; and while two thirds had received some formal training in the previous five years, it was largely short-term, workplace training of a highly specific kind.

We know, from previous research (see e.g. Jenkins *et al.* 2003) that engagement in formal adult learning is the strongest single predictor of future engagement; but it is always hard to know whether this is just because some people 'like' learning, or whether engaging in it creates an appetite for more. And previous studies have looked largely at data relating to formal classes in further and adult education, rather than in the workplace.

This study allowed us to examine whether or not involvement changes trajectories; and at both follow-up interviews, we obtained detailed information on whether respondents had undertaken any further learning since the end of their course. Table 5.8 summarizes post-course participation; but was any of this learning a *result* of the course? Put differently, were participants more likely to continue learning once they had returned to it, and than they would have been in its absence?

To estimate whether or not participants had increased their propensity to participate in learning, we created a comparison group from the LFS (Labour Force Survey), matched on occupation and age. This was used to assess the impact of attending the literacy course on subsequent participation in education and training. As Table 5.8 shows, at first follow-up, a year after course completion, participation in further education and training was significantly higher than for the matched LFS samples. In other words, it appears that participation in the course did increase the sample's propensity to engage in further learning.

We were able to test this proposition further because of the 'natural experiment' alluded to above. A sub-group of our sample were 'involuntary' learners, who were effectively obliged to take a course, whereas the majority were motivated volunteers. Involuntary learners were significantly less likely than voluntary learners to engage in follow-up education or training; their exclusion from the sample makes the higher participation rate (compared with the LFS base) highly significant ($p=.003$) (Table 5.8) The results at the last follow-up were broadly similar, although the significance levels of differences between the sample of learners and the matched LFS sample were lower. The LFS data did not give a good match for ESOL learners and comparisons there must be treated very cautiously. Note also that a negligible proportion of ESOL learners were in the involuntary category.

In the final questionnaire, we also collected other learning-related data. Respondents were asked about their attitudes towards education and 75 per cent of participants stated that they felt differently about education after their course, in uniformly positive ways. Many respondents felt more confident about engaging in learning.

The reading habits of learners also showed substantial changes two or more years after completing the literacy course. About a third reported

Table 5.8 Participation in training (%)
Learner sample in year following completion of basic skills course compared with matched Labour Force Survey sample* for the same period

	Learner sample		LFS sample
	All	Omitting involuntary learners	
Non-ESOL	44.5	51.9	37.5
ESOL	45.8	n/a	33.7

Differences are significant at 10% level for the full non–ESOL sample. Omitting involuntary learners, p = 0.003 (for non-ESOL learners). For ESOL learners p = 0.041. The number of ESOL learners who were involuntary was negligible.

* Cases with complete data only.
Note: The LFS sample of ESOL respondents almost certainly under-represents (in total and on specific characteristics) the total ESOL working population and these comparisons should be treated with caution.

Table 5.9 Participation in training (%)
Learner sample participation during the period between first and second follow-up (one to two years after completion of basic skills course) compared with matched Labour Force Survey sample*

	Learner sample		LFS sample
	All	Omitting involuntary learners	
Non-ESOL	34.9	44.3	37.5
ESOL	34.2	n/a	33.7

* Cases with complete data only.

Differences for non–ESOL participants with involuntary learners excluded, and LFS estimates, significant at 10% level. Other differences not significant.

that they were reading newspapers more and around a quarter were reading books or magazines more (see Table A.15 in the Methodological Appendix). Once again, a comparison of 'voluntary' and 'involuntary' learners is instructive, and strongly confirms the importance of motivation. Overall, at final interview, just over half the sample reported reading more of at least one category of material, but this was significantly less true for 'involuntary' than for voluntary learners.

Finally, Table 5.10 summarizes respondents' preferred areas for future learning. Once again, what is striking is their interest in general and developmental learning, rather than in supposedly 'vocational' skills which will lead (supposedly) to greater productivity and greater earnings.

Table 5.10 What learners would like to learn if able to choose completely freely (answers at final interview)

	%
'Nothing in particular'	23
One or more specific answers given	77

Distribution of positive choices (some respondents gave more than one answer)

	N	%
ESOL classes	26	15
IT-related*	41	23
Specific vocational skills **	24	14
Driving lessons (car)	4	2
General education	80	46
(of which, answers from non-ESOL learners relating to maths/English/writing)	(6)	(3)

* Answers ranged from 'Learn CAD', 'Learn a new programming language' to 'More advanced IT', 'Internet use'.

** e.g. plumbing, HGV licence, social work, NVQ Care.

Conclusion

One advantage of workplace-based courses is that they have the potential to draw in people who would be unlikely to attend formal college courses. The demographic profile of learners on Skills for Life college courses has been very heavily skewed towards young adults. Over two-thirds were aged 16 to 18, and a mere 8 per cent over the age of 45 (Metcalf and Meadows 2004). Workplace-based courses have redressed this balance to some extent, with a much more even spread of ages evident in our learner sample. Moreover, many of the learners in our sample had not done any learning in the recent past and very few of them might have been attracted to a basic skills course at an FE college. So workplace basic skills courses can reach people who are not normally involved in continuing education or training.

However, the results reported here underline the limitations of a top-down approach to course delivery, within a context of short-term contracts and high up-front costs. This has been discussed in previous chapters (see especially Chapter 4) and we return to it in detail in Chapter 7. In concrete terms, we find that learners' reading performance a year and two years after the course showed a very small average gain in performance; but that for native English speakers the improvement did not reach conventional statistical significance levels. The larger improvements were among ESOL

(English as a Second Language) learners. It is quite likely that this simply reflects longer time in an English-speaking environment.

On balance, there is little to suggest that, the Skills for Life courses had any substantial impact on skills. Given their nature, this is not really surprising. They were very short, and not necessarily well suited to learners' objectives and needs; although it is also true that most participants felt that they had gained something significant from them. Where gains in skill were found, they seemed as or more likely to be the result of 'extra-curricular' activity – in speaking English, or, for native speakers, of workplace opportunities to reinforce and increase skills.

More positively, we found that the experience of formal learning can have a lasting effect on participants' attitudes and activities. Most of the sample had done very little previous, formal post-school learning. Following their courses, there was a modest but statistically significant increase in the numbers undertaking additional formal learning (compared with what would have been expected from national data). Three quarters reported feeling differently about education, and over half reported reading more. There were major differences here between the large majority who participated voluntarily, and those who were obliged to study by their employers; and this gives us confidence that the reported changes are genuine, and that *voluntary* adult learning, in the workplace, can indeed change learning trajectories.

Taking our findings alongside the evaluation by Meadows and Metcalf of college-based courses (Chapter 3), the conclusion must be that the Skills for Life policy has not delivered any readily identifiable improvements in economic outcomes for individuals. It could be that, in the longer-term, increased participation in learning will feed through into enhanced economic outcomes for learners. However, the learners themselves – with a clear grasp of their own circumstances – appear far more interested in other outcomes and benefits from learning.

Chapter 6

Literacy learning, workplace practices and lives beyond work

This chapter examines literacy learning at work from the perspectives of the learner 'trajectories' involved, the workplace practices in which employees are engaged and specific life situations that arise in and out of work. It shows how 'social ecological' approaches lead us to consider the relationships between the processes of literacy learning, the features of the workplace environment that invite people (or act as impediments to them) to engage and learn, and the diversity of employee motivations. As such, it sheds light on the actual experiences of 'learning individuals' that underlie the summary results reported in Chapter 5.

The concept of learner 'trajectories', as exemplified by the research of Gorard *et al.* (e.g. 1998, 2001, Gorard and Rees 2002), represents an important attempt to theorize learning episodes through the life course by aggregating individual experiences into sets of typologies. Though representing an important theoretical advance in conceptualizing a diverse range of learning experiences and highlighting some key social parameters and constraints that shape these experiences, Gorard *et al.*'s approach allocates a minimal role for individual agency over the life-course.[1]

Models of adult learning that heavily emphasize structural determinants rooted in the individual's early life become increasingly challenging in light of a diversified, post-industrial economy, dramatic advances in communications technology, globalization and shifting patterns in family, class, ethnicity and gender. The 'reflexivity' of 'high' or 'post-modernity' outlined by theorists such Anthony Giddens (1990) and Ulrich Beck (1992) in which individuals, groups and social institutions routinely engage in self-examination and change in response to incoming flows of information signals the dangers of over-reliance on the 'predictive determinants' of an individual's life. As highlighted by Richard Edwards 'reflexivity signifies the increased options available ... Previously structured choices and opportunities are no longer held to be as determining of biographies as was previously the case' (Edwards 1998: 377). Indeed, in an attempt to predict the determinants of workplace learning, Gorard *et al.* (1999) noted the complexities involved in doing this, 'especially with regard to differing views of its role' (p.15).

We focus here in detail on the shifting 'learning orientations' of workplace learners, on personal agency, and the ways in which employees use what they have gained from participation in the literacy programme both in their day-to-day work practices and in their lives outside work.

Adults learning in and through the workplace

The concept of trajectories is typically used in work on transitions of young adults into the labour market, providing ideal type models of segmented routes that can be used to understand a variety of personal histories (see Evans and Heinz 1993, 1994). In adult life, routes diverge. Experiences diversify still further and new contingencies come into play (a process termed individualization by Beck (1992) and Giddens (1990)). In researching adults' life and work experiences, initial career trajectories take on historical significance.

Several different lenses can be brought to bear on the relationships between adult employees' individual behaviours in relation to learning and the opportunities afforded to them through their workplaces. The social processes that start, for young adults, with educational achievement, occupational 'choice' (however restricted), applying for and taking up jobs, and establishing independent personal and family lives continue in adult life as individuals strive to maintain employment, change jobs, balance work and family life and find personal fulfilment.

Behaviours in relation to learning are the patterns of activity that people adopt in relation to workplace programmes and varying degrees of opportunity to learn through new workplace and life experiences. These do not indicate enduring personal attributes such as personal flexibility or initiative, but reflect complex sets of motivations, beliefs and attitudes towards learning and their own capabilities. These we term 'orientations to learning'. These orientations can change according to specific experiences of success or failure, opportunities or setbacks at any stage. Orientations towards work and career are similar.

Participation in workplace basic skills programmes: the potential for workplace courses to respond to shifting attitudes to learning

As we saw in Chapters 4 and 5, the learners in the study were predominantly male, with an average age of just over 40. Fifty-four per cent of the learners had left full-time education with no qualifications; and many spoke English as a second language. Nearly all engagement was on a voluntary basis. The generic motivation of 'learning new skills' was the most commonly cited, and the courses surpassed expectations on this measure. Thirty-five per cent of learners cited the improvement of work performance as important and rather fewer listed this as an actual outcome. 'Promotion' barely figures.

The in-depth interviews corroborate and expand on this picture of learner motivation. They involved 66 learners, and highlight a whole range of factors behind engagement; from 'curiosity', to wanting to make up for missed earlier opportunities; from wanting specific help with job-relevant skills, to wider career aims; from a desire to help children with school work to wanting self-improvement and personal development (Evans *et al.* 2007). Overall, this suggests that, for the majority of learners, motivations for learning are not tied narrowly to expectations of advancement at work, or an aspirational career trajectory.

The in-depth interviews also explored the potential advantages and disadvantages of learning in the workplace rather than a college. Just under half the learners referred to the relative convenience and accessibility of workplace learning. For example, one ESOL learner at a bakery told us: 'workplace is better for us because we are here ... Because when you go home you've got to see children and you've got to cook and that ... and then people don't bother'. An employee of an engineering factory told us: 'I used to go to the college, I'd be working ... look at my watch, got to go in a minute, got to go in a minute'.

The benefit of learning with colleagues in a familiar setting was also frequently cited as an advantage of workplace learning (see also Chapter 4). A bus driver mentioned that he preferred undertaking a course in the workplace, 'because at least it's in familiar settings as opposed to I've got to find a room, J49 and Fred Bloggs will be in there waiting for you'. Similarly, an employee of an engineering company told us that he preferred 'learning at work because you're working with the people you're learning with ... they can have the chats, and ... conversations and ... discuss it amongst yourselves if they're struggling with anything'. Disadvantages of workplace learning that were mentioned included shift work interfering with the learning (in the bakery and care home); possible embarrassment with colleagues; preferences to separate studying from the workplace and preferences for longer courses.

Transitions through the life-course: perspectives from individual case-studies

From the 66 learners in the in-depth sample, 12 of these cases have been selected here to exemplify some of the diversity of individual experiences of literacy learning in and through the workplace (see Table 6.1). No claims are made about the representativeness of these cases, given the complexity of factors involved. However, our research design allows us, in the discussion which follows, to 'benchmark' all of our cases against the patterns and regularities found in the wider samples.

Table 6.1 The twelve selected cases

Arjan Singh Sandhu (b. 1950) moved to the UK at the age of 11 with his family who were originally farmers in the north of India. He worked on the track at Southern Transport Systems, supporting repairs, before taking on an administrative role at the same company. He undertook a GCSE in English at STS for two hours a week for one year. He is currently unemployed having taken voluntary severance from STS systems.

Bennie Thomas (b. 1945) was brought up in the West Indies and came to the UK when he was 19. Brought up by a mother who had no formal education and a father who showed no interest in his children's education and suffered from alcohol addiction, Bennie suffered from extreme educational disadvantage and left school at 15 with no qualifications. He has been working at STS for over 40 years and currently undertakes the role of ticket machine engineer. Bennie's supervisor encouraged him to undertake English and maths courses so as to cope with the increasing paperwork in the workplace. Bennie proceeded to embark on over 100 hours literacy and 50 hours numeracy courses over a three year period at one of the company's learning centres.

Bill Williams (b.1961) has been working at Coopers food processing factory (most recently as a seasoning technician) since leaving school. He was brought up by his mother who worked as a cook at a primary school and managed to gain a few lower-grade CSEs despite an indifferent school education. He has previously studied the Greek language at evening college in the local town, having visited Greece on holiday, but found it difficult to combine attendance on a formal course with work. Bill has completed Learndirect (online learning) literacy and numeracy courses at the company's learning centre.

Kathleen Croft (b. 1956) had a disrupted education as a result of arriving in the UK at the age of 7 from the West Indies. Until recently taking voluntary severance, she worked at Southern Transport Systems as a support manager. She undertook an English course at STS which culminated in her gaining a GCSE English B grade. She is currently combining looking after her children with undertaking a computer course and plans to return to work when her children are older.

Mary Gallagher (b. 1960) was brought up in Ghana where she received an elementary education before undertaking vocational training in embroidery. She moved to the UK with her husband and studied at an FE college for one year but had to leave the college when her son was born. She worked as a cleaner at Thorpton Local Authority where she was given the opportunity to undertake a communications and literacy course (paid outside working hours). She has subsequently become a care-worker at a psychiatric hospital where she has also completed an NVQ Level 2 in care work.

Melanie Taylor (b. 1968) has been working at Brightland Bakeries since she left school at the age of 16. She had previously studied sociology and criminology (both at Level 2) at a centre for lifelong learning. Melanie undertook Level 2 literacy and numeracy qualifications at the Brightland Bakeries learning centre. She was subsequently promoted to the position of hygiene coordinator and currently supervises approximately 20 people.

(continued)

Table 6.1 continued

Mike Philips (b. 1953) has been working at HLN Manufacturing (a large engineering company specializing in the manufacture of parts for cars) for the past 30 years, most recently as a forklift driver. He left school at 15 with no qualifications. He was one of eight learners who took part in a Skills for Life course that ran from May 2005 to July 2005, consisting of 90-minute sessions for ten weeks. The course was set up by three ULRs in the company (with the support of the management) who approached the local college. He has subsequently proceeded to undertake two computer courses at Level 1 and Level 2 at the company's new learning centre (established by the company's ULRs).

Mike Swan (b.1973) is a machine tool fitter at the Weapons Defence Establishment (WDE) where he has worked since leaving school at the age of 16. He took part in an ICT and English course consisting of one and half hour sessions over 22 weeks at the company's learning centre. He has subsequently been promoted to the role of works supervisory officer which entails increased responsibility and use of computers and has proceeded to undertake an ICT Level 2 course at work as well as computer programming NVQ Level 1 course at a nearby college.

Roger Taylor (b. 1954) works as a machine tool fitter at the Weapons Defence Establishment. He left school at 16 with a number of CSEs before undertaking an apprenticeship with his current employer. He took part in an ICT and English course consisting of one and a half hour sessions over 22 weeks at the company's learning centre. Since undertaking the course, Roger has continued to undertake the same duties at work. He plans to continue working at the WDE until retirement.

Tracy Beaumont (b. 1968) works on the shop floor of Coopers food factory as a quality assessor. Previous jobs include working as a machinist in a clothes factory and as care assistant in a psychiatric hospital. She left school at the age of 16 without any qualifications and has not previously engaged in adult education. Tracy has undertaken a variety of Learndirect literacy and numeracy courses at the company's learning centre.

Trevor Woodford (b. 1982) left school at 16 with no qualifications. He undertook a variety of casual jobs before becoming a caretaker at the London Borough of Thorpton where he embarked on a communications course for three hours a week over a five week period. He has subsequently taken on a more supervisory role as caretaker and plans to become a housing officer.

Victoria Appiah (b. 1950) works as a receptionist at Southern Transport Systems (STS). Victoria came to England from Ghana, where her education had been interrupted as a result of her parents' transient lifestyle. She has spent much of her adult life in England, bringing up her children as a single parent. Workplace courses at STS Systems allowed her to gain a GCSE in English followed by maths and ICT. She has subsequently undertaken a one year course in creative writing at a London college despite the difficulties of attending a college after work.

* All the individual and organizational names cited are pseudonyms.

Orientations to learning

The cases illustrate adults' complex sets of motivations, beliefs and attitudes towards learning, and towards their own capabilities. They show how these learning orientations are rooted in prior educational experiences. They also show how these orientations can shift over time, how they influence engagement with workplace activities and how they can be supported through learning opportunities offered in and through the workplace.

The influence of early educational experiences on learning orientations

Reflecting the broader sample, the majority of these selected individuals spoke about their early educational experience in largely negative terms. Victoria Appiah felt she had suffered from her parents' uprooted life style and her parents' lack of concern for her education, describing herself as her 'mum's handbag'. Although Arjan Singh Sandhu reveals that he enjoyed the experience of being at school, his education was severely disrupted by the process of moving from India to the UK at the age of 11. Mary Gallagher enjoyed her experience at school but regrets that she received only an elementary education in Ghana as a result of her parents' insistence that she undertake vocational training at an early age in response to economic pressures: 'I did like school, yes. But you know when you are young, everyone wants you to do this, do that, so I went to the wrong direction.'

By their own admission, Trevor Woodford, Mike Swan and Roger Taylor's education suffered from a lack of application at school. Trevor revealed that 'when I was a kid I was always the clown of the class'. Mike Swan and Roger Taylor look back with some regret: 'I didn't really try that hard, and it didn't really interest me ... I look back and think well I should have done a bit better really ... I know I could have' (Mike Swan).

Melanie Taylor felt that her confidence was adversely affected by the school environment, as did Tracy Beaumont: 'I think that's what puts me off going to college ... because I would love to go to college but I think that's what really puts me off'. The advantages of workplace learning in being accessible, convenient and (most importantly) less loaded with intimidating associations had been particularly important for Tracy.

Despite these mixed starting points, the learners spoke of a shifting attitude to learning over the life-course (Box 6.1).

Many of these adult workers perceived the value of education for their children. Bennie Thomas sought to encourage his six children (five of whom have now gone on to university and moved away from home) to take advantage of the educational opportunities that were denied to him: 'because I pushed them to make sure they get what I didn't get'. had this

---

Box 6.1   Shifting attitudes to learning over the life course

Bill Williams talked about the significance of a shifting attitude to learning:

> At school you have to go. I was only 16 when I left school. I'm 43 now. I just got older and dafter, some people say wiser ... you start to realize now that these things are worth teaching at school, you try to instil into your child they're not just teaching you these things to make life boring, they're teaching you because you need them in the future.

Kathleen Croft commented both on her alteration in attitude towards learning over time as well as the significance of generational changes: 'because my generation was different, my mum didn't believe in us doing homework, we were just there to cook and clean ...'. She is consequently keen to adopt a more involved approach with her own children (aged 8 and 11 in 2004).

---

edge of wanting to learn. But ... working and having children is another issue.'

Despite his indifferent school education, Mike Philips made a point of encouraging his own children to study seriously at school and they (and his wife) had subsequently gone on to study at university. Roger Taylor has similarly sought to ensure that his own children benefit from an extended education: 'So we've always encouraged our children to do well at school ... as a stepping stone to prove that you can do something and get a degree, it's something that you always have.'

The effect of workplace courses on learning orientations

The individuals' involvement in workplace courses had an important effect in consolidating and expanding these shifting learning trajectories. One aspect of this is a willingness to take on more educational challenges (see Box 6.2 and Box 6.3).

Melanie Taylor had already undertaken courses at adult colleges, but appreciated the workplace courses as a means of overcoming further the legacy of previous school experience:

> Doing the courses at work ... it sort of made you feel that going back to the classroom wasn't as daunting as you think it would be. Do you

Box 6.2   Aspirations to move on ...

For Mary Gallagher, the communications and literacy course at Thorpton council gave her the confidence to leave her job as a cleaner and embark on a new career as a care-worker in a psychiatric hospital:

> You know, I was working as a cleaner if it was not for the course ... I couldn't have done any better. But because of the course that helped me to take that ... 'I can do better' ... 'I go somewhere else'. Not the same as a cleaner all the time. That course pushed me to go for that.

The course was also important in giving her the confidence to embark on further learning in the form of a NVQ in care work at her current employer.

Both Mike Swan and Roger Taylor attended the ICT and English course at WDE. Mike Swan revealed that: 'it mainly gives more confidence to try and improve, try other courses as well, work and things like that.' He has proceeded to undertake an IT Level 2 course at the Weapons Defence Establishment and a computer programming NVQ Level 1 course at a nearby college. Roger Taylor was also encouraged to embark on further self-study: 'Yeah it's kicked you off really to think about moving on and doing a little bit more'.

Box 6.3   A 'critical understanding of the English language'

Arjan Singh Sandhu's participation in the GCSE English course at STS had bolstered his confidence through a more critical understanding of the English language.

> It gives you more confidence because you are aware of how words are put together, you are more aware of when you make a mistake ... It helped me a lot with confidence ... when I'm reading anything I can analyse it better ... You get more confidence because of the way of looking from different angles which I was taught on the course.

The course has encouraged him to embark on further learning; he has undertaken an ECDL course run by the local council and is hoping to undertake a course to study the French language. He regards the course at STS as laying an important foundations: 'you need English for everything ... English is the basis of everything.'

know what I mean? I suppose I thought they'd treat you like a child but they didn't. I didn't like school.

For Victoria Appiah, growth in self confidence was the most significant personal outcome. 'You know I wish I could describe it stronger than what I'm saying, it's like you've been caged and set free. That's how I feel.' Such a sentiment prompted Victoria to embark on a year-long creative writing course after the completion of the workplace courses at STS.

For Kathleen Croft the course had provided more 'impetus, to go further and do more, that's really made me feel right, you can do this and try and do something else … It's encouraged me to move on … even yesterday I bought a course book to see what else is out there, what else is available for me to study.'

Not everyone experienced big increases in confidence. Tracy Beaumont said her confidence was still low despite having completed the literacy Level 2 test. She felt that she struggled with reading, especially in public situations:

it's like if you go in a meeting and you read things I panic, I panic, you know what I mean, I'm really like conscious about it … because like, a lot of people take the mickey because you can't read, and now I'm really self conscious of it.

Tracy's case is an example both of the potential advantages of workplace learning (her fear of formal learning means that she would not have engaged with other forms of educational provision) as well as the limits that exist in addressing deep-seated anxieties in some individuals.

Orientation to careers and career development

In upholding the importance of literacy and numeracy skills for economic advancement, Skills for Life discourse assumes a particular career trajectory for those individuals who are involved in workplace programmes; that of enhanced performance at work and increased potential for promotion at work. Yet, our interviews with both managers (see Chapter 7) and learners suggest that participation is motivated, on an individual and organizational level, by a far wider range of factors than merely the wish to improve performance at work. Moreover, involvement in such courses does not, in the majority of cases, relate to what may be described as an 'aspirational' career trajectory.

Of the 12 learners selected above, three (Bill, Tracy and Mike) were motivated by factors that were entirely unrelated to the workplace. Tracy felt that there was little need for developing her literacy skills for her current job on the shop floor of the factory. Though she deals with

---

Box 6.4   Motivations unrelated to the workplace

Bill's main experience of literacy in the workplace is through recording faults in machinery. However, he feels that his literacy skills have not impeded him in the workplace since he can 'muddle through'. 'I only put flavour on crisps ... they give you the flash title 'seasoning technician' but all I do is put a bit of dust on some slices that I fry on a table.' Bill's main reason for signing up for the courses was that he was 'just curious ... I mean I left school with no qualifications to speak of, CSE things, which are probably in museums now ...'. The literacy courses have helped him with writing letters and have improved his capacity to help his child with homework but have not impacted substantially on the workplace. 'You have sheets to fill in every day, but there's very little writing involved, it doesn't matter if it's grammatically correct or not.' Bill is planning to stay with his current company in more or less the same job: 'I've only got 16 years to go until I'm 60 ... at my age and my qualifications I'm getting double the minimum wage, ... I'm relatively happy in what I do.'

---

graphs at work, 'I just get the computer to add them up for us'. She learnt how to use this technology at work without going on a formal course. Her participation in workplace courses is motivated by a wish to bolster her confidence which (as mentioned above) has been sorely bruised by negative educational experiences. Bill (see Box 6.4) also did not feel that developing literacy skills was relevant to his job.

Mike's motivation for doing the course was 'For general interest, general knowledge, and to improve myself. I think as long as you're stimulated by learning different things, seeing different things then you'll always stay active and your brain's always alert....'. He took great pleasure in his newly acquired computer skills which allowed him to book his holiday online. 'I still want to learn [another] language. It's arrogant of us to think that everybody should speak English, we should be able to communicate in their language also, you know, to be fair.'

For Victoria Appiah, Mary Gallagher, Mike Swan and Roger Taylor career-oriented considerations were significant but not always dominant. The experience of undertaking the English course gave Victoria a greater appreciation of reading and a love of writing. The courses boosted Victoria's confidence at both home and work, underlining the difficulty of making clear-cut distinctions between 'job-specific' and 'generic' outcomes and motivations for learning: 'you know you go to your work, or doing whatever you're doing, with your head up'.

Mary Gallagher regarded the communications and literacy course as having minimal relevance to her work as a cleaner at Thorpton Local Authority: 'It's got nothing to do with my work. We don't write ... just

> **Box 6.5   Developing wider language competences**
>
> Arjan Singh Sandhu was motivated primarily by learning for its own sake since he felt he was coping sufficiently with the literacy requirements for his job as an administrator at STS: 'I could have got by … It's a hobby.' The course also allowed Arjan to maintain closer ties with his colleagues, reflecting the potential of workplace courses to have important social capital effects:
>
> > It helps you get to know your colleagues better you see their personal side… When you are on the course you are working with colleagues, working with colleagues you can learn more about them at the same time as learning more about subject.
>
> Having taken voluntary severance, Arjan is considering studying the French language: 'there's a love hatred relationship with English and French so I wanted to… look through the French eyes what they think about the English people. I know through the English eyes what the English people think of them, so I wanted to think you know through the French eyes, just you know. I want do that.'
> However, Arjan maintains that the course may also have an important effect in facilitating any new jobs that he may undertake:
>
> > Nowadays you have to write all these essays for interviews for a job … In workplaces without English you can't achieve half the things you can with English. With English the future is unlimited.

when we are off sick some time, just fill in sick form that's all.' Rather, the course played an important role in allowing her to assist her son with his homework and prepare for her future career aspirations.

Mike Swan and Roger Taylor were motivated to undertake a course at WDE for a variety of job-specific and generic reasons. But whereas Mike Swan was promoted to works supervisory officer and offered the chance to undertake an NVQ Level 2 in ICT within the company, these opportunities were denied to Roger Taylor. 'We were waiting for something to happen and all of a sudden Mike's doing it and nobody else is … if that had been available I'd have gone and done Level 2 but it wasn't available.' Frustrated with the lack of opportunities for promotion within the workplace, Roger Taylor feels the literacy component of the course had little connection to his daily work practices. By contrast, Mike Swan, who initially attached little importance to literacy aspects of the course, now regards the literacy component as being important in paving the way for his new responsibilities in the workplace: 'I realize that it [the literacy component of the course] was quite an important part … before I wasn't really writing too much,

Box 6.6 Multifaceted learning

Kathleen Croft, having taken voluntary severance from her company, subsequently emphasized the value of knowledge and potential career benefits; though not necessarily in the short term. She is undertaking a computer course funded by the local council and is planning to stay at home, whilst also undertaking temporary jobs, in order to support her children. She is planning to embark eventually on a course in psychology:

> I've never stopped learning which I've said to the kids until you're buried you're still alive so do something, so you know, keep your brains ticking ... Now I've got this qualification behind me I feel more confident ... If anyone's pushing, questioning me 'have you got the qualification for this' or whatever, I could say well 'yes. I've got something to show that I've been through the wheels and I've done this'.

Bennie Thomas outlined an appreciation of learning for its own sake accompanied by job-specific considerations. The increasing 'textualization' of health and safety in the workplace has challenged his previous capacity to cope: 'everybody have to read and write or fill forms in which we never use to do before ... I was struggling a bit.' The course 'just came ten years too late but it helped a lot'. Though Bennie has subsequently taken early retirement (following back problems) he plans to maintain his educational interests. He set aside a room which he uses as a study for both himself and his 14 year old son:

> Now I'm preparing a room, I'm doing it up properly for ... my son and I to actually do our study there ... I've already told my son ... his name is Alex, I said this room will be Alex and Bennie room, it's true so all his work he will do there, his paper work, I will show him how to file it and everything ... so it (the course) helped me a lot you know.

Melanie Taylor was motivated by general interest, a wish to alleviate negative educational influences and an awareness that literacy and numeracy skills were important for advancement within the workplace. She was promoted after the course to the position of hygiene coordinator and currently supervises approximately 20 people, writes incident report forms, undertakes audits and uses email. She also uses maths in relation to meeting Key Performance Indicators (KPIs): 'it's just like adding up how many hours in the day you've worked, how many trays you've produced, and what's your average trays per minute per hour and like, the percentage of your down time and the labour.' Melanie's participation in workplace courses had helped her to undertake public presentations: 'I can stand up in front of a load of people and talk or read or something and I could never have done that a long time ago.'

Table 6.2 Future plans at time of second interview

Future plans	Frequency	Percentage
Same job at same company	127	48.1
Promotion in same company	46	17.4
Similar job at different company	17	6.4
Different job at different company	44	16.7
Retired	13	4.9
Full–time education	2	.8
Other	15	5.7
Total	264	100.0

and now obviously I use it a lot more, do more handwriting as well as on the computer.'

Trevor Woodford experienced substantial job-specific outcomes from his workplace course, which had improved his capacities to fill in reports about accidents or incidents of graffiti on the estate. He regarded the course as being useful in preparing him for the next stage of his career as an estate officer which would entail more office administration and contact with contractors

More generally, few of our respondents saw their futures in terms of steady progress at work as a result of better literacy-related performance. At the second sweep of data collection, we asked learners: 'In terms of your working life, where do you see yourself in two to three years from now if things go according to plan?' As shown in Table 6.2, only 17 per cent anticipated promotion within the same company, and well over a quarter expected to leave their current workplace.

Changing learning orientations

The longitudinal nature of the study allows us to track the working lives of those who are exhibiting changing learning orientations. While we cannot generalize on the basis of relatively few cases, our cases were selected carefully to provide varied prior experiences and current work position. This, along with step-by-step analysis of interviews, enables us to form a coherent picture of how these adults' orientations to learning changed through workplace engagements, how they are acting to realize their goals, and what happens when external factors such as redundancy intervene. Once again, these cases can be benchmarked against the larger samples.

Distinctions can be drawn between those for whom changes in learning orientation are seen as specific to current work and career goals, and those for whom they must be related to wider personal development terms.

Turning to the career behaviours of the wider sample of employees engaged in the workplace basic skills programmes, these can be categorized as:

- aspirational – seeking skills development and wider experiences;
- content with status quo at work (often associated with family and other out of work priorities);
- struggling to overcome barriers in day-to-day work.

In these terms, Trevor Woodford, Melanie Taylor, Mike Swan, Arjan Singh Sandhu, Mary Gallagher, Kathleen Croft and Roger Taylor can be described as 'aspirational'. These individuals revealed a commitment to skills development and self-improvement that incorporates (to differing degrees) a commitment to advancement within the workplace. Victoria Appiah, Bill Williams and Mike Philips can be described as being 'content with status quo'. Bill's mockery of his job title (seasoning technician) together with his perspective on retirement betrays a career disposition in which priorities are invested heavily in life outside work. And Tracy Beaumont and Bennie Thomas may be described as 'struggling to overcome barriers'. Bennie's struggles are related directly to poor literacy and numeracy skills which have been increasingly exposed as a result of the greater use of report-writing in the workplace.

The actual career events that can potentially follow engagement in learning can also be categorized, building on Evans and Heinz (1993, 1994) typology, as:

- progressive (promotion, planned move to a better job);
- upwards drift (gradual enhancement of work, overcoming difficulties, increased responsibilities);
- downwards drift;
- stagnation;
- interruption.

Trevor Woodford, Melanie Taylor, Mike Swan and Mary Gallagher's career events in the period after their participation on the workplace course may be described as 'progressive' in nature in so far as they have taken on more supervisory roles. Victoria's career events may be described in terms of 'upwards drift' since participation in workplace courses has bolstered her position at work and increased her confidence. Tracy Beaumont, Bill Williams, Mike Philips and Roger Taylor's career events fall into the category of 'stagnation'. Previous participation in workplace courses have assisted Kathleen Croft, Bennie Thomas and Arjan Singh Sandhu in their current phase of career 'interruption' (see Boxes 6.5 and 6.6).

Far from being propelled along the long term pre-determined learning trajectories proposed by Gorard et al. (1998), these cases have shown how adult workers can change orientations over time. This underlines the point that orientations are not manifestations of deep rooted personal characteristics but are shaped by learning and labour market experiences, both positive and negative. Furthermore, these changes are best understood not simply as outcomes of individual agency, nor of organized programmes, but as part of a social ecology of learning.[2]

There are affordances for (and impediments to) learning in all workplace environments, some more accessible and visible than others. Employees' intentions to act in particular ways in pursuit of their goals and interests make the affordances for learning more visible to them. In this case shifting orientations to learning, and efforts to compensate for early educational disadvantage, allowed the individuals described here to recognize and seize affordances for learning within the workplace.

The know-how associated with literacy practices such as report writing or finding better ways of expressing oneself, and the confidence of 'knowing that you can' often develop further as the person engages with the opportunity. For example, Trevor Woodford experienced a surge of confidence in response to his enhanced capacity to cope with writing letters and reports at work, which provided enhanced learning opportunities through increased exposure to these duties. The process of making the affordances for learning more visible itself can generate some employees' will to act. For example, Coopers' open learning centre has developed a wide range of learning opportunities (e.g. online courses and the loan of laptops) that can be flexibly incorporated into the employees' lives at work and home (see also Chapter 8). As orientations to learning shift, both the changing levels of know-how, and the confidence that comes from 'knowing that you can', stimulate action and the seeking out of affordances within and beyond the workplace in the form of further opportunities. Mike Philips' progression to a computer course, Victoria's involvement in a creative writing course and Tracy and Bill's participation in a large number of on-line courses at Coopers' learning centre, as well as Mary Gallagher, Mike Swan, Roger Taylor and Arjan Singh Sandhu's participation in further learning are examples of an increased yearning for learning that has grown out of initial participation in workplace courses.

The advantages of workplace learning in being more accessible, convenient and free from negative associations of formal learning, have been significant in engaging learners who have been failed by previous forms of provision. The poor experience of school described by such individuals as Tracy Beaumont and Melanie Taylor is mirrored by many other employees in our broader sample. There is often a greater proclivity for learning among older employees than in previous stages of their career. The timing of workplace courses is therefore key to their potential effectiveness in responding to shifting attitudes to learning on the part of the individual since leaving school.

In promoting literacy and numeracy skills, the Skills for Life strategy is driven by highly economic imperatives (see Chapter 1). Yet the motivations of employees, both when first engaging, and in subsequent changes over the life-course, are rarely focused exclusively on the development of job-specific skills. Half of our selected cases – Bill, Victoria, Tracy, Bennie, Mike and Arjan – have chosen not to follow a promotion-oriented career path. These differences in life, work and career priorities are broadly reflective of the larger sample.

'Use it or lose it': the significance of employing literacy skills in the workplace

The longitudinal dimension of the research has also allowed us to trace the impact of shifting organizational structures on the uses of literacy and numeracy at work. It is apparent that those employees whose literacy assessment scores have increased since engagement in the course are also people who have continued to use their literacy and numeracy skills whether at work or at home.

Those learners we interviewed in-depth who had made most literacy gains between the first and second literacy assessment[3] had generally continued to develop their skills in the workplace as well as beyond. The case described in Box 6.7 illustrates how strongly the development of such skills is related to their employment in practical work settings. This finding, which is entirely congruent with general learning theory, is further substantiated by the positive relationship between literacy improvement and 'job change' found in the wider sample. Table 6.3 shows the results of regressing job change on change in reading scores, controlling for score level and test form. 'Job change' here refers to taking on new responsibilities or additional tasks within an existing role as well as taking on a completely new role at work.

As discussed in Chapter 5, employees in general made modest or no literacy gains as a result of engaging in literacy courses. This finding is understandable in view of their relatively light exposure to employment of literacy and numeracy skills in the workplace. Those for whom English was not their first language ('ESOL') made larger, significant gains in their measured literacy. This, too, is consistent with the 'use it or lose it' principle, since these employees are on a rather different 'learning curve' from native English speakers. They experience challenge and opportunity in practising their developing English language skills in everyday activities in rather different ways. Those learners who made significant changes in their personal use of literacy could also strengthen their skills (see Box 6.8).

Box 6.7   Literacy skills at work – use them or lose them

In WDE – the Weapons Manufacturing Company, the learner whose level of literacy had improved most substantially in that organization had been promoted after the course and now actively used a wider range of literacy skills as part of a broader organizational shift towards the delegation of responsibility to lower level employees. Whereas during the Time 1 in-depth interview he attached little significance to the literacy component of the course, at the Time 2 in-depth interview he retrospectively valued his participation in the course in the light of his recent promotion.

Other learners we interviewed in this organization who had not benefited from these structural changes within the organization and had not been promoted and continued to engage in the same working routines (which entailed minimal use of literacy) made either no progress or negligible gains in their literacy scores. For example, Roger Taylor, who was doing the same type of job, continued to have minimal exposure to literacy practices and whose literacy score declined between Time 1 and Time 2 literary assessments reported the following:

I've never been particularly good at the English side of things. I feel like I'd like to improve it but I don't find it necessary in what I do. I don't do an awful lot of writing …

Table 6.3 Relationship between growth in reading score (between first and second interview) and job change

(a) All cases	Coef.	Std. Err.	t	P>|t|
Time 2 reading score	−.38	.05	−6.98	0.000
Version A*	−12.34	2.66	−4.64	0.000
Job change	5.31	2.57	2.07	0.040
Constant	24.12	3.30	7.31	0.000

Number of observations = 182, R^2 = 0.2292

*The *Go!* Reading tests have two overlapping question papers, one intended for very weak readers and one for stronger readers. Receiving version A of the test means that a learner is a very weak reader. (Readers were allocated tests on the basis of tutors' own pre-testing. In the event that this had not occurred, a short screening test was used.)
See Table 5.7 for fuller data.

> ## Box 6.8   Using new literacy skills in personal lives beyond work
>
> Victoria Appiah was asked whether and how she uses her newly developed literacy skills outside work:
>
> A: I'm more into reading. I want to, I want to you know and I've found reading enjoying, to be able to read, and I have the aid of finding words, if I don't know the meaning I'll go and look for it, so it has improved a lot.
>
> Interviewer: So what sorts of things do you like reading now, that you didn't read before?
>
> A: I read newspapers, and I pay particularly attention to the construction of the sentences and that sort of thig ...
>
> And I love to write, that is my *main issue,* share my experience with other people, even between friends you know.
>
> Interviewer: Have you changed your mind about anything, since, as a result of going on the course?
>
> A: Changed my mind means wanting to do more. You know wanting to do more.
>
> Victoria is engaged in voluntary work as a befriender:
>
> Interviewer: So these learning experiences that you've been through has it had any effect on that aspect of your life [counselling/befriending} or was that something you've always done and you've always felt the same way about?
>
> A: Oh this time I have confidence.
>
> Interviewer: The confidence comes through in that as well?
>
> A: Yes. You know I wish I could describe it stronger than what I'm saying, it's like you've been caged and set free. That's how I feel, so I think ...

Further insights into workplace learning and working practices

The majority of learners participating in in-depth interviews self-reported that they coped adequately with their existing literacy and numeracy skills in the workplace. Approximately one third mentioned that they struggled with aspects of literacy or numeracy in general (whether at work or home); with half of these revealing that poor literacy or numeracy skills had either adversely affected their work or prevented them from fulfilling career plans. These included three caretakers at a local authority who had encountered increasing use of report-writing in order to document instances of damage to property and two residential care-workers at an old people's home who had encountered increasing documentation in the workplace (mainly in the form of 'care plans' for the residents of the home). Among our case-studies, Tracy Beaumont, the quality assessor in a food processing company, admitted to poor spelling but felt that poor literacy skills were only exposed on training days when she would dread the experience of being asked to read material out loud. Similar anxieties beset Bennie Thomas, a ticket machine operator at STS, who struggled with reading and writing (and admitted that this had curbed his opportunities for promotion) but managed on a day to basis and only felt 'caught out' on training days.

ESOL[4] learners, for understandable reasons, tended to see a more direct link between participation in workplace learning and job-specific considerations but only two learners in our in-depth sample (an operative at Brightland Bakeries and an admin officer at STS) reported that their existing levels of English adversely affected their current job responsibilities. An instructor at the transport company STS felt that his career prospects had been impeded by severe dyslexia but had become adept at employing various 'avoidance strategies' in order to cope with his existing job.

Many learners commented that their capacity to cope with their existing literacy and numeracy skills reflected their relatively light exposure to literacy in the workplace (e.g. bus drivers who only occasionally had to fill in an incident report form). It is important to note that organizational contexts differ widely; whereas some jobs have been affected by increasing report-writing in response to auditing demands and increasing health and safety regulations as well as the 'levelling out' of management structures, there are also many jobs and organizational contexts which entail negligible use of literacy practices.

The introduction of new technologies (frequently cited in Skills for Life literature as necessitating higher level literacy and numeracy skills) can often pre-empt or circumvent employees' use of literacy and numeracy skills; as in the case of a worker at Coopers, another food processing company, who told us she no longer used maths at work because 'the computer does it all for me'.

Not only do our findings conflict with prevailing policy assumptions about the existence of large-scale literacy and numeracy skills deficiencies in the workplace; they also resonate with the results of Livingstone's (1999) large-scale surveys. They are indicative of the capacity of employees to 'make do' with their existing skills and competencies and develop these in response to the exigencies of the workplace, frequently taking advantage of 'informal' learning opportunities of different kinds. Such informal learning most frequently takes the following forms (Taylor and Evans 2009):

- observing 'knowledgeables';
- practising without supervision;
- searching independently for information;
- focused workplace discussions;
- mentoring and coaching.

Box 6.9 illustrates how this may occur in practice; and these dimensions of informal learning are also explored through case-studies in Chapter 8.

Box 6.9   Union Learning Representative supports skills use in work practices

In the case of HLN, the large West Midlands engineering company, the workplace literacy and numeracy enhancement programme was a grass-roots initiative on the part of Union Learning Representatives with the wider support of the company and local college. Though the company has undergone major organizational change, embracing new technology and implementing surveillance procedures which entails increased documentation, the vast majority of learners were coping adequately with their existing skills. The employees used numeracy (averages, working with diameters) without having formally acquired these skills on a course. Informal learning processes had equipped all the learners (with the exception of one employee who struggled with the metric system) with the necessary skills to undertake their work.

Trevor Stephens (a Union Learning Representative) described the significance of what he termed 'hands on learning' in which employees were shown how to use new technology and develop their skills whilst working:

> I think a lot of people though, probably a lot of people on the shop floor, they've been there for years and years, probably are very good mathematically although they haven't done it at school, but by using, through engineering and one thing and another they probably are quite good. We're sort of more advanced maths than sort of basic, sort of equations and working out surface areas and stuff like that but probably having to put it down on paper that's where they could struggle.

Although employees had to cope with an increasing volume of paperwork as a result of more stringent company surveillance procedures and production quotas, they reported that this was largely of the 'tick box' variety and did not challenge their existing literacy skills. Two of the learners who were interviewed in-depth made a point of expressing their appreciation of the course as a means of practising skills which they would otherwise not have the opportunity of developing in their everyday work.

Summary and conclusions

A 'social ecology' of learning in the field of adult basic skills leads us to consider the relationships between the affordances of the workplace (or those features of the workplace environment that invite people to engage and learn, or act as impediments to them) and the agency or intention to act of the individual employee, reflected in their diverse motivations.

These reflexive relationships, as epitomized by the cases considered in this chapter, illustrate the significance of workplace programmes in supporting shifts in adults' learning orientations. In avoiding an undue stress on the structural constraints on learning trajectories, a social ecological approach explores the interdependencies between individual action and the affordances and constraints of workplace environments. Companies that aim to expand and enrich job content in jobs at all levels are likely to find employees working to expand their capacities accordingly. However, those who send employees on 'basic skills' courses only to return them to a job and work environment that provides no opportunities for their use are likely to see the benefits of their investment eroded over time.

Although Gorard et al. (2001) acknowledge the lack of weight accorded to individual agency, and have sought to address such a weakness through their work on 'learner identities' (e.g. Gorard et al. 2001), they still cling to an overarching theoretical model in which individual choices fall within structural determinants that are predictable from the individual's early life.

These findings are also consistent with Evans and Heinz's (1994) findings on young adults' transitions, which showed that while trajectories and behaviours had structural foundations in gender and social class, young people could move out of their 'predicted' trajectory and this was dependent upon the interplay of transition behaviours with organizational structures and environmental influences.

Chapter 7

The organizational impact of literacy learning at work

Introduction

In this chapter we turn to looking specifically at the impact of workplace programmes on the host organization as a whole. As discussed in Chapters 1 and 3, one of the major justifications for targeting subsidies to workplaces is the argument that employers will tend to under-spend on relevant but 'general' training; and, conversely that additional training will therefore have a direct impact on productivity.

This impact may be direct, via the trained workers' own greater skills; and the focus of both government policy, and of prior research, has been on the direct impact of skill changes. However there may also, in theory, be additional and wider benefits. Untrained workers may become more skilled, as a result of working with those who have trained. In other words, learning may extend beyond those who attended formal courses to those with whom they work. Or, the introduction of training, and a training culture, may have an impact on the whole way an organization functions; on its 'social capital'. This, too, may have a major impact on productivity; and in our research we attempted to measure whether or not any changes in social capital were occurring.

Employers and 'market failure'

As we also discussed in Chapter 3, the underlying rationale for subsidizing workplace training derives from arguments about 'market failure' and the likelihood that employers will under-invest in general training. It is hard to think of anything more 'general' in applicability than basic skills, and especially literacy; and core human capital theory therefore suggests that employers will be unwilling to invest in paying for literacy classes as much as the potential benefits to them would justify. The theory does not, however, predict that there will be no such investment at all. On the contrary, if improving their employees' literacy would indeed have direct pay-offs, one would expect to find a substantial amount of employer expenditure – though a lot less than is optimal for the economy.

There is some evidence that sizeable numbers of employers are now making some provision for their workers to improve their basic skills where necessary. The 'Learning and Training at Work 2001' survey (Spilsbury 2002) asked a sample of over 3,000 employers in England which among a number of learning opportunities they offered to employees at the location. Among all workplaces with five or more employees some 59 per cent said that they offered at least one of the eight types of learning opportunity listed. Basic numeracy was offered by 11 per cent of employers and basic literacy by 10 per cent. (Learning in information technology (40 per cent) and working with others (37 per cent) were the forms of learning opportunity most commonly available).

Unfortunately, there are no further details in the Learning and Training at Work survey about how basic skills courses were delivered, or the number or type of employees who had taken advantage of the learning opportunities on offer. We also do not know how many of the employers who did offer courses did so with their own, or with government funds.

The government's motivation for funding workplace basic skills courses is, as we have seen (Chapter 1), overwhelmingly economic, especially in England. It has consistently emphasized the potential financial gains from raising employees' basic skills. The research evidence does, however, indicate that the literacy of semi and unskilled workers is not, in fact, a major issue for most employers, whether or not it should be (Chapter 3). A number of things follow.

First, one might reasonably hypothesize that employers who do engage in workplace basic skills provision will be drawn from the minority for whom serious 'skill gaps' exist; perhaps because of changes in workplace demands, involving increased requirements for literacy (including writing).

Second, one might expect that, having probably under-invested before, they will be very satisfied with the results of the schemes. This satisfaction will, of course, depend on the success of the schemes in improving workers' skills.

Third, if improvements are experienced by employers, and can plausibly be ascribed to Skills for Life provision, they should then be persuaded of the benefits of basic skills training and more willing to spend larger amounts of their own money than before. Subsidized Skills for Life provision should, in other words, provide exactly the sort of demonstration effect needed to increase employer understanding of, and demand for skills, in line with government intent (see e.g. Performance and Innovation Unit 2001). Skills Minister David Lammy, at the 2008 Skills for Life and Work conference (Lammy 2008), dangled before employers the 'unambiguous' benefits of participation, as exemplified by Ford in Dagenham – 'a 22 per cent reduction in energy consumption since the implementation of its Skills for Life strategy'. How could any manager resist paying to repeat and extend such outcomes?

Funding basic skills in the workforce

As noted earlier (and see also the Appendix) recruiting an adequate sample of workplace schemes proved harder than we had expected from either government documentation and reports on Skills for Life, or large companies' public announcements about their involvement with basic skills provision. Of the sample that we finally established, *every single employer with one single exception,*[1] was receiving substantial government funding, although there was considerable variation in the proportion of costs covered. Box 7.1 summarizes the funding sources used.

Box 7.1   Major funding streams supporting workplace basic skills provision

Learning and Skills Council support for 'Skills for Life'

In England, the Learning and Skills Council (LSC) pays 'providers' of courses largely on a fee-per-student basis. Its funds are capped and particular types of course, identified in a yearly grant letter from the Secretary of State, receive priority. Basic skills courses were extremely high priority in the period 2002–2007. They were among the most generously funded courses, and providers – colleges and private training companies – were encouraged to recruit widely (DfES 2003a).

Courses were duly offered to employers, by providers who were then paid by the LSC in exactly the same way as for classroom-based learners. In the majority of sites in our sample, the provider – typically a college – was receiving funds from the LSC on this basis.

Employer Training Pilots (ETPs)

Between 2002 and 2005, the Treasury financed 'Employer Training Pilots'. These were the forerunner of 'Train to Gain', which is now absorbing increasing proportions of the adult education and training budget. ETPs (like Train to Gain (T2G)) were intended to address the supposed 'market failure' in training which leads to under-investment by employers. Nationally, around 10 per cent of ETP learners were engaged in stand-alone basic skills courses (Hillage and Mitchell 2004: 61).

Both 'ETPs' and 'T2G' are designed to deliver formal qualifications in the workplace, primarily at 'Level 2'. Although in principle, money can be made available under T2G for courses that do not lead to formal qualifications, and are 'non-target-bearing' (sic), this is currently not common (Linford 2008); under ETPs it was more so.

Four of the study sites had basic skills provision funded through Employer Training Pilots.

European Social Fund

The European Social Fund channels money to eligible parts of the EU in order to improve employment opportunities, increase social and economic cohesion, and reduce differences in prosperity between different parts of the EU. In England, money is distributed through the Regional Development Agencies (RDAs) for a number of purposes that include, specifically, 'developing a skilled and adaptable workforce'. One site was receiving courses funded by the European Social Fund, via a contract between the local RDA and a local college.

Scottish Adult Literacy and Numeracy Strategy

In Scotland, local authorities receive block grants under the strategy, and have a major degree of control over their own priorities. Two sites in the study were funded through local authorities in this way. In one, the grant was to a major public sector organization, which then ran in-house courses; the other was to a not-for-profit organization which then worked with local WEA tutors and a range of companies.

Learndirect

Learndirect (run by UfI, originally the 'University for Industry') provides courses which are entirely IT-based, and can be accessed on a drop-in basis by registered learners. While most of these are in colleges, major efforts were made to encourage companies to house centres. Two companies in our sample had Learndirect centres.

Fifty-two of the 53 establishments studied (so all, with that one exception) had the full cost of the tuition covered: that is, they did not make direct payments to the provider of the instruction. Some also received direct payments to underwrite some time off work for learners. Some either matched that with their own funds or fully funded some time off work (although these were a small minority). Some put a good deal of time into recruitment and support of learners, and/or used their own funds to create a dedicated learning centre. Others did not.

In addition to this direct funding for tuition, there were two important sources of additional support for workplace basic skills.

Union Learning Fund

The Union Learning Fund was established in 1998 in order to encourage the take up of learning in the workplace. Grants to unions through the Fund pay for the training of Union Learning Representatives (ULRs), and also support full-time field officers who can help set up and organize workplace learning. (Courses themselves can then be funded in the normal way). Many of the sites in our sample, 19 in all, had active ULRs, who persuaded and encouraged managers to approach providers and sponsor courses, and some sites were involved in special projects with full-time staff.

Adult Basic Skills Strategy Unit (DfES)

From 2002, the Skills for Life strategy was promoted by a special unit within the DfES. Developing basic skills in the workplace was a major theme; for example, the Workplace Basic Skills Network, based at Lancaster University, was funded to provide specialist courses and support for tutors and trainers teaching in the workplace. Funds were also provided for special demonstration projects. Two of our sites were involved in such a project, organized through the Basic Skills Agency.

Employer motivations

In discussing why employers might have a strong motive for supporting basic skills provision, we noted the widespread belief that the 'knowledge society' was changing and increasing literacy demands at work. Participants, we suggested, were likely to be drawn from among employers where there had been changes in the skill demands of the enterprise; and who were experiencing serious skill gaps.

Our results indicate no such thing. Only a small minority of managers reported any significant changes in workplace literacy requirements. More generally, *the motivation of the employers in our sample was overwhelmingly non-economic.*

Figure 7.1 shows the relevant questions which we asked managers at the first interview.

In their responses,

- managers, on average, selected seven of the ten possibilities as relevant in their case;
- in only half the cases was the option 'job-specific skills' chosen at all;
- only three managers – out of 53 sites – selected job-specific skills as their single most important motivation.

The absence of economic motivation is underscored by the content of the courses offered. We had expected workplaces to ask for and receive

Q29a Can you please look at this list and tell us which of these outcomes you think your company is hoping to achieve through this course/training programme? Please select all that apply. *PLEASE PROMPT FOR ANY OTHER ANSWERS. SHOW CARD.*

1. Improve job-specific skills of staff   [ ]
2. Improve 'soft' skills of staff (e.g. team-working, communication)   [ ]
3. Offer general development to staff   [ ]
4. Increase staff morale   [ ]
5. Reduce number of errors at the workplace   [ ]
6. Reduce absenteeism   [ ]
7. Reduce staff turnover   [ ]
8. Improve health and safety   [ ]
9. Increase staff confidence   [ ]
10. Help staff to be receptive to change   [ ]
11. Other (please specify)   [ ]

_____

_____

_____

Q30a Which of the above would you say is the most important and why?

_____

_____

_____

_____

_____

Figure 7.1 Questions used to determine employers' motives for sponsoring basic skills classes

specifically tailored material, designed to improve job skills: only one did so. In three sites, the courses were Learndirect, so pre-programmed. In 26 cases the content of the learning was entirely decided by the provider. In the remaining 23, content was determined by combinations of the provider with management and/or unions; but the large majority reported that it was 'mostly' the provider who decided.

Since the courses were offered free to learners, this might make economic issues irrelevant (though that is hardly the policy intent). However, in a number of cases, employers underwrote participation in paid working time. All sites incurred organizational costs, not least in negotiations with line managers over shifts; many provided equipment and furnished teaching space. The lack of interest in direct economic pay-offs is therefore striking.

In the case of ESOL employees, there was, it is true, interest in improved communication, though it was rarely seen as central to job performance. But where employees were English-speaking, far and away the most important motivation was to offer general development as a way of showing that employees were valued. A common theme was put succinctly by one manager: 'It's a crap job. This means we can offer them something.'

As discussed elsewhere (Wolf et al. in press), employees also participated largely for reasons which had nothing to do with their current jobs or work plans. These findings are quite at odds with the analysis underlying government policy, which assumes that employers and employees alike are economically motivated. It is, however, consistent with recent findings from an American study of workplace literacy, where researchers also expected that employers and employees would be financially motivated, and materials contextualized to serve current job demands. In fact, the opposite turned out to be the case (Hollenbeck and Timmeney 2008).

Of the three exceptions to the general rule in our study – the managers who wanted job-specific skills – two were from the care sector. This sector is heavily regulated and all care facilities have to ensure that a high proportion of their staff are qualified to NVQ2.[2] Since NVQs require the completion of substantial document-based portfolios, basic skills assistance was welcomed for employees who might have problems with NVQ evidence completion. The third employer was a large public sector organization which was primarily involved in NVQ training, using ETP funds, with basic skills provided as an add-on.

Organizational outcomes A: employer satisfaction and responses

Two years after the courses, we re-contacted the host enterprises in order to find out what impact the tuition had on participants, and the wider workplace.

As discussed in Chapter 5, learners had been highly positive about the courses. On a scale from 1 (lowest) to 7 (highest), 40 per cent gave a

	Number	%
'A little' successful	5	10
Moderately successful	5	10
Very successful	11	23
Manager currently in post knows nothing of the course and/or is unable to provide any feedback on its effects	21	43
Site no longer exists because of reorganisation or total closure of company	7	14

Note: Four sites were excluded from the analysis because they involved dedicated learning centres within the organiser, where the manager involved was also organising and running the training rather than forming part of the management team of the enterprise itself.

Figure 7.2 Employers' feedback on courses, two years later

grade of 7, 72 per cent one of 6 or 7, and only 12 per cent less than 5. Nonetheless, the measurable impact on them had been very modest. What about the employers? In every interview, we asked for a general evaluation, and then both the specific ways in which the course had produced good outcomes, and for concrete examples. Figure 7.2 summarizes the general evaluations given.

We return below to the implications of the last two rows (showing that in *well over half the cases* it was impossible to ascertain what the impact or perceived impact on the enterprise had been). What of the feedback provided in the other cases?

Eleven (or just under a quarter) judged the course to have been very successful. In five cases, the improvement in the communication skills, and especially the verbal skills, of ESOL learners was the main valued outcome. In the other six sites, learners were native speakers, and two offered individual stories of individuals who had progressed to further learning. In four, there was a general conviction that it had improved morale, openness to change and confidence but no specific examples could be offered: one manager replied that 'It must have been a real success, or I'd have heard!'

The ten cases where responses were less positive included a couple where the literacy had been embedded in an NVQ, and no distinct literacy-related outcomes had been noticed. In other cases, either attendance had been poor, or tutors had chopped and changed, or there was simply no particular positive impact that the employers had observed.

These rather mixed responses, given in the course of quite extensive, one-to-one interviews, contrast quite markedly with most programme evaluations. Most people, when asked their opinion of something they have received for free, tend to tick the 'highly satisfied' box. In general, people do not like to look gift horses in the mouth (especially if there might be more coming), nor, for the most part, do they want to hurt people's feelings for no good reason or return. Equally, no-one likes to feel they have wasted their own time and effort to no good purpose (Baron and Byrne 2004, Cooper 2007).

As a result, formal evaluations of interventions commonly find that an overwhelming proportion of participants report positive outcomes *even when the evaluators can find no independent evidence of impact*. It seems likely that the responses of the employer sample may thus over-state and certainly are unlikely to understate, satisfaction levels.

The real test of employer responses to training outcomes is, of course, where they subsequently put their money. If workplace basic skills had the impact that government expected, one would predict subsequent changes in employers' training activity. The then Skills Minister David Lammy, at the 2008 Skills for Life and Work conference (Lammy 2008), dangled before English employers the 'unambiguous' benefits of participation, as exemplified by Ford at Dagenham – 'a 22 per cent reduction in energy consumption since the implementation of its Skills for Life strategy'. How could any manager resist paying to repeat and extend such outcomes?

Our sample produced no such heady reports, and no major changes in training expenditures. Among the 46 sites which were still extant at the time of our follow-up interviews:

- Only six were still actively involved in programmes that offered workplace basic skills provision to employees.[3]
- Every one of those six had become involved in basic skills provision quite independently of, *and prior to*, receiving SfL funding; although SfL funding had, in two cases, enabled them to increase the scale of provision and secure better, and dedicated, premises. This prior involvement was the result of the commitment and initiative of internal permanent staff. It included expenditure from the organization's own budget, although five of the six were also, at our final visit, still obtaining substantial public funding from a variety of sources.
- Four of the six had an internal learning centre that was itself a provider (and therefore had not been involved with an external provider).

None of the 40 organizations which had ceased offering basic skills had actively rejected the idea. Most had stopped because neither 'free tuition' courses nor subsidized courses were being offered any longer to them by providers. (Several volunteered the information that they had employees currently taking NVQs: these were being offered free under Train to Gain). None of the 'drop-outs' was inclined to offer a course at full 100 per cent cost to themselves; equally, five of the six who did still offer basic skills were doing so contingent on a continuing and substantial subsidy.

In other words, there is no evidence to suggest that a dedicated programme offering free basic skills training has had any effect whatsoever on employers' later training practices. This is consistent with the findings of the quantitative analysis of Employer Training Pilots overall, conducted by the Institute of Fiscal Studies. This concluded that 'Our estimates are consistent with a small positive effect of ETP on the incidence of training among eligible employers. However the confidence intervals around the estimated effects show that these effects are generally not statistically significantly different from zero' (Abramovsky et al. 2005: 7).

Organizational outcomes B: social capital

Although the major focus for basic skills policy has always been the individual learner, in the case of workplace provision, possible benefits stretch beyond learners themselves to the organization as a whole. As noted above, enterprises may benefit because individuals become more productive; because people working alongside them also become more productive via more efficient work practices and informal learning; or because the culture of the organization changes in a positive way.

The second and third of these phenomena are aspects of 'social capital' or 'organizational capital'. Coleman's work is seminal here: he argues that 'Social capital is the set of relationships between individuals and within groups which make ... possible the achievement of certain ends that would not be possible in its absence' (Coleman 1990: 302). If an organization has high levels of social capital it will also exhibit high levels of trust among its members, and strong shared informal values and norms. It will be more effective and it will have higher levels of a certain type of intangible capital on which it can draw productively.

The idea of such social capital has been extensively discussed in recent years and in this context relates specifically to 'factors which influence productivity, yet are not directly related to the individual skill levels of employees' (Aspin 2004: 2). With small groups of workers, taking short courses, it is clearly unlikely that basic skills programmes will have a major impact on enterprise culture and social capital. Nonetheless, as we have seen, the most important motivation for employers was, in fact, 'social capital' related – in other words, they wanted to demonstrate to employees that they, the employers, had employees' interests at heart, and were trustworthy, rather than hostile and ungenerous.

We therefore looked in some detail at indicators of social capital and at whether they had changed at all as a result of basic skills workplace

Box 7.2   Questions relating to social capital

- Are your workmates also your friends?
- To what extent do you feel part of a team at work?
- Do you feel valued by your co-workers?
- Do you feel valued by your employer?
- In the last few weeks, have you volunteered to do anything at work over and above your normal day-to-day tasks?
- How easy would you say it is to do that at your workplace?
- In the last few weeks, have you made any suggestions for changes or improvements in how your work is organized?
- How easy would you say it is to do that at your workplace?

provision. The indicators we selected related first, to employees' attitudes to their employer and employment; and second, to their fellow-workers whether they saw them as friends, and if this was an inclusive and pleasant workplace. Third, we asked some questions which related directly to how people actually behaved at work, and specifically to whether they felt able to act in ways which might increase productivity – for example, by making suggestions for change. Making such suggestions is risky for low-level employees: equally, risk taking and experimentation characterize firms with robust relationships (Aspin 2004:5).

Box 7.2 summarizes the measures used. Learners were asked the relevant questions at a first interview (before the courses) and at a second interview (a year later). Were there any changes?

If so, they were not discernible from our measures. We found no significant changes, in either direction, in learners' characterization of their workplace as one in which workmates were friends, or they felt part of a team. There was some increase in the numbers feeling highly valued by their co-workers; but no significant changes at all in how many felt valued by their employers, or in how easy they found it to make suggestions for change, or how easy it was to volunteer to do something extra at work.

As Figures 7.3 and 7.4 illustrate, there were also no significant changes in how learners rated their jobs, and in their general satisfaction levels. Figure 7.3 shows how people felt about the 'personal' aspects of their job – remuneration, individual prospects. Figure 7.4, by comparison, examines those aspects which are most directly related to productivity and social capital; and here, again, we find no significant or noticeable differences.

The disappearing provider

At our follow-up interviews with managers, we were frequently told that they were no longer being offered free basic skills courses. Yet the English government still regards basic skills, in the workplace, as a major

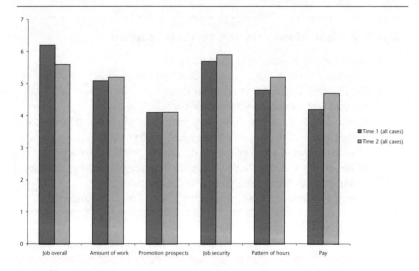

Figure 7.3 Satisfaction with extrinsic rewards (7 = very satisfied, 1 = very dissatisfied)

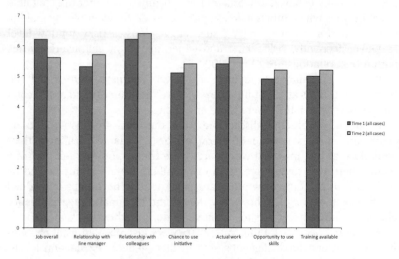

Figure 7.4 Satisfaction with job context and demands (7 = very satisfied, 1 = very dissatisfied)

priority and there are targets for basic skills qualifications obtained in the workplace, within 'Train to Gain'. So are the managers correct?

In some sites, all or almost all eligible learners had already received their entitlement. In a few, harsher economic conditions had reduced managers' willingness to host courses of any sort. But in others, there were many employees who had not yet received a basic skills course, and their managers would have liked to offer one. It is impossible to know how many FE colleges, adult education centres and private training providers are in fact soliciting employers to sign up for basic skills courses. But at follow-up meetings, tutors who had been heavily involved in outreach when the study began (2003) confirmed that their institutions had indeed stopped trying to recruit large numbers of employers for Skills for Life.

There seem to be two reasons for this. The first is that the courses were never very profitable. Time and again, when locating sites, we would be told about companies which were going to sign up to activities involving large numbers of learners – 100 here, 200 there. However, the courses that actually ran were almost all very small – typically well under ten employees signed up even for the first session, and there was often high drop-out thereafter. The only exceptions were the three workplaces where attendance was effectively compulsory.

When providers' teaching and administrative costs are fixed, but payment is per learner, small classes are generally not sustainable. A within-college course which had fewer than ten recruits would normally not run, and even with generous Skills for Life funding, workplace provision thus turned out not to be very attractive. In addition, the model which was being promoted by government was very expensive, as discussed in the next section.

The second reason is a change in the funding environment. This was flagged up very clearly by one manager whose company was no longer offering basic skills courses, but whose employees were receiving NVQs free under Train to Gain. 'We have to guarantee the College at least 6 attendees, and if it drops below 5 completing, there's a £600 per person cancellation fee,' he explained. Previously, his staff – all with extremely limited English – were offered an NVQ1 plus literacy/ESOL . Now they were doing a Level 2 NVQ (notionally the same level as a GCSE grade A–C) with no additional literacy tuition.

Why? Because government targets and policy were emphasizing 'full Level 2' qualifications to the exclusion of most other provision. Level 2s were what providers contracted for with the Learning and Skills Council; and Level 2s were what employers were offered. It was also critical that the company not drop 'below 5 *completing*' (italics ours). As noted earlier, when the study sites were recruited, it was still relatively easy to obtain funding for courses that did not lead to a qualification. That is no longer the case. Moreover, a substantial amount of the funding is 'output related', received only once the learner actually achieves the qualification.[4]

At another site, part of a large not-for-profit care organization, the manager told a similar story. She was also no longer hosting basic skills courses, but had a provider who regularly offered free courses with which assistants could obtain the required NVQs. The provider also worked with the manager to try and organize other training which the organization was interested in. As she explained, 'The provider (a college) has put together a training course to cover what we want and need, but everyone also has to take a different Level 2 qualification at the end so that we can get the funding.'

It is impossible to identify basic skills courses and enrolments in the workplace if they are funded under what was, in 2003–2005, mainstream LSC adult funding, as they were not counted separately.[5] It is, however, possible to identify funding for Skills for Life distributed under Train to Gain. From this, we know that the workplace basic skills course does still exist in some form: Siôn Simon, for the government, informed Parliament that at the end of March 2008, 41,000 T2G learners were enrolled for SfL awards, compared with a target of 73,470 (Simon 2009).

Whether or not T2G-funded basic skills are stand alone or combined with an NVQ, the mode of delivery is likely to be very different from most of the courses we observed. Thirty hours of tutor-delivered group teaching was the common pattern in our study, outside Learndirect sites; and only a minority were intended to 'deliver' formal qualifications. However, T2G funding (at the *higher* rate) requires that learners receive a minimum of 15 hours 'underpinning knowledge ... or substantial skills development' (Linford 2008: 97): in this context a minimum is generally a maximum. Under ETPs, which were generally somewhat more generously funded than T2G, the evaluators found that, on average, and for the whole of their programme, participants only spent 17 hours in direct training of any sort (Hillage *et al.* 2006: xv).

Such a funding regime makes it almost impossible for a provider to enter learners for a literacy qualification unless they are already effectively at the standard involved. Among adults, effective literacy improvement – moving up the equivalent of a grade or school year – typically requires almost ten times as much instruction time as this (Comings 2004); while teaching for a GCSE will typically total around 100 hours.

Train to Gain – like ETPs – is dominated by private training providers, and in 2007, the chief executives of the two largest companies gave evidence to the House of Commons Select Committee on Education and Skills explaining how the programme works. There are 14 forms required when they take on a learner, which take about two hours to complete. Hence:

> we lose a number of people because they just cannot be bothered to go through the process, even though we hold the pen for them ... To put it into perspective, I have got something like 50 people who are employed full time on processing bits of paper, which is inordinate waste.
> (House of Commons Education and Skills Committee 2007: Q273, Q274, supplementary memorandum from Dan Wright)

This, and the 'output-related funding' regime, mean that companies can only make a profit if they concentrate on ensuring that qualifications are indeed completed, as efficiently and quickly as possible; which implies assembling portfolios for NVQs rather than spending time on training and, for basic skills, offering test preparation at the individual's current level. Very few managers in the study were aware of the funding complexities which drove provider activity. Nor were union officials and learning representatives. There would, typically, be a highly dedicated and committed individual, working to promote learning and persuade management to collaborate. Uninformed about the labyrinthine funding mechanisms which underlay course provision, they were sometimes angry at colleges' behaviour. At one site where provision had ceased, a ULR complained that

> The main problem was with the college. They wanted to meet their own targets and draw down government funding for SfL courses. But that was not necessarily what the employees wanted. They were not listening to the individual. In the end they didn't want to enrol more students because they were more bothered about the completion of the course.

Even sites with histories of large-scale provision complained that it was becoming increasingly difficult to maintain on-site education. One company, while still providing courses at the time of follow-up interviews, was planning to close its own on-site Learndirect centre because of demands from the national office for ever-more expenditure, record-keeping and oversight, and a negative Ofsted report which they felt entirely misunderstood the nature of workplace provision. At another of the still extant learning centres, our interviewee – the most experienced and longest-standing in our sample – was also pessimistic. After 24 years of basic skills provision, she explained,

> we are able to keep going because we have been around for a very long time. Up to now we have been giving the learners more than 30 hours. But I can see the writing on the wall – these learners just don't fit in with today's methodology.

Trying too hard? The dangers of gold-plating

Current funding arrangements clearly make it unattractive for most colleges to continue with workplace provision; and impose a model on those still in the market which is of highly dubious value educationally. But could the basic model have worked, without the funding and qualification changes of recent years?

Our data suggest that even without these, the approach developed by Skills for Life will tend to be extremely, if not prohibitively, expensive. In advance of the full-scale launch of Skills for Life, the government supported a number of 'Pathfinder' post-compulsory education projects in deprived areas, one of whose objectives was to develop workplace learning. Their reports indicated that it typically took 20–30 hours of negotiation with an employer before active in-house basic skills training could be organized and underway.[6]

The total cost to an institution of a 'cheap' professional employee (salary + on-costs + administrative overheads) is, in 2008 prices, on the order of £52 an hour.[7] So a course incurs costs of £1,040–£1,560 before it gets under way. Tutor and administrative costs for the course itself then follow. On top of that, however, the revenue for the courses that do run must cover *the 'deadweight' costs of the negotiations which did not result in a course starting up at all.*

More detailed information on the recruitment process was collated and supplied to us by the full-time Workbase Coordinator for one of the Pathfinder projects. Over the course of a (full-time employed) year she would typically:

- target 150 employers with a mailshot;
- follow up the mailshot with individual phone calls;
- obtain an initial positive response from 30 employers (20 per cent) and visit each one individually;
- arrange to set up a course in 15 workplaces – i.e. *one in ten of those originally contacted.*

Moreover, 'good practice', as recommended by, for example, the Workplace Basic Skills Network (DfES-funded), emphasizes the need to tailor content to the workplace and the individual learners. This means carrying out both an 'Occupational Needs Analysis (ONA)' (clarifying the literacy and numeracy requirements associated with the company's jobs) and a 'Training Needs Analysis (TNA)', clarifying how many post-holders are likely to need training. For our Pathfinder contact, with an independently funded coordinator, this latter stage involved two more extensive visits to the company. Between the second and third, a course would be designed to fit the findings of the ONA and TNA. The total number of preparatory hours per 'realized' course was thus around 120 rather than the 20 to 30 average reported to the DfES (see above); to which would be added, typically, 30 hours of teaching.

As we have seen, numbers enrolling on workplace courses tend to be very small – typically six or seven. At the current price of £750 per 'full' Level 2 basic skills qualification delivered in the workplace, that means £4,500–£5,250 (possibly less if output-related funding is imposed). But that covers only between 87 and 101 hours of (relatively low cost) professional time in total. Allowing for a one in ten success rate in getting courses up and running, this looks unmanageable even without a full needs analysis.

Not surprisingly, as we reported in Chapter 4, few of our sites had carried out any form of formal needs analysis, let alone both an ONA and a TNA. A number of centrally supported projects, in both England and Scotland, piloted alternative approaches which, it was hoped, would yield economies of scale. One model funded coordinators within a large organization, who could, in principle, cascade information and assistance (including needs assessment) through existing management channels. Individual managers would then be informed of the availability of LSC funding and of local providers and could organize courses directly. Good practice could be preserved, but deliver far larger numbers of learners than through discrete approaches to large numbers of enterprises. This, too, however, proved problematic and highly expensive, as the case-study in Box 7.3 illustrates.

Box 7.3   Embedded basic skills: a failed attempt at economies of scale

In 2003, one of the big RDAs initiated a project entitled 'Embedding Basic Skills in Local Authorities', managed for them by the now-defunct Basic Skills Agency and designed to embed 'sustainable literacy, language and numeracy policies ... within their HR structures to meet employee LLN needs'. The project funded qualified practitioners within the selected authorities, who could work with senior management and with providers, as well as 'empowering key members of internal staff to run the project in the long term'.

The actual cost of tuition/learning undertaken could be covered by LSC payments in the normal way and was not included. Activity would include full Organizational Needs Analysis and evaluation of results, including comparisons of participants and control groups. Three authorities were selected for initial two-year funding following a competitive tendering process.

One authority conducted and submitted a full evaluation of its scheme and was able to locate spending details. It received £142,000 over two years from the BSA. £15,000 went to providers for development costs (and the latter also enrolled enough learners to draw down an additional £36,500 from the LSC). The rest was spent internally. Ninety-five learners enrolled on the courses for which LSC funding was available; a further 26 attended short courses run by the project practitioner. Total spending was £178,000 (RDA + LSC funds) or £1,471 per learner. Spending per learner excluding the LSC fees (the 'normal' expenditure per learner) was £1,174. Although some SfL activity is continuing elsewhere in the borough, with involvement from LA employees, this developed totally independently, with completely different personnel and funding sources; and there has been no follow-on from this project.

One authority failed to establish any viable internal courses or learning under the project and the practitioner recruited to run the scheme left part way through the period.

The third spent a total of £119,018. Large numbers of employees were given information and offered a needs assessment; one course started for 20–30 employees; all but three dropped out. There is no continuing activity.

The RDA as a whole spent £772,400 on the project (including payments to BSA to establish the project and provide oversight and support). No final report or comparisons of participants with controls can be located.

Source: Project notes and papers. (Two of the authorities participated in the research: as with all others, they did so under a guarantee of anonymity).

Discussion

In England, total expenditure on Skills for Life between 2001 and 2008 is estimated at over £5 billion (House of Commons Public Accounts Committee 2009). In the workplace, at least, there seems little to show for it all; we found no stable legacies, either in the form of ongoing provision, or in changes in employers' training activities. Our findings are, moreover, consistent with those of both the other researchers who have examined the institutional impact of workplace-oriented initiatives in the skills sector (Finlay *et al.* 2007) and of evaluations of their impact using national datasets (Abramovsky *et al.* 2005). Like Prospero's cloud-capped towers, these schemes have vanished into thin air, and 'leave not a wrack behind'.

There were a number of reasons for this, some of which are directly attributable to government policy. First of all, a good deal of provision was funded in ways which were intrinsically short-term. Union Learning Fund and European Social Fund money was of this type; recipients could only expect one project, one tranche of funding. The Pathfinder Projects provided levels of funding which could not be sustained and on a one-off basis. This is an approach which cannot – and does not – help a long-term infrastructure to develop. It is anti-institutional, when what is needed is a set of sustainable institutions to deliver the *lifetime* learning to which governments are officially committed.

Second, these problems have been compounded by the nature of government funding policy, its constant changes, and the domination of quantitative targets. As we have seen, bureaucracy, output-related funding, and the ever-greater difficulty of obtaining money for non-qualification bearing courses combine to generate workplace provision which cannot possibly be 'improving' anyone's skills significantly, and which is unlikely to convince employers of the value of direct contributions from their own resources. Government policy has also meant the disappearance of the types of course promoted and supported by the Union Learning Representatives to whom the very same government has given legislative backing and funds.

These are aspects of policy which could be changed; but other problems are more intractable. First of all, the workplace itself is not a good location in which to develop stable learning institutions. In the space of just over two years, we found that 14 per cent of our sites had closed altogether. In over half, there was no manager in post who had any recollection of or knowledge about the courses which had taken place. National figures on company start-ups and closures show that this is quite typical, while the public sector is also characterized by constant reorganization. (For example, in just eight years, the British government department responsible for Skills for Life has changed its name several times, from the DfEE to DfES, and then to DIUS, and finally to BIS).

Second, workplace provision which uses anything like the model we tracked is extremely expensive. Top-down provision, on a workplace-specific pattern, involves, as described above, multiple contacts for each course operated; small groups; and heavy fixed costs.

Overall, therefore, the model of workplace provision used in this country over the last decade appears to us to be non-viable as an effective, long-term approach. Equally, it is apparent that, in many workplaces, there are committed and enthusiastic learners, and also many individuals (notably many current Union Learning Representatives) who are able and willing to promote and facilitate learning, given the right infrastructure. More effective approaches, we would suggest, need to find ways of putting control and funding much more clearly in the hands of the learners themselves, rather than treating them as passive recipients to whom providers offer ready-made wares. We return to this argument in our concluding chapter.

Chapter 8

The interplay of 'formal' and 'informal' learning at work

Introduction

This chapter looks in detail at the way in which *formal* learning which took place in literacy courses might be carried over to the workplace, and the extent to which there were synergies between it and the *informal* learning which is so central to all workplaces. It does so through detailed case-studies of four sites; and in the process sheds light on a number of our own key findings, and on the more general training literature.

As we saw in Chapter 3, the training which most consistently leads to wage returns and promotion has been developed and provided by employers directly. This reflects the need for effective skills development to respond to the particular circumstances of individual workplaces; and this chapter will illustrate how formal literacy training might or might not generate synergies depending on circumstances. It also illustrates in concrete terms how it could happen that, as described in Chapter 7, organizations that had supported literacy provision in the workplace nonetheless largely ceased to offer courses after a short period. Of the four cases described here, which include companies nationally acclaimed for their training, only one came to the end of the research study period with provision ongoing and secure.

As Billett (2002) points out, the more worksite activities a worker can access and engage with, the more learning that may result. Nevertheless, these learning opportunities are not distributed equally across a particular organization; those individuals confined to routine work, and whose roles may be less valued may have fewer chances to expand their learning. Evans and Waite (2010) have focused particularly on the experiences of 'routine workers' at the lower end of the earnings distribution showing how learning will depend crucially on organizational environments and the extent of distribution of opportunities for informal learning. The tacit dimensions of knowledge and skill are also germane to the exploration of informal-formal learning relationships (Evans *et al.* 2004). To illustrate in more detail the interplay of formal and informal learning at work, we look in turn at four of the workplace sites included in the study.

Coopers: food processing company

Coopers is a large food manufacturer in the north-east of England, employing 460 core staff and 120 agency staff. The company has previously attracted national acclaim for its provision of courses for employees and the community.

The first learning centre was set up in 2001 within the main factory, on the initiative of senior management. Initially consisting of a small room with five computers, the learning centre became a Learndirect centre in 2002, and then moved to a large purpose-built building in 2004. The company paid the salary of a full-time tutor and assistant and provided the funds for the new building, whilst Learndirect finances the computers and resources. The main room in the learning centre is now equipped with 15 desk-top computers and an interactive class whiteboard. There are three other meeting rooms, one of which is equipped with video-conferencing facilities and plasma TVs. In the main hall, various cabinets showcase awards made to the company for its training activity.

As of May 2005, 300 employees of Coopers have undertaken courses at the learning centre. All learning takes place in the employees' own time.

The centre is also open to, and visible in, the local community. In addition to computer and Skills for Life courses, and job-specific training, the centre also offers courses of general interest. These courses, which are well attended events, are also used as a 'hook' by the tutor to attract individuals to Skills for Life courses.

The tutor is fully aware of the challenges of enlisting individuals on literacy and numeracy courses:

> I've been here since August 2003 and I knew that I couldn't just go out on to the factory floor and say 'do you want to come in and learn how to read and write?' I mean no one would ever dream of doing that so I had to be quite clever and put on activities that weren't related at all to reading and writing, just to build relationships to get people in to the centre.

Computer courses are an important means of overcoming barriers to developing literacy and numeracy.

The development of training opportunities within the company has led to a shift in emphasis from 'informal' to 'formalized' learning within the company. Bill Williams, a technician noted that when he first began working at Coopers over 25 years ago 'I used to come to work on Monday and there'd be a nice piece of equipment appear and you had to figure out how it worked. While now it's a lot more, you do get trained for the jobs.'

Each employee at the level of technician and above also undergoes the Performance Development Process (PDP) which reviews their work and sets learning objectives linked to the learning centre. According to the manager

Now the goal is to roll that out across all our employees, so the GOs (General Operators), would have the same type of objectives, and that's when ... you can start to see links coming in, at the moment we don't do that in a structured way as such but it's another, it's another tool to use.

The company sets aside formal space for informal learning. As part of his performance development process (PDP), Bill Williams was given time off to find out about other sectors of the company and learn from their work through observation and questions: 'I did two days walking around where they fried the crisps to learn how they do their job so I found out how my actions impact on them.' Hilary Benton was actively encouraged to engage in an ongoing process of informal learning as part of her Front line Employee to Front Line Manager programme (a fast-track promotion scheme for graduates).

The company also makes use of so-called 'huddles' in which employees gather to share their working experiences and listen to company updates. Such events allow the management to disseminate formal learning opportunities – notably courses at the learning centre – facilitate the pooling of collective experiences to enhance performance at work. Such meetings allow employees to enhance their working practices via routine workplace meetings (a form of 'observing knowledgeables', see Chapter 6). They also allow for the critical questioning and exchange of working practices and therefore represent important sites for informal learning by 'focused workplace discussions' (Chapter 6).

According to the Human Resources manager:

when we've done huddles, we've done various activities on site, there's people you'll find won't participate in it, and the reason they do that is because ... they're not very good at reading and writing, some of the arithmetic, numeracy skills are lacking so this has helped bring some of them people on (the course).

The tutor at the company's learning centre similarly expressed the view that those with poor literacy and numeracy skills were less equipped to take advantage of staff development opportunities.

There's a lot of people who can't even read the communications put out, so a lot of people miss the opportunity to say like trips or awards or things because they don't understand the posters or they don't understand the literature that's like flying about within Coopers.

The increasing 'textualization' of the workplace means that those who have literacy and numeracy needs are particularly vulnerable. As noted earlier (Chapter 4) not all organizations involved in our research, report an increasing use of literacy, numeracy and technology in the workplace; but some, like Coopers, have had major changes. In the words of a production manager: 'if somebody cut their finger 10–15 year ago we'd stick a plaster on and say 'there there there'. Now there's a four page document we've got to fill in and how can we stop somebody else from doing it again?'

Courses are promoted through the 'huddles', notices, the company bulletin as well as through PowerPoint presentations in the canteen. The learning centre is an important site for the complex interweaving of formal and informal learning opportunities. The learners have the opportunity to undertake a variety of formally accredited Learndirect courses in Skills for Life and ICT but are also given scope to engage in independent 'self-directed' learning. In addition to guiding learners through SfL courses, the tutor also lent laptops to learners so that they could experiment and develop confidence with the technology in their own time. For Maggie Taylor, a General Operator, such an opportunity was vital in allowing her to overcome her fear of using technology and experiment with the computer in her own time 'I'm very nervous with computers, very nervous ... but George loaned me an old laptop and I was okay with that, I could just pick it up when I had a spare couple of hours'.

As noted earlier, the company was well known and recognized for its training and learning culture. However, increased formal requirements for government-funded programmes were implemented during the period of the study. The publication of a critical Ofsted report in 2007[1] brought to a head various tensions between the company and Learndirect that had been simmering for some time.

According to the HR manager at Coopers, Learndirect were keen to increase the ratio of community to company learners (currently 60 per cent from company and 40 per cent from the community) in order to increase the potential pool of learners signing up for courses. The company felt increasingly 'restricted' by compliance with the Learndirect national contract and had already begun to seek alternative provision. The company felt aggrieved that Ofsted had not taken account of the type of provision that was offered at the learning centre and claimed that Ofsted criteria were too restrictive and college-centred.

As a consequence, the company, at the last research visit, was changing its approach and support. It was making arrangements for a local college to provide courses in the learning centre (utilizing the two tutors who are currently based at the centre). From the company's perspective this will provide more 'flexibility' in terms of allowing them to offer a wider range of courses, including those at a higher level. Such an arrangement has the additional advantage of protecting the learning centre from separate external inspection as a provider. In the meantime, the learning centre is open for employees to engage in learning without embarking on formally accredited courses.

Summary: formal and informal learning opportunities at Coopers

Coopers provides for a range of formalized learning within the company structure but also accords official space for the opportunities for informal learning (observation of other employees, sharing of ideas in huddles, etc.). The increasing 'textualization' of the Coopers work environment has made employees who struggle with poor literacy and numeracy more prone to miss out on formal training opportunities and increases the significance of 'informal' learning for these particular employees.

The learning centre represents an important site for the inter-weaving of formal and informal learning opportunities. It is noticeable that the popularity of the learning centre has rested partly on it not being too closely associated with formalized learning, and allowing informal self-directed learning ('searching independently for information', another key aspect of informal learning, Chapter 6).

The learning centre initially attracted national acclaim from institutions such as Business in the Community for its innovative efforts to provide learning opportunities that straddled the company/community divide. Yet, the centre's incarnation as a recognized Learndirect centre has generated problems. The Ofsted inspection highlighted a failure to conform with nationally recognized standards and assessment procedures, which emphasize formal learning; whereas the company had embraced a vision of learning that included both formal and informal elements.

HLN Manufacturing

HLN Manufacturing is a large engineering company specializing in the manufacture of parts for cars with a global workforce of approximately 50,000 employees. In its West Midlands site (the focus of this case-study), the company has 323 employees, including 15 managers, 40 technical staff and 260 operatives. The number of employees on the site has shrunk from over 2000 in the early 1980s as a result of the introduction of computerized technology.

As part of their everyday work, machine operators monitor and calibrate computerized machinery. Their work entails the use of 'basic averages' to monitor output as well as the filling in of in production plans. Several machine operators remarked upon the increasing prevalence of target-setting and report-writing, manifested in the introduction of 'lost-time' analysis in the last two years in which forms have to be filled in on an hourly basis if production quotas have not been met. In the words of one of its Union Learning Representatives, Bill Renfrew:

> everything is around production now and you have to hit targets, without the targets you're not making a profit so you know, it's all

around that now. And there are some visual sheets, big sheets that you have to write down so anybody can walk past and say why didn't you hit the target ... there is a lot more paper work now.

ULRs were key in the development of a workplace course, as described in Box 8.1. For the majority of employees, the motivation to embark on such a course was tied to generic rather than job-specific factors (see Chapter 6). For example, Mike Philips, who had worked for the company for 30 years, embarked on the course 'for general interest, general knowledge, and to improve myself'. The human resources manager cited general development for staff and increasing staff morale as the key objectives.

Box 8.1   Union Learning Representatives in action

Union Learning Representatives (ULRs) were instrumental in the establishment of a 'Skills for Life' 15 hour course. Bill Renfrew found out about the Union Learning Fund (ULF) through the company union committee, and volunteered to train as a ULR.

He sent out a questionnaire to all employees asking them about learning needs and preferences, 10 per cent of which were returned. The majority of those who returned the questionnaire expressed a preference to undertake a computer course: 'there were very few that wanted the basics in literacy and numeracy'.

Frustrated with his efforts to gain funding from the Union Learning Fund, Bill Renfrew and the other ULRs decided to establish a course on their own initiative. 'I just knocked the union on the head and I went my own way and I got in touch with the college, and that's how the course started off.' The ULRs were advised that they should set up a literacy course as a 'first step' to learning. They encouraged employees to embark on this to pave the way towards an ICT course, but encountered a frustrating 18-month delay as a result of complications over funding which meant that 'expectations, enthusiasm of learners were let down ... we've had to build them up again'.

The course was eventually launched as Key Skills Communication – Level 1 and 2, and Key Skills Application of Number – Level 1 and 2. It consisted of two classes lasting 90 minutes for ten weeks in the employees' own time. The classes were run in the middle of the day on Thursday in order to fit in with employees' shift patterns. The company has been supportive of Bill Renfrew's involvement as a ULR, giving him time off each Thursday to be on the course and help other learners. A total of eight employees, six machinists, one forklift driver and one craftsman undertook the course which was run in the 'union room', a cramped room without windows.

Despite the increased use of report-writing and computerized machinery, all the employees felt they coped adequately with their existing skills in the workplace, with the exception of one who struggled with the metric system and who was subsequently dissatisfied with the course since it failed to respond to his specific requirements.

The lack of job-specific motivations for undertaking the course becomes more understandable when one considers the significance of informal learning within the organization. Through a variety of informal learning processes, including 'observing knowledgeables', 'focused workplace discussions' and 'mentoring and coaching', the employees had developed proficiency in the specific skills that were needed for their job. More formalized one-day training would take place in such areas as health and safety as well as in response to the introduction of new technology. Two of the learners who were interviewed in-depth appreciated the course as a means of practising skills which they would not normally develop in their working lives. Tim Roberts explained his situation as follows:

> when I was at school we did essays and constant work since I've left school I'm just manual, I'm just making stuff you know, there's nothing really lengthy that I have to write anymore, and I like to write but I just don't get the chance to.

Similarly Bill Renfrew appreciated the opportunity to reawaken skills that had been largely dormant since his time at school.

> I thought it was really good, especially the numeracy and literacy, I'd left school 40 odd years ago and you use some of it but you don't use a lot of it, so going back to the numeracy and the literacy was really hard to begin and I did want to start learning again which I did do.

All the learners undertook Literacy Level 1 and Level 2 tests at the college at the end of the course. The undertaking of the exams in a college environment was a source of concern for some learners. Trevor Stephens said 'the older you get, to sort of walk in to college … You suddenly feel as though you're being stared at … by the young kids'.

Summary: formal and informal learning at HLN Manufacturing

The establishment of a learning centre, and an SfL course, was a grass-roots initiative on the part of ULRs with the support of the company, as described in Box 8.2. The learners' motivation for engaging in the course was underpinned by the high value placed on learning for its own sake.

Though the company has undergone major organizational change with new technology and increased use of documentation, a majority of learners have coped adequately with their existing literacy and numeracy skills. The employees used numeracy skills (averages, working with diameters) without having formally acquired these skills on a course. Informal learning processes had equipped all the learners (with the exception of one) with the necessary skills to undertake their work.

The Weapons Defence Establishment (WDE)

The Weapons Defence Establishment is a weapons manufacturer with three and a half thousand employees. The company was approached by Cloville College who offered to run basic literacy and ICT courses with

---

Box 8.2   A new company learning centre: ups and downs

At the request of the ULRs, the company built a new Learning Centre in 2006. Funded by the company at a cost of £10,000, the learning centre consists of a large training room and additional room equipped with four computers. Three of these were donated by company employees whilst the fourth was purchased on the basis of money the learners won from a NIACE Learners Group Award.

The majority of learners from the literacy and numeracy course continued on to NVQ Level 1 and Level 2 computer courses in the new learning centre. In April 2007, the number of learners on these ICT courses, which were taught by a tutor from college who also provided additional laptops, had declined from 18 to 10.

Mike Philips who had completed Level 1 and embarked on NVQ Level 2 in computers spoke with great enthusiasm about his new found skills:

> and now I can do it myself, fantastic, I switch the computer I can do whatever I like now, send emails you know its absolutely brilliant. I mean it doesn't affect my job but if I needed a job it's there.

Trevor Stephens, who had proceeded to study a CLAIT course at college was considering the possibility of training as a social worker through the Open University at the time of the second follow-up interview. For Jon Barker the course had the additional advantage of facilitating his work as a union convener. The other learners had embarked on computer courses as a result of 'general interest'.

Bill Renfrew continued to pursue additional funding. He felt disillusioned by his inability to gain any funding from Union Learning Fund. He was also contemplating ways of promoting the courses more effectively.

---

funding from the South East England Development Agency (SEEDA). The ICT and English classes consist of one and a half hour sessions over 22 weeks with approximately seven learners in each class. The courses take place at the company's impressive training centre which is located several miles from the main site amidst pleasant parkland. Each learner was assigned a computer at the beginning of the course. According to the course tutor, the goal of these courses was to 'learn basic computer skills and brush up on English'. WDE involved the unions representing lower-level employees (at that time, Transport and General Workers Union and Amicus).

The training manager saw the ICT and English courses as a useful opportunity to rebalance the distribution of training within the company:

> At the end of the day, we're in a competitive market place for some very clever physicists, mathematicians, engineers, metallurgists, so inevitably if we end up getting our hands on those individuals we often give them all the development within reason that they need ... possibly at the expense of some of the people at the lower end. As a result, this programme has given us the opportunity to give those individuals some development as well.

Most importantly, the ICT and English courses facilitated the company's bid to encourage employees to take on more responsibility within their existing job roles as part of an overall trend towards the 'levelling out' of management structures, as discussed in Box 8.3.

In a course offered over 22 weeks, the majority of learners were machine tool fitters involved in the maintenance and supply of machinery parts. Most were motivated by the need to develop their ICT rather than literacy skills. In-keeping with the 'learning by stealth' approach, most of the learners were not aware of the literacy component of the course.

For Gary Thompson, the concealed literacy component had various advantages: 'I think it was probably good, the fact that I didn't know before, because I probably wouldn't have gone otherwise.' He explains his reluctance to go on a more explicitly literacy course: 'Basically because I'm not very good at spelling. So sort of a fear in that area would have put me off.' As in other sites, the learners emphasized the advantage of learning in the workplace as opposed to a college. For Gary Thompson, undertaking a course at college involves more of a risk of 'getting somewhere and finding that you're a bit of an idiot. Where as locally it seems quite acceptable to say, right that's it, I can't do it I've had enough. There's less embarrassment.'

The longer-term impact of the course has been shaped by individual opportunities for career development within the company. On follow-up Mike Swan and Gary Thompson had been promoted to the position of Works Supervisory Officer. Both employees expressed the view that the

---

Box 8.3   Increasing responsibility at work

WDE Manager:

> There are fewer people within our organization than there were ten years ago. As a result of that we have been asking those people to take on more, but er ... because we weren't developing them often they've said 'I want to stay where I'm comfortable', 'No I'm not prepared to take on more'. But in light of us giving some of this additional development to them we have seen more of a ... 'I'll have a go at that' attitude from them. You've given me something so ... yeah I've got that little bit more confidence to have a go at it.'

All the learners remarked that they had taken on increasing responsibility in recent years, including such tasks as filling in self-appraisals, dealing with contractors, sending emails and writing risk assessments, all of which also increased their exposure to technology. Employees are encouraged to sign up for courses through their appraisal meetings which are also tied to pay and promotion prospects. Equally, employees are encouraged to 'show initiative' in taking on more responsibility in the form of more challenging tasks that depend on informal learning 'on the job'.

Liz Andrews, a Health Physics Surveyor described this company ethos as follows:

> We've been more responsible for ourselves and looking after our own work, we've been given a bit of slack too, to use our own initiative ... whereas in the past they would book everything in for us ... and we'd say yes or no, whereas now we can more or less go off and do it.

Roger Taylor highlighted the significance of 'Focused Workplace Discussions' as being a particularly important component of informal learning in this workplace:

> Well we work as a team, and ... I mean you could be on a job and somebody might have had a similar type of job so you always have a chat with somebody, did you know about this? Or have you had any experience of this? so ... we exchange knowledge between each other all the time. It's part of your job.

Box 8.4   Formal course triggers informal learning opportunities

The course also allowed for the development of a variety of informal learning opportunities. Oliver Green was one of several learners who bought a computer during the course so that he could consolidate his newly acquired skills at home: 'I used to finish off what we were doing in class at home'. Mike Swan similarly commented on his increased capacity to experiment with ICT: 'if you're waiting for a job and you think well I'm waiting for that bit of paperwork here and you think right well I'll have a go at that, and see if I can get it checked.' The impact of the course was extended further into the workplace through the employees' informal pooling of experiences and recollections. Roger Taylor described this process as follows

> we've got a computer we can use at work, ... it's one we share, I mean all the guys in the office have got their own, but there's one in the workshop that we can share and Ralph's doing spreadsheets and stuff ... so he says yeah can you remember how we did this? So we sit down together and work it out, from the course that we did, the training that we had, somebody might remember something.

course had helped them prepare for their current job which involves extensive use of ICT in order to undertake risk assessments and deal with contractors (see Chapter 6).

The other employees had also taken on more responsibility, whilst undertaking the same job roles, as part of the company's strategy of delegating more demanding work to lower-level employees. Undertaking the course and a willingness to undertake higher level tasks had allowed Ralph Welsey (b. 1953) to be positively assessed in his PDG (peer development group) which had led to a 5 per cent pay increase. But he still felt disgruntled by his salary of £14,800 a year (in 2006). The computer course had facilitated his capacity to take on increased administrative duties: 'it adds to the variety',

> obviously it's more interesting than sweeping up, but then you've got the thing going, at what point do you say I'm doing this additional work and I think I should be earning more and I'm not. And that's going to start eating away, it's not worth doing.

Although Gary Thompson viewed the course as a 'very good step up', he expressed a more negative view of the company's motivations for running the course:

since their training is very much to suit themselves, they send us on these courses and they get work done that they would normally have paid higher grades to do ... so it's beneficial to us but I think they get more out of it, and the other thing is with this company, they like their perception of Investors in People, their little logos etc, so I think its part of their plan but overall I think they get very good value out of what they put us on.

Some learners were frustrated that increased responsibility had not been accompanied by increased pay and promotion opportunities; and this was accompanied by a degree of perplexity over opportunities for further learning.

From a management perspective the courses have been a success. By October 2006, 400 learners had completed the IT and literacy courses. The training manager claimed that

> The course has been helpful in our efforts to make the workforce 'feel as one' so to speak. Previously ... there was much more of a hierarchical structure. Those at the top are skilled and then there is the rest. The courses have given people more confidence and opportunity to engage with computers.

The courses have helped to 'broaden people's horizons ... people are now more willing to take on new roles'.

Summary of formal and informal learning opportunities at WDE

The levelling out of management structures within the Weapons Defence Establishment has increased the significance of both formal and informal learning opportunities. As part of taking on more responsibility, employees are encouraged to commit themselves to training opportunities through the appraisal system. Whereas previously salaries were uniform within grades of the organization, in the current system promotion and pay depend on individual performance. In this context, employee involvement in formalized training has the potential to bring benefits in terms of promotion and pay.

The IT and English courses at this organization have been a success in so far as they have recruited a large number of learners over the long-term. The popularity of these courses indicates the importance of workplace courses being tailored to the priorities of the organization in question.

The levelling out of management structures also has major implications for informal learning. The expectation that employees should 'take on more' and 'show initiative' means that employees are frequently given greater scope for learning about new duties through 'on the job' experience at work.

Thorpton Local Authority

In the borough of Thorpton, which employs between 1,500 and 1,800 staff, Union Learning Representatives (ULRs) have played an important role in implementing a series of Skills for Life courses at the local authority's learning centre – located on the premises of a refuse centre – in partnership with the learning centre manager and two colleges.

The courses, entitled 'IT and English' and 'Communication Skills at Work' last for six hours a week over a five-week period and are designed for a range of front-line staff including cleaners, caretakers and refuse collectors. Funded by the Learning and Skills Council (via the local colleges) and facilitated by the local authority's release of employees during working hours, the courses aim to give the learners a chance to 'brush up' or improve their literacy skills with the chance to take national tests at Level 1 or 2. Jane Richards (learning centre manager) met individuals in small groups and also discussed the courses at staff meetings. Dave Michaels, a ULR, was instrumental in setting up the courses.

This case-study focuses on caretakers and cleaners who undertook a communications course, involving literacy and ICT for three hours a week over a five-week period. An increase in report writing in order to document damage, accidents and instances of vandalism provided the underlying rationale (see Box 8.5). In the words of the learning centre manager:

> We've just run a course for caretakers. Now in theory they virtually tick boxes, but they're finding that they're having to write a little bit more information on forms, and I think that does worry some of them because they all say well my spelling's terrible, my handwriting is terrible – so they are aware that perhaps they're having to … write more and they're being, and their handwriting and their spelling is being, noticed more than perhaps it was five years ago.

Several of the learners who were interviewed in-depth felt the course had improved their use of literacy in the workplace. Trevor Woodford maintained that the course had improved his capacity to fill in reports and use writing skills in everyday life. He gave the example of writing an email to the council complaining about the tiles in his kitchen:

> Without putting it nastily I wrote a decent sort of email to them and I got a reply back with the same sort of manner I wrote the email in. Whereas before I suppose I wouldn't have even bothered, you know.

In follow-up Trevor Woodford revealed that he had taken on a more supervisory role as a caretaker and had proceeded to undertake various computer courses at the local civic centre. He regarded the course as being useful in preparing him for the next stage of his career as an estate

---

Box 8.5   Mentoring and coaching in caretaking

The caretakers had learnt how to undertake their current roles by a combination of formal and informal learning. Each newly appointed caretaker is formally assigned to a more experienced colleague who guides them through key duties, such as cleaning and keeping records of damage to the property, through an informal process of 'mentoring and coaching'. In addition caretakers periodically undertake one day training in such areas as health and safety, manual handling and 'dealing with violent people'. Abdul Nazif emphasized the importance of skills developed through work experience:

> I didn't know how much was involved in cleaning, until I got this cleaning job, it's not an easy thing, it's complicated, there's chemicals, water, amounts, substances ... there's certain things you have to really get to know, of course – you learn from experience.

---

officer which would entail more office administration and contact with contractors: 'when I do move on I'll have the confidence to do it'. Trevor would also engage in 'self-directed learning' by referring back to his course notes in response to specific tasks at work: 'if I'm doing something that was related to that course then I would look at my notes to help me'.

This is another example of an employer establishing a newly refurbished learning centre, with a specialized computer room. A ULR who has played a particularly important role in the development,[2] maintains that learning opportunities are now much more entrenched. When he first sought to set up courses for front-line staff he encountered a degree of resistance on the part of some middle managers; one manager proclaimed 'Why do they need training? They know how to use a broom.' He now feels that managers are considerably more supportive, having seen the benefits of training in terms of increased confidence (manifested in individuals being 'much more verbal' in meetings) and employees' increased capacity to deal with health and safety and other material.

The communications courses are ongoing for front line staff and have now incorporated more health and safety and appraisal training alongside ICT. Jane Richards, the learning manager maintains that 'those who have done the course will speak up more' and are more likely to become involved in local steering groups. She also feels the courses have been successful in encouraging learners to embark on further learning.

Box 8.6   Limits to informal learning

Abdul Nazif provided a less sanguine view than some of the capacity of one course to make a substantial impact on working practices: 'putting something good into something that's spoilt for so long it's not going to make it right, so much damage already, Colin [the tutor] did a great deal of work on me, but it didn't really put the picture right.' Yet, Abdul Nazif underlined the significance of literacy to fulfil his goal of gaining promotion: 'I wanted to better my position at work, cos I don't always want to be doing manual work'.

Abdul developed informal, self-study techniques in recognition of the importance of developing his literacy skills: 'I've adapted at work lately a little notebook which I write down all the incidents down and I'm getting really into that, because it's like identifying problems and putting it down, expressing myself and dates and time and all that.' Re-interviewed later, Abdul Nazif was still undertaking a lower-level caretaking role which was effectively a job as a cleaner (though also involving basic documentation). He saw his poor literacy skills as holding back his career development: 'it's my responsibility, I shouldn't be expecting anyone to do that, I should actually use my wages, pay for it and get the English higher and to move forward in life ...'. Substantial progress in this area depended ultimately on formal training.

Summary: formal and informal learning at Thorpton Local Authority

Caretakers at Thorpton Local Authority have acquired job-specific skills and knowledge through a combination of formal and informal learning. The local authority formally allocates more experienced colleagues to guide recently appointed caretakers, but the mentoring process itself is largely unstructured and informal.

The increasing use of report-writing amongst caretakers has underlined the significance of literacy skills and has highlighted a skills deficiency in this area amongst some employees. With the exception of Abdul Nazif (Box 8.6), most caretakers have employed various strategies which involve 'getting by', and informal learning has not provided ways for major literacy gaps to be addressed. The courses have helped some employees improve their literacy skills and has facilitated progression within the workplace. Yet the most significant outcome, highlighted by learners, the tutor and manager alike, has been an increased confidence on the part of employees which has led to development of further formal learning opportunities (through willingness to embark on further learning).

Significance of the wider organizational environment

Greater day-to-day job satisfaction was apparent in many of the UK employees who had participated in formal workplace courses, and had developed a greater awareness of the learning potential in their jobs as well as their own abilities to learn. Longer term follow-up is indicating, through, that without advancement or some kind of external recognition of learning and development, this satisfaction can be eroded over time.

Employees' personal and educational backgrounds as well as skills they had learnt from a variety of experiences in and out of paid employment influenced the ways in which they carried out their duties and responsibilities and dealt with various workplace situations. There is a need to consider how the wider organizational environment itself needs development if it is to support rather than undermine investment in learning. Promotion prospects/strategies can be important in sustaining employee motivation to take up formal courses in the longer term; this is less so for engagement in informal learning, where the focus is on current job satisfaction.

Informal learning that results from 'mentoring or coaching' as well as participating in 'focused workplace discussions' is a complex process that involves the interplay of employee agency, workplace relationships and interdependencies and the affordances of the wider environment. These practices can in some cases promote rich informal learning, for example opportunities to expand and share knowledge and skills in supportive workgroups. In other cases, workplace discussions and mentoring/coaching can have unintended negative influences on learning, for example where the interdependencies of the workplace are undermined by feelings of lack of trust.

In particular, confidence to take on new challenges is dependent on the extent to which workers feel supported in that endeavour. Eraut (2004) has pointed out 'if there is neither a challenge nor sufficient support to encourage a person to seek out or respond to a challenge, then confidence declines and with it the motivation to learn' (p. 269). Rather than focusing on supposed productivity gains as a direct outcome of formal and informal training it may be more advantageous to understand better employee job satisfaction and engagement with the workplace. The wider framework for understanding the organizational context provided by Evans *et al.* (2006) shows how interventions need to take account of both employee and employer interests, recognizing that these often represent different rationalities and follow a different logic about what matters at work; and that the work environment fundamentally affects how far formal learning can be a positive trigger for further learning. A short-term timeframe and a narrow of view of learning, will not enhance the learning environment (Evans *et al.* 2006).

Summary and conclusions

Workplace learning centres represent important sites for the inter-weaving of formal and informal learning opportunities. It is noticeable that in the cases described here, the popularity of the learning centres rests partly on their not being too closely associated with formalized learning. Employee participation in a formal programme can act as the catalyst for various informal training activities that occurred back on the shop floor. Participating in an organized class or in a tutorial session heightened employee awareness of the importance to learn. This interplay between formal and informal training was synergetic. There are advantages and disadvantages of workplace-based formal courses: such training offers accessibility but also can potentially be negatively affected by pressure from managers/supervisors on employees to miss learning sessions in order to fulfil their duties in the workplace.

Care should be taken not to confuse strategies for 'getting by' at work with informal learning. Supervisors taking pre-emptive or 'circumventing' action over tasks involving literacy skills can create a vicious circle of employees' over-reliance on supervisors to fill in forms, for example, thus missing the opportunities for informal 'mentoring and coaching' and reinforcing underlying skills deficiencies instead of helping to solve them. While increasing textualization of the workplace is often cited as a motivator and stimulus to learning in the workplace, our cases also reveal another consequence. Employees with poor literacy and numeracy tend to be the ones who miss out on the formal training opportunities linked to textualization, thus falling progressively further behind others in the workplace and becoming more vulnerable as a consequence. Informal learning is only a partial answer.

Part 3

The wider context
International collaborations, social ecology and policy implications

Chapter 9

The findings in international context
Continuities and emerging themes

Introduction

The research project that forms the centre of this book examined a large scale policy initiative inspired by a very particular view of the national and global economy, an equally particular view of individual motivation (whether that of employers or learners) and a confidence in the capacity of governments to design effective top-down interventions. We have presented our findings on programme outcomes, at both individual and enterprise level, and also related them to more complex views of individual agency and the social ecology of learning. In this chapter, we relate our findings to those emerging in other countries, and in particular to three collaborative partnerships developed by the project with research teams working from a similar perspective.

Governmental concerns over adult basic skill levels are by no means confined to the UK: for example, the IALS results which led to the Moser report and Skills for Life were also greeted with dismay by a number of other participating countries (Carey ed. 2000). Critiques of resulting policies have also articulated similar themes, and have highlighted the tensions between governmental strategies and adult education's long-standing purposes and traditions.

In a comparative study of state sponsored literacy programmes Torres (2009) has identified three common policy models: (1) therapeutic (2) recruitment and (3) forced modernization. The first of these gives experts and professionals the major role in determining how literacy training can most effectively integrate people into the labour market. The second 'recruitment' model refers to policies which aim, above all, to enrol large numbers of learners in adult education programmes, with the rationale of incorporating the disadvantaged into the dominant political and social regime, whatever that may be. The driver for the third 'forced modernization' model is to enhance national prospects for integration into the world market economy.

Any of these can in principle incorporate literacy development in and through the workplace; although in practice workplace provision has come to the fore in advanced economies (see Heidegger 2004, Evans *et al.* 2006). Incentives for work-based learning as well as the 'roll-out' of large-scale employer-focused programmes have characterized the policy framework in nations such as the USA, Australia, Canada, New Zealand as well as the UK.

Moves towards workplace provision should, ideally, foreground the importance of better understandings of the social practices involved in learning, which, as we saw above, are very evident in workplace contexts. However, despite the global influence of Lave and Wenger (1991), this is not apparent in most government policy – and indeed much North American literature and research has continued to reflect an individualistic framework (see Lee 2007).

By contrast, Lonsdale and McCurry (2004) in their highly influential review for the NCVER in Australia, provide an overview of current conceptions of literacy for policy-making and teaching and learning, showing how conventional approaches to the development of literacy as sets of more or less technical skills are challenged by widened accounts of literacies as constituted in practice. And Roberts and Gowan's (2007) literature review for the Canadian Council on Social Development (pp. 2–5) acknowledges the effects of not just human capital but also social practices literature.

Across the world, researchers are adopting a wider treatment of learning at work which highlights the connections between the conditions and entitlements that govern the wage relationship, the environments that workers experience and the learning dispositions that adults themselves bring to their work. Such an approach emphasizes that even the best individualized approaches to learning are only partially successful; just as, in the TLRP Gateway Book *Improving Workplace Learning*, Evans *et al.* (2006) showed the importance for workplace learning of informal learning through everyday working practices.

International collaborations

During the course of our research, three significant international relationships have been forged with researchers working within such paradigms. The first was with NCSALL, the Harvard-led US National Research Centre; the second with the New Zealand Department of Labour-commissioned national study of workplace literacy programmes; and the third with the Social and Humanities Research Council sponsored research on teaching and literacy learning led by the University of Ottawa, Canada. Each of these collaborations focused on a different part of the literacy learning landscape and had contrasting insights to offer our own research. We summarize their work and findings below in order to illustrate a developing international dialogue among literacy researchers.

The benefits of longitudinal research: Collaboration with the US National Centre for the Study of Adult Language Literacy and Numeracy (NCSALL)

In the USA the National Centre NCSALL, has conducted longitudinal research into literacy practices, motivations and successes of adult learners for over a decade. When a corresponding National Research and Development Centre was established in 2002 in England, collaboration between these two national centres afforded links between large longitudinal surveys yielding evidence on adult literacy development through the life-course.[1]

As shown in Chapter 2, taking a life course perspective can ensure that educational trajectories are studied in ways that recognize their 'complex intertwining' with social institutions and social roles. A life-course perspective also explores the ways in which individuals' work and family roles influence their learning trajectories, including learning that takes place outside formal systems. Most importantly, Reder and Bynner (2009) have used a combination of statistical modelling methods to analyse changes over time in measured literacy proficiency, literacy practices, programme participation, employment earnings and other variables.[2] Literacy (literacy proficiency; literacy practices) programme participation (formal adult education programmes, community-based programmes and self-study activities) socio-economic outcomes (labour market activity, educational progression and attainment, SES) are included in models which address how far adults' literacy abilities continue to develop in adult life. Statistical modelling has shown that a two-step process is taking place. Both programme participation and self-study positively impact on engagement in literacy practices and this in turn may lead to increases in literacy proficiency.

In discussing implications for programme evaluation and improvement, Reder argues that looking for short term proficiency gains at or shortly after a programme has ended is very problematic. The findings suggest that, for detecting 'relatively short term literacy gains', programmes should assess literacy *practices* rather than literacy *proficiency*. Proficiency measures may be more reasonable measures of programme impact only if longer term follow-up is possible. Reder concludes that a broader picture is needed of adult basic skills learners than just as participants in programmes – active learners deploying different resources in and out of the workplace in efforts to improve basic skills over time are the ones who will improve. Overall, Reder concludes that there is strong evidence that many adults experience literacy gains in adult life and that literacy programmes do have a positive effect on literacy growth curves.

Reder does not investigate workplace engagement directly; but an inference from the research that Reder himself draws, though tentatively, is that 'better jobs', that may engage a broader range of workers' literacy skills, are likely to support the development of literacy proficiency. More generally, both Bynner and Reder, in comparing US and UK findings, have shown that adults' persistence in literacy learning, irrespective of whether support is provided in episodic forms or in sustained longer-term programmes, is key. This is important, given the very short programmes provided by UK governments and the many barriers to mounting longer-term literacy programmes of study at work in systems that are voluntaristic and market-led. The finding that the 'hours' necessary to achieve increases in levels of literacy can be hours gained in episodic learning, through self-study, supported practice and other means, opens up the prospect of following up what are essentially introductory 30 hour courses.

Inclusion of literacy, language and numeracy (LLN) in-house training programmes: collaboration with New Zealand Department of Labour, John Benseman and the University of Auckland

A series of research visits sponsored by the New Zealand Ministry of Labour and National Research and Development Centre (NRDC) facilitated connections between our research and parallel research into workplace programmes in New Zealand (Benseman *et al.* 2010). The latter has focused on the inclusion of literacy, language and numeracy development (LLN) through interventions in a range of companies and the *Go!* tests were made available for their use.

Questions that guided the research had some important overlaps with our own, in focusing on:

- how workplace literacy programmes[3] are viewed by participating employers;
- issues that arise in relation to policy, funding, organization, curriculum and pedagogy;
- identifying learning gains from participation.

The New Zealand research differed from our own research in a number of key respects. Direct comparisons were made with companies choosing not to participate in programmes; testing of gains in literacy proficiency took place once, immediately after the programmes, rather than at yearly intervals thereafter; and the nature of the programmes offered was different. As Benseman *et al.* note (2010: 143), 'all except one of the Upskilling courses was contextualized to the needs and settings of the participating workplaces, but only one out of the 53 UK training programmes was contextualized to the workplace'.

Table 9.1 summarizes key similarities and differences between the two learner groups. The New Zealand study involved 15 programmes (compared with 53 in the UK for a similar sample size) and were diverse in terms of the industries involved, company size, location, programme formats (e.g. 1:1, small group), duration and types of learners. The learning gains were on average much greater than those in the UK sample, although it must be emphasized that the results are not directly comparable since the New Zealand tests were administered one week after the course

As discussed in Chapter 3, this contrasts with UK results where, measured one or two years later, only ESOL learners recorded any significant gains, and the mean score for all learners with complete data rose by only three points on the 100 point *Go!* scale. Few learners improved enough to move up a level. (The proportion at Level 1 or higher did move up slightly, from 69 per cent pre-enrolment to 71 per cent at second follow-up.)

The New Zealand team found particular resonances with the findings of *Improving Workplace Learning* (Evans *et al.* 2006), the TLRP forerunner of the present research. This has argued for an approach to workplace learning, which connects the individual employees, their immediate working environments and the wider framework that governs the employer-employee relationship. This framework stresses the importance of learning taking place informally through everyday working practices,

Table 9.1 Comparison of New Zealand and UK participants in workplace programmes included in the research

New Zealand respondents	UK respondents
66% male	67% male
Average age 39 years	Average 38 years
34% ESOL	41% ESOL
Average of 3.6 years secondary schooling: 51% do not have a school qualification; 16% have a qualification at NCEA Level 2 or equivalent.	39% of the sample had no formal qualifications, or none. 34% of non-ESOL and 49% of ESOL learners had qualifications at Level 2 or above.
They have worked for their companies for an average of 5.3 years and been in their current job an average of 3.5 years.	They have worked for their current employer for an average of 7.5 years.
Most had not done much workplace training previously.	Most had done little workplace training previously.
41% were at IALS/ALL Level 1; 45% at Level 2;* 14% at Level 3+. (Level 1 equates to all UK Entry levels combined: 9% of the sample were Entry level 1; 18% Entry level 2; 24% Entry level 3.)	At start of courses, 11% at or below Entry 2, 22% Entry 3, 43% Level 1, 24% Level 2 or above.

* People at Levels 1 and 2 are likely to have difficulty with aspects such as reading and understanding

an aspect embraced by the New Zealand research. As already noted, the Upskilling Partnerships Programme placed heavy emphasis on contextualizing learning in the participating workplace, creating more potential for synergies than in the UK programmes observed.

In common with the UK findings, Benseman's team found that many research informants in companies saw LLN development only in terms of formally structured courses or identifiable 'training' involving the inculcation of a body of knowledge and sets of skills. Interestingly, the New Zealand team showed that new programmes (ELNPs) were beginning, slowly, to change this and some case studies indicated that if work – embedded forms and development through enhanced work practices 'are not taken into account and a continuum of learning opportunities provided, it is possible that companies will not take up LLN as a factor in workplace learning' (Kell 2009: 26).

The New Zealand research has concluded that workplace learning does indeed need to be conceptualized as learning through, in and for the workplace (Evans et al. 2006). If this is done, it is argued learning can address adult learners' needs as individuals for skills and possibly qualifications that will give them security and mobility; at the same time as it addresses their needs as employees and their employers' needs for them to be able to engage successfully in workplace tasks and demands (Kell 2009: 26).

It follows that enabling frameworks are therefore needed that will provide a range of opportunities and support, such as new forms of financial support,[4] training subsidies for time release, performance incentives for peers who act as mentors, or tax credits aimed at the company as a whole. We suggest that lessons could be drawn from the superior sustainability of US literacy programmes (Nelson 2004).[5]

Both the New Zealand and the UK research suggest that the view of LLN as 'foundational and therefore, general,' has unintentionally fostered the perception that LLN is not the responsibility of firms. Benseman et al.'s recommendations have led to a re-framing of New Zealand LLN Action Plan (2008–2012) asking whether an understanding of LLN as closely linked with business processes and outcomes can become associated, in the minds of employers with the learning that is necessary for production and innovation to take place. In the UK, continuing work on challenges to sustainable workplace programmes is addressing similar issues.[6]

Facilitating literacy learning at work through collaborative learning: A Canadian-UK exploration sponsored by the Social Sciences and Humanities Research Council of Canada (SSHRC)

So far, we have shown how international cross-referencing of our research has underlined the importance of the longer-term development of literacy proficiency and the need to recognize the interplay of formal and informal literacy learning. Such interplay may be facilitated by collaborative learning. This requires teacher development.

Early indications that collaborative learning was a preferred model by some practitioners experienced in workplace programmes led to Anglo-Canadian cooperation between the Institute of Education and the University of Ottawa. A UK practitioner researcher (Sue Southwood) was supported by NRDC to work with counterparts in Canada.

One purpose of this Anglo-Canadian inquiry was to investigate how adult students learn collaboratively with other and what teaching styles best support this learning. The multi-site case-study research design involved several sites in Ontario, Canada, and in London, United Kingdom. Both Canada and the United Kingdom share similar literacy challenges, policy initiatives and program delivery systems. For example, at the national government policy level, in Canada, a Parliamentary Committee Report entitled *Raising Adult Literacy Skills: The Need for a Pan-Canadian Response* (2003), recommended the development of a federal literacy policy. A report to the Minister of State for Human Resources Development titled *Towards a Fully Literate Canada* (2005) advocated a national strategy that focuses on the adult learner, seeks community solutions and supports learning communities. This viewpoint was the basis for the new Adult Literacy and Life Skills Survey (Statistics Canada 2005).

The key questions for the joint study were: (1) 'How do adult students use collaborative learning with other peers in a wide range of adult literacy provisions?' and (2) 'What teaching styles best support collaborative learning practices among adult students?' Insights from the UK work were set out and discussed in detail in Chapter 4.

A model of collaborative learning and teaching model shown in Figure 9.1, was constructed by the research team. It reflects literacy practices that are embedded in a specific cultural context and mediated by the personal circumstances of both the learners and the instructors (see Taylor *et al.* 2007c). A central component in the model is the tutor/instructor's philosophy which was identified using a 'Teaching Perspectives Inventory': a questionnaire which identifies and classifies pedagogical philosophies. Tutors have certain conceptions of their roles and the nature of learning, and ideas about how student learning can be supported in particular

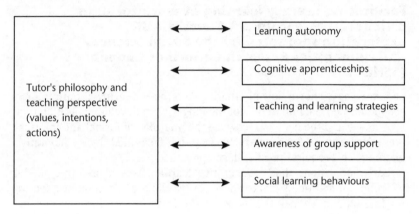

Figure 9.1 Building blocks for a collaborative learning and teaching model in adult literacy

contexts and settings. The TPI addresses these (and is described in the Methodological Appendix).

There were some interesting differences in the TPI profiles. The UK tutors, all work-based tutors supporting literacy learning in workplaces, shared a nurturing profile on their Teaching Perspective Inventories and a belief in building trust and confidence amongst learners to create a climate conducive to learning. However, while nurturing was dominant, it was not massively so: profiles were relatively flat, with significant scores in all other categories except social reform. This contrasted with the Canadian tutor profiles where individuals typically showed one or two highly dominant perspectives. The more mixed UK profiles may be explained by the effects on practice of workplace cultures and constraints, together with the more structured, mandatory literacy curriculum frameworks in which UK literacy tutors have to work. These combine to influence tutors' beliefs, intentions and scope for action.

The components of Figure 9.1 are fundamental to how adult students use this learning approach, whether in small, large and 'tutorial' groups. The set-up of a collaborative environment encourages social learning behaviours. Simultaneously, certain types of teaching strategies that favour collaborative learning are chosen by the tutor. Over time and with group support and feedback, learners model these teaching strategies with other peers in the style of cognitive apprenticeships. In the process, the roles of the instructor and the student change; learners move from a position of being guided in their learning to one where they experience some sense of growing independence.

UK observational data confirmed these dynamics of learning. It also showed (see Chapter 4) how work relationships outside the classroom impact on how adults learn collaboratively; workplace peers play an important role in helping those who are lacking in self-confidence, and employee-learners can adapt their behaviour to work collaboratively. Collaborative learning strategies can, it appears, help to overcome some of the barriers that adult learners encounter. The international evidence provides further support for Reder's practice engagement theory (1994) that individuals acquire literacy through participation in a variety of literacy practices and participate in these practices in different ways.

Summary and conclusions

This chapter has introduced three international collaborations which indicate that the following factors appear to apply cross-culturally.

The provision of instruction and support has to be available in episodic forms or in sustained longer-term programmes, to build literacy proficiency. At work, building literacy proficiency may depend crucially on the extent to which skills are taken up, utilized and expanded through workplace literacy practices. The development of collaborative models and practices in learning and teaching can connect general literacy development with workplace processes and the expansion of employees' capabilities to participate in and carry out workplace tasks and roles. As workplace processes can restrict as well as expand employees' learning, as much attention has to be given to the workplace environment as to teaching philosophy and values. Collaborative models of learning and teaching, when investigated in depth, also lead us back to 'practice engagement theory' and the importance of skills use. Literacy proficiency is built by multiple engagements. Short courses can be gateways to further learning and the building of proficiency; but better skills utilization at work, as well as opportunities beyond the workplace is crucial.

Chapter 10

Improving literacy learning in and through work

In this concluding chapter we summarize the implications of our research. We discuss these with respect to government policy on improving literacy in the workplace, but also address, more generally, the lessons learnt about how best to promote effective workplace learning.

As discussed in Chapter 1, our research took place in the context of unprecedented expenditures on adult basic skills provision. In England, total expenditures on Skills for Life between 2001 and 2008 are estimated at over £5 billion (House of Commons Public Accounts Committee 2009). Although the government's most recent spending reviews have reduced somewhat, the preferential funding for basic skills and workplace provision generally remains a high priority.

As a result, the 'Train to Gain' programme (T2G), which pays for workplace-based programmes leading to a formal qualification, has absorbed increasing amounts of government funding over the last few years. Within this programme, basic skills provision received a considerable amount of money. Siôn Simon, for the government, informed Parliament that, at the end of March 2008, 41,000 T2G learners were enrolled for Skills for Life awards (Simon 2009). This meant that 12 per cent of enrolled T2G learners were enrolled for a basic skills award, either alone or with a vocational qualification.

More generally, Train to Gain is driven by the need to meet targets (and contracts) for numbers of qualifications awarded.[1] Low levels of funded hours per learner, and payments tied to 'outputs' (i.e. qualifications), mean that providers can only make a profit by ensuring that qualifications are indeed completed, as efficiently and quickly as possible. This creates a very strong incentive to enter learners for qualifications at levels they are already close to achieving. At the time that we recruited sites and learners, T2G had not yet become the main programme of funding for workplaces. However, its creation has further intensified rather than altering many of the characteristics of earlier funding and provision. Hence, we believe, the policy and organizational lessons of our findings remain highly relevant, rather than outdated as a result of policy reform.

Policy implications

In one key sense, the workplace programmes studied confirmed an underlying policy assumption. They were successful in reaching adults who do not normally participate in formal learning, and who would find it difficult to do so without the convenience of workplace provision.

However, our findings call into question every other assumption made in the design and funding of workplace basic skills programmes. The 'deficiency model' at the heart of policy was one of adult learners who lacked the skills to do their jobs well, and would benefit economically from improving them; and of employers faced with basic skill 'gaps', who would secure higher productivity as a result of the programme.

Neither the learners nor the employers in our study fitted this description. Learners were motivated by a far wider range of factors than the wish to improve job performance – helping children with their homework, pursuing interests outside work, learning new skills as a form of personal development. And we have shown how managers were also motivated largely by factors other than the desire to 'plug' skill gaps or improve productivity. The main impulse was to strengthen the psychological contract between employer and employee – to demonstrate to employees that they were valuable and valued.

Managers believed the courses improved staff confidence and morale, but reported very few examples of direct impact in narrowly economic terms. Nor did they particularly want them: they did not, for the most part, feel that there were substantial 'basic skills gaps' in their workforce. Policy makers' adoption of a 'deficiency model' fails to take account of individuals' capacity to make do with their existing skills and competencies and tailor them to the actual demands of the workplace; and ignores evidence that employers do not, in fact, report skills gaps as a major problem.

It is just as well that 'skill gaps' are not a huge problem, given that the workplace courses studied did not, in general, have any substantial impact on participants' literacy skills. Among learners for whom English was their first language, there were no statistically significant improvements in literacy attainment. Among ESOL learners, there were small but statistically significant gains, but it is very likely that these resulted from continued exposure to an English speaking environment. (This hypothesis is supported by the finding that the features which were associated with improvement for first-language learners, such as feeling that the course was the 'right' level for them, were not significant for ESOL learners.)

Moreover, in the host organizations, there appears, once direct funding ends, to be very little left to show for it all. As described above, our longitudinal research found no stable legacies or outcomes at all that could be ascribed to government activity, either in the form of ongoing provision, or in changes in employers' training activities. Our findings are, moreover, consistent with those of both other researchers who have examined the institutional impact of workplace-oriented initiatives in the skills sector (Finlay *et al.* 2007) and of evaluations of their impact using national datasets (Abramovsky *et al.* 2005). Like Prospero's cloud-capped towers in *The Tempest*, these schemes have vanished into thin air, and 'leave not a wrack behind'.

There were a number of reasons for this, some of which are directly attributable to government policy. First of all, a good deal of provision was funded in ways which were intrinsically short-term. Union Learning Fund and European Social Fund money was of this type; recipients could only expect one project, one tranche of funding. The Pathfinder Projects which were meant to develop good practice for the future provided levels of funding which could not be sustained on a one-off basis. This is an approach which cannot – and does not – help a long-term infrastructure to develop. It is anti-institutional, when what is needed is a set of sustainable institutions to deliver the *lifetime* learning to which governments are officially committed.

Second, courses were themselves very short. They were typically 30 hours in total in the sites we studied; since then, average provision will have shrunk further, since Train to Gain typically allows for a total of 17 hours' contact time. The domination of quantitative targets also places enormous pressure on providers to ensure that learners are not stretched, but on the contrary, entered for qualifications they will pass. Meanwhile, learners' own publicly-funded entitlements are expressed in terms of qualifications – they can be funded for only so many, of a certain level and type. The restrictions which these rules generate have grown even worse in recent years, and make it increasingly difficult to secure funding for the sort of developmental programme supported by managers, union representatives, and learners alike.

These are aspects of policy which could be changed; but other problems are more intractable. First of all, few individual enterprises are in a position to develop stable learning institutions. In the space of just over two years, we found that 14 per cent of our sites had closed altogether. In over half, there was no manager in post who had any recollection of or knowledge about the courses which had taken place. National figures on company start-ups and closures show that this is quite typical, while the public sector is also characterized by constant reorganization. (For example, in just eight years, the British government department responsible for Skills for Life has changed its name from DfEE to DfES and is now to DIUS. See Wolf 2009.) Second, workplace provision which uses anything like the model we tracked is extremely expensive. Top-down provision, on a workplace-specific pattern, involves, as described above, multiple contacts for each course operated, small groups and heavy fixed costs.

This argues for an approach which emphasizes entitlements for individual learners, not for employers and workplaces; and for demand driven by individual learners, not by government preconceptions about skill gaps and skill needs (Wolf 2010). There are lessons to be learnt from countries such as the US, where tuition assistance from employers is non-taxable; where employers correspondingly provide assistance as a way of motivating and retaining staff; and where a very high proportion of community college students get full or partial employer support for courses which they select (Cappelli 2002; Lerman *et al.* 2004). There are lessons, too, closer to home, in some of the lifelong learning initiatives piloted by local authorities in the 1990s, using individual entitlements and vouchers for adults (Jarvis *et al.* 1997). The Union Learning Representative structure needs to be developed and strengthened rather than, as at present, undermined by a system that routes all expenditure through contracts between employers and providers.

In sum, our research indicates that current policy is misconceived in a number of fundamental respects. There are major disjunctions between policy assumptions about large scale literacy and skills deficiencies in the UK and the reality of employees' capacity to cope with their existing skills and competencies. Problems are compounded by vague assumptions about the increased significance of literacy and numeracy skills in a post-industrial 'knowledge' economy, and an obsession with quantitative targets and central control of training agendas.

However, the research also provides a number of important positive lessons about the drivers of effective adult learning; and it is to these that we now turn.

Adults learning

The research has confirmed that there is a strong appetite for learning among many adults who have not found it possible to attend conventional classes. Participants were more likely to continue with formal learning than would otherwise have been the case; the large majority felt differently, and more positively about education and learning; and many also reported increasing the amount they read. Their strong levels of satisfaction with the courses they had taken reflected these underlying responses. The changes in their learning trajectories were not dramatic – but nor would one expect this from what was, in every case, quite a limited experience. But the changes were discernable and clear for a good number of participants.

By using a social ecological approach we were able to elucidate the dynamics of learning in and through workplace environments and confirm the importance of whether, and how, work-related experiences reinforce and build upon skills addressed in formal learning. The interdependencies already mapped by Evans *et al.* (2006) in other TLRP research were confirmed here, for different scales of activity – macro-organizational, political, regulatory, cultural.

The fact that so many adults want to learn means that companies that aim to expand and enrich job content in jobs at all levels are likely to find employees working to expand their capacities accordingly. Conversely, employees who attend courses, only to return to a job and work environment that provides no opportunities for their use, are likely to see the benefits of their investment eroded over time. If employees attend literacy courses while continuing to engage in day-to-day tasks which have little or no literacy content, then their jobs are unlikely to sustain, let alone increase, any gains in literacy skills.

Much of the policy debate at governmental level assumes that what is good for business is also good for employees and for society. Conversely, the pluralist framework of industrial relations (Rainbird *et al.* 2003), recognizes the conflict inherent in the relationship between workers and managers. This conflict, held to be inevitable, stems from different interests, trajectories and power bases. Both Geary (1995) and Hyman and Streeck (1988: p4) are sceptical that participative management strategies can achieve more harmonious industrial relations.

Achieving cooperation in the context of potentially conflicting relations certainly requires active management (Edwards 2003: 12) from middle managers who frequently find themselves in positions of having to foster creativity while controlling performance. However, we think there are genuine opportunities and potential for employee development in the workplace. Geary (1995) believes that winning over employees by encouraging more active forms of participation in organizational matters can also lead to the re-shaping of some aspects of work organization, and to promotion of skills development, particularly in the case of generic skills. Green's research (2009) provides support for this view. And in the workplace literacy programmes that we studied, it is noteworthy that managers were most interested in the potential of programmes to raise morale and strengthen the 'psychological contract' between firm and employee.

Improving workplace learning means paying attention to what people want and need; and to the different expressions of interests that come from work groups differently located in the social landscapes of the organization and labour market. Employee voice plays a greater part in new management strategies, and can enable managers to bring about a better equilibrium of interests.

In the end however, expanding and improving learning at work in these ways involves a cost-benefit analysis for all involved. They must evaluate the potential advantages in enhancing the qualities of the broader environment, while recognizing that the organization's *raison d'être* is the production of goods or services rather than promoting learning *per se*. As Hodkinson and Rainbird in the final chapter of Evans *et al.* (2006) have noted 'the eventual decisions about precisely how a particular learning environment can be improved will entail recognition of these different interests and whether mutual benefits can be identified' (p. 172).

In summary, there are real possibilities for enhancing learning in and through the workplace – but realism is required. And a major implication of our study is that policy-makers should be more realistic about the motivations for and benefits of workplace provision. It makes far more sense to see workplace provision as one milieu among others in which citizens can make use of an entitlement to learning; and as a form of provision which may have multiple benefits, over a long period of time, rather than an immediate productivity-enhancing intervention.

Methodological appendix

Data collection

Possible sites for data collection were identified and contacted using a wide variety of different sources:

Formal Skills-for-Life-affiliated networks

The principal and co-investigator (Wolf and Evans) had close links with the National Research and Development Centre for adult literacy and numeracy, which was funded until 2008 as part of the Skills for Life strategy. Wolf and Evans both served at various points on the NRDC executive board: and NRDC provided co-funding for the project during 2004–2007. Contact sites and individuals were obtained from a variety of sources within the Skills for Life networks, including the DfES' own staff, the Workplace Basic Skills Network, based at Lancaster University, and individual practitioners attending NRDC/SfL events.

Informal contacts and non-SfL networks within the further and adult education community, and employers

These included NIACE and LSDA and the Scottish Executive. Some large companies were contacted directly after we were informed, through published literature or word of mouth, that they were offering basic skills courses.

Individual FE colleges

Individual colleges were contacted both through prior contacts and by 'cold calling'.

Union Learning Fund

The Union Learning Fund was established in 1998 in order to encourage the take-up of learning in the workplace. TUC staff provided us with contacts for project leaders in individual unions which had been funded to help establish workplace learning centres and activities.

Sector Skills Councils

Contacts were made with the SSCs responsible for the occupational areas selected for the study. One of these (Asset Skills, the Sector Skills Council for facilities management, housing, property, planning, cleaning and parking) was also the designated SSC with responsibility for leading on basic skills and provided us with a number of useful contacts.

In addition to the above, all of which yielded concrete possibilities, we also contacted the following organizations without receiving any concrete leads:

- All Learning and Skills Councils (central and area)
- All RDAs
- SfL Brokers

Sectors

Our original research design provided for explicit comparisons between sectors, on the assumption that courses would be contextualized and that it would be appropriate to measure progress both on sector-related and general literacy materials. In the event, this was not the case – with one single exception, the courses studied did not use customized material, and most did not even contextualize materials very much.

Occupational sector was included in a number of the analyses, and some significant differences were apparent between sectors on some measures. These reflected differences in the recruitment patterns of the sectors (notably the proportion and educational level of ESOL employees); and also differences in the range of occupations held by learners in different groups.

The overall distribution, by sector, was as follows. (Mixed groups were found in Scotland, where the patterns of recruitment and provision was different; and in some large employers, notably local authorities, where learners from different parts of the authority were in the same class.)

All participating employers were guaranteed anonymity, as were all participating learners.

Table A.1 Recruitment of sites and learners

Sector	Sites	Learners
Cleaning	9	103
Food processing	12	104
Health care	8	66
Transport	16	224
Mixed	8	77

Instruments

With one exception, courses were in literacy or literacy and IT, not numeracy. Although we attempted to create a numeracy sample, hardly any numeracy provision was located. We also expected programmes to use sector-specific materials, related to job-specific skills, and proposed to sample on this dimension. (Previous work on adult literacy had suggested that such materials are highly effective pedagogically: see Sticht and Mikulecky 1984.) In fact, use of such materials was almost non-existent.

As a result, although we had originally expected to use two types of assessment instrument – one measuring general skills, and one modified to reflect the site-specific characteristics of each enterprise, and its basic skills teaching – we were only able to test general skills, and, for analysis purposes, only *general literacy skills*. (We did measure numeracy skills at the one numeracy site but numbers were too small to provide any meaningful results.)

The following instruments were used:

- Learners' Questionnaire Occasion 1
- Learners' Questionnaire Occasion 2
- Learners' Questionnaire Occasion 3
- Managers' Questionnaire Occasion 1
- Managers' Questionnaire Occasion 2
- Tutors' Questionnaire
- Union Learning Representative Questionnaire
- Workplace Supervisor Questionnaire
- *Go!* Magazine literacy assessment (2 levels, 2 parallel versions, plus a pre-test for level placement)
- Effective Lifelong Learning Inventory (ELLI)
- Teaching Perspective Inventory

Questions from Learners' Questionnaire 1 and Managers' Questionnaire 1 are reproduced below. All questionnaires are available from the ESRC Essex Archive (http://www.data-archive.ac.uk/).

Go! magazine literacy assessment: The *Go!* magazine assessments were developed by the National Foundation for Educational Research for NRDC and specifically designed to identify and measure small changes in proficiency. They are also designed specifically for an adult audience. They are based around authentic-seeming magazines (two parallel editions). For each of these two editions of *Go!* there are two overlapping literacy assessments, requiring written responses: one for very poor readers, one for more accomplished readers. (These provide parallel forms across the two magazines.) The raw marks can be standardized allowing all candidates, whichever version they took, to be given a mark on a scale of 1 to 100. Each broad category in the government's relevant qualifications framework (Entry 3 through Level 2) is associated with a range of marks on *Go!* A sample of the *Go!* material is shown in the Introduction.

The Effective Lifelong Learning Inventory (ELLI): was developed by Deakin Crick *et al.* (2004) to capture individuals' 'capacity for lifelong learning'. In the form used for this study it contained 44 items. Each makes a statement about learning. For example:

I like to question the things I am learning.

When I'm stuck, I usually don't know what to do about it.

and asks the learner to state how far that statement applies to them.

The ELLI instrument was administered to learners at the first and second interviews and the data are currently being analysed.

The Teaching Perspectives Inventory: Identifies teachers' views on what is 'good teaching'. Respondents are given 45 statements and asked whether this describes them always/usually/sometimes/rarely never. For example:

I ask a lot of questions while teaching.

I want to provide a balance between caring and challenging as I teach.

The answers are related to five possible underlying philosophies of teaching: transmission (effective teaching requires a substantial commitment to the content or subject matter); apprenticeship (effective teaching is a process of socializing students into new behavioural norms and ways of working); developmental (effective teaching must be planned and conducted from the learners' point of view); nurturing (effective teaching assumes that long-terms hard persistent effort to achieve comes from the heart not the head); and social reform (effective teaching seeks to change society in substantive ways). Some teachers have profiles which show a very marked commitment to one of these philosophies; others do not.

Questions from Learners' questionnaire at time 1

What is your official job title?

Is your job: permanent/on a fixed-term contract/seasonal, temporary or casual?

Do you work full-time or part-time?

How many hours per week?

Do you work overtime at all?

If yes, how many hours per week on average?

What times of day do you usually work?

How long have you been working for your current employer?

Do you manage or supervise any colleagues at your current job?

If yes, how many colleagues do you manage or supervise?

Could you please briefly describe your work history in the last five years (including periods out of work)?

At what age did you leave school or formal education?

Did you leave with any qualifications?

What were they?

Have you attended any courses or formal training since school?

Were any in the last five years?

Were any of these courses at the workplace?

Did you gain any further qualifications?

What were they?

Do you know if your parents had any formal qualifications?

If yes, what were their highest qualifications?

Is English your first language?

What is your first language?

Were you educated in your first language?

Can you read in your first language?

Can you write in your first language?

Is English the language you normally speak at home?

Which (other) language(s) do you normally speak at home?

How many children under 16 are you responsible for or looking after?

How old are they?

Do you have any other caring responsibilities at the moment (e.g. relatives)?

Who are you caring for at the moment?

Can I just ask you your date of birth?

In which of the following ethnic groups do you consider that you belong?
   White/Black or Black British/Asian or Asian British/Dual Heritage/ Other

For each aspect that I am going to read out to you I would like you rate it between 1 and 7. Ratings towards 1 indicate that you do not like that aspect of your job very much; ratings close to 7 indicate that you like or feel positively about that aspect of your job; ratings around 4 indicate that you are rather indifferent about that aspect of your job.

   The amount of work you have to do
   Your promotion prospects
   Your relationship with your line manager or supervisor
   Your relationship with your colleagues
   Your job security
   The chance to use your own initiative
   The pattern of working hours/shifts
   Your pay, including any bonuses or overtime
   The actual work itself
   The opportunity to use your skills and abilities
   The training opportunities available

Using the scale from 1 to 7 again as before, how would you rate your job overall?

Are your workmates also your friends?

To what extent do you feel part of a team at work?

How many of the people you work with did you talk to yesterday?

Was that a typical day?

If yesterday wasn't a typical day, how many of the people you work with do you talk to on a typical day?

Which of the following best fits your situation?

> I know most of the people at my place of work
>
> I know many of the people at my place of work
>
> I know a good number of people at my place of work
>
> I know a few people at my place of work, but most are strangers
>
> I know only one or two people at my place of work

Do you feel valued by your co-workers?

Do you feel valued by your employer?

In the last few weeks, have you volunteered to do anything at work over and above your normal day-to-day tasks?

How easy would you say it is to do that at your workplace?

In the last few weeks, have you made any suggestions for changes or improvements in how your work is organized?

How easy would you say it is to do that at your workplace?

How likely are you to leave your current employer in the next year?

Why do you think you will or might leave?

> The firm will close down
>
> You will be made redundant
>
> You will reach normal retirement age
>
> You will take early retirement
>
> Your contract of employment will expire
>
> You will decide to leave and work for another employer
>
> You will decide to leave and work for yourself as self-employed
>
> You will leave to look after home/children/relative
>
> You will decide to be unemployed/take time off for a while
>
> You will leave the country
>
> Other reason

In terms of your working life, where do you see yourself in two to three years from now if things go according to plan?

> Same job at the same company
>
> Promotion within the same company
>
> Same/similar job at a different company

Different job at a different company

Not working

Retired

Other

Is this the first time that you are attending a course/training programme at the workplace with your current employer?

How come you got involved in the training?

Using the scale from 1 to 7 again, how happy are you to be going on this course?

Why are you doing this training?

Which of the above would you say is the most important reason for doing this course/training?

Now I'd like to show you a list of possible benefits from training like this. What would you would you say are the TWO main benefits for you personally?

It makes work more interesting

It will help you to earn more money

It helps you to do your current job better

It improves your chances for promotion

It improves your chances of getting a better job

It enables you to learn new skills

It is good for meeting new people

Other

And what benefits, if any, do you think there will be for your employer?

Do you hope to gain a qualification at the end of this course/training programme?

What qualification?

Would you say that you are more or less likely to come into work on the days that you have a class/training session?

Are you following an online course within a learndirect centre at all, in addition to the course/training you are following at the workplace?

Will there be an opportunity to do another course at work, once this is finished?

How likely is it that you will be attending such a course?

What kind of course will that be?

How likely is it that you will do another course outside work (e.g. local college), once this course is finished?

What kind of course?

Questions from managers' questionnaire at time 1

How many different literacy, numeracy, ESOL or basic IT courses are currently taking place within your company/organization? [If more than one course is mentioned, then questions should be repeated.]

When did/will this course/programme start?

What kind of employees is this course/programme intended for?

Which of the following types of skills would you say the course/programme gives more emphasis to?

  Basic skills (literacy, numeracy or ESOL)

  IT skills

  Vocational skills

  Other (specify)

What type of basic skills would you say this programme/course gives more emphasis to?

  Literacy

  Numeracy

  ESOL

  Literacy and ESOL

  Literacy and numeracy

  Other (please specify)

Is the course/programme leading to a particular qualification?

Can you please tell us which of the following qualifications the course/programme is leading to?

  Adult Literacy/Key Skills Communication (please specify level)

  Adult Numeracy/Key Skills Application of Number (please specify level)

  ESOL/EFL qualification (specify which)

  NVQ (specify subject and level)

  IT qualification (specify which)

  Other (specify)

Is the course/training programme taking place during employees' normal working hours?

In which of the following ways was the course/programme set up?

> You were approached by the current provider directly
>
> You were approached by a BSA approved broker
>
> It was an initiative of a trade union representative
>
> You/other member of your company approached the current provider
>
> Other (please specify)

Was there an Organizational or Training Needs Analysis (ONA/TNA) carried out before the start of the course/programme?

Who carried out the ONA/TNA?

Who decided on the specific content/scope of the course/programme?

How were staff recruited to the course/training programme?

Can you briefly describe how the course/programme was advertised to staff and how staff were recruited to it.

When an employee enrols on the course/training programme, who else knows about it:

How is the course/programme funded?

Can you please look at this list and tell us which of these outcomes you think your company is hoping to achieve through this course/training programme? Please select all that apply.

> Improve job-specific skills of staff
>
> Improve 'soft' skills of staff (e.g. team-working, communication)
>
> Offer general development to staff
>
> Increase staff morale
>
> Reduce number of errors at the workplace
>
> Reduce absenteeism
>
> Reduce staff turnover
>
> Improve health and safety
>
> Increase staff confidence
>
> Help staff to be receptive to change
>
> Other (please specify)

Which of the above would you say is the most important and why?

Is this the first time that your company/organization has offered this type of training/course for this type of employees?

If not, what other courses of this type have been offered in the past (please specify how many and in what subject)?

When were (was) these (this) course(s) offered?

Would you say that the current course/programme is a continuation of these previous course(s)/programme(s)?

How successful would you say the previous course(s) was (were) in meeting its (their) objectives?

Can you briefly explain why?

Could you please provide us with a list of other formal, off-the-job, training programmes that your company/organization has offered to non-managerial/non-professional staff in the last year (e.g. health and safety training, technical skills, 'soft' skills).

Which of the following statements best describes your company/ organization's approach to filling vacancies?

    Internal applicants are only source, no external recruitment

    Internal applicants are given preference, other things being equal, over external applicants

    Internal and external applicants are treated equally

    No recruitment in last 5 years

What percentage of vacancies in the past 12 months have been filled by employees from within this organization?

Thinking about the last two years, would you say there has been a lot of change, some change, a little change or no change in the nature of people's jobs within your company/organization?

Again thinking about the last two years, would you say that there has been a lot of change, some change, a little change or no change in the type of skills that people need to carry out their jobs within your company/ organization?

Does your company/organization have a formal appraisal system for staff?

If yes, is this system linked to professional development?

If yes, could you please briefly explain how the system works?

Background Tables

The learner sample

Table A.2 Characteristics of learner sample compared to overall adult learner population: 2005–2006 (%)

	Study learners	FE learners in publicly supported further education institutions 2005–6	Adult and community learners in publicly supported provision 2005–6	All forms of adult learning (self-reported and including workplace training) 2006
Male	67	41	23	48
Female	33	59	77	52
Under 25	6	51	35	15
25–34	22	17		16
35–44	32	15	58*	20
45–54	23	9		20
54+	17	8	7 (60+)	29

* Ages 25–59.

Sources: Learning and Skills Council Learner 2007, DfES First Statistical Estimates 2007, Aldridge and Tuckett 2008.

Table A.3 Qualifications held by learners (pre-enrolment) Non-ESOL learners (%)

	Total	Under 25	25–34	35–44	45–54	54+
Below level 1/ none	40	28	27	40	42	49
1 or 2 (unclear)	10	2	13	12	5	6
1	16	10	17	16	20	10
2	25	60	25	27	23	22
3	6	–	11	5	8	7
4 or 5	3	–	7	–	2	4

continued ...

Table A.3 continued

ESOL learners (%)

	Total	Under 25	25–34	35–44	45–54	54+
Below level 1/ none	38	64	34	24	46	43
1 or 2 (unclear)	5	6	–	2	3	3
1	8	0	3	16	11	9
2	12	10	12	8	14	20
3	23	10	27	30	17	15
4 or 5	14	10	24	20	9	10

Table A.4 Language characteristics of sample

	%
First language English	59
ESOL	41

Table A.5 Time spent with current employer

	%
Less than 1 year	13
1–2 years	24
2–4 years	18
4–7 years	12
7–12 years	10
More than 12 years	23

Table A.6 Percentage feeling valued by employer and colleagues at time 1 (full sample)

	Employer	Colleagues
Not at all	13	3
A little	19	7
To some extent	34	51
A lot	34	39

Correlations of reading scores

Table A.7 Factors affecting initial reading score: non-ESOL cases

	Coef.	Std. Err.	t	P>|t|
Female	6.68	2.72	2.45	0.15
Age	0.059	0.10	0.57	0.57
Qualifications (base=none)				
Level 1 or 2	9.83	2.52	3.89	0.00
Level 3 or above	12.05	3.95	3.05	0.00
Quals missing	3.50	4.64	0.75	0.45
Sector (base = transport)				
Cleaning	–13.03	5.91	–2.20	0.03
Food	–2.09	4.35	–0.48	0.63
Health	–2.42	7.27	–0.33	0.74
Mixed	–1.53	4.26	–0.36	0.72
Occupation (base = routine manual)				
Managerial	3.26	5.41	0.60	0.58
Skilled	1.12	6.46	0.17	0.86
Personal service	–6.39	6.39	–1.00	0.32
Sales	–19.08	8.22	–2.32	0.02
Elementary occupation	2.19	6.03	0.36	0.72
Constant	51.64	55.5	9.30	0.00

Number of observations = 276, R^2 = 0.1985

Table A.8 Factors affecting initial reading score: ESOL cases

	Coef.	Std. Err.	t	P>|t|
Female	6.45	2.85	2.27	0.02
Age	–0.15	0.12	–1.28	0.20
Qualifications (base=none)				
Level 1 or 2	0.04	3.40	0.01	0.90
Level 3 or above	1.85	3.23	0.57	0.57
Quals missing	–0.89	5.15	–0.17	0.86
Sector (base = transport)				
Cleaning	–20.86	6.22	–3.35	0.01
Food	–21.68	3.61	–6.01	0.00
Health	–9.87	6.64	–1.49	0.14
Mixed	–11.72	4.58	–2.56	0.01
Occupation (base = routine manual)				
Managerial	19.91	6.38	3.12	0.00
Personal service	7.26	6.54	1.11	0.27
Sales	27.08	5.12	5.29	0.00
Elementary occupation	5.99	3.68	1.63	0.10
Constant	43.02	6.28	6.85	0.00

Number of observations = 181, R^2 = 0.4705

Table A.9 Factors affecting improvement in reading between initial and first follow up test (non-ESOL)
Dependent variable: change in reading score between time 1 and time 2

	(1)	(2)	(3)	(4)
Time 1 Standardized score	−0.348	−0.357	−0.342	−0.332
	[5.30]***	[5.39]***	[5.18]***	[5.17]***
Highest qualification (base none or below Level 1)				
Level 1 or 2	7.747	6.865	6.706	6.647
	[2.95]***	[2.62]***	[2.58]**	[2.51]**
Level 3 or above	3.268	3.248	5.733	4.326
	[0.77]	[0.73]	[1.33]	[0.98]
Go version A (Time2)	−10.020	−9.050	−9.570	−8.829
	[2.47]**	[2.19]**	[2.35]**	[2.20]**
Go issue 1 (Time2)	−0.624	−1.439	0.025	−2.063
	[0.26]	[0.55]	[0.01]	[0.82]
Attended all sessions of initial course		3.883		
		[1.31]		
Obtained qualification at end of initial course			5.918	
			[2.12]**	
Any subsequent training since initial course				1.880
				[0.76]
Constant	17.848	16.494	13.282	16.314
	[4.56]***	[3.90]***	[3.21]***	[4.10]***
Observations	151	147	148	139
R-squared	0.1895	0.1963	0.1857	0.1901

Absolute value of t statistics in brackets

* significant at 10%; ** significant at 5%; *** significant at 1%.
Model controls for score at Time 1
Note: None of the relationships held for the ESOL subsample.

Table A.10 Outcomes of the course and reading scores, non-ESOL cases (Models control for score at time 1)
Dependent variable: change in reading score between time 1 and time 2

	(1)	*(2)*	*(3)*	*(4)*
Enabled me to learn new skills	4.144			
	[1.66]*			
No particular benefits for me		–6.210		
		[1.89]*		
Course was too easy			–6.784	
			[1.90]*	
Course met expectations a lot				1.128
				[0.44]
Constant	15.518	18.019	17.767	16.917
	[3.75]***	[4.64]***	[4.53]***	[3.92]***
Observations	151	151	149	148
R-squared	0.2048	0.2092	0.1889	0.1835

Note: all models control for highest qualification, Time 1 standardized reading score and Time 2 Go! version and issue.

Absolute value of t statistics in brackets.
* significant at 10%; ** significant at 5%; *** significant at 1%.
Note: None of these relationships held for the ESOL subsample.

Table A.11 Relationship between growth in reading score (between first and second interview) and job change: age controls introduced

	Coef.	*Std. Err.*	*t*	*P>|t|*
Time 2 reading score	–.43	0.74	–5.77	0.000
Version A	–18.19	4.17	–4.36	0.000
Job change	5.43	3.22	1.69	0.095
Female	–4.20	3.37	–1.25	0.215
Age	–.17	.15	–1.10	0.276
constant	37.37	8.80	4.25	0.000

Number of observations = 107, R-squared = 0.3013

Younger learners are more likely to change jobs; but the relationship between job change and reading improvement remains significant at the 10% level even after introduction of controls for age.

Course outcomes

Table A.12 Outcomes of course

	Yes (%)	No (%)
Learnt new skills	49	51
Good for meeting people	27	73
Qualification gained?	67	33
Any benefits from it for you?	88	12

Table A.13 Overall evaluation of course: did it meet your expectations?

	(%)
Not at all	5
A little	12
To some extent	33
A lot	50

Table A.14 Attitudes to work, colleagues and supervisors and working conditions

	Time 1 (all cases)	Time 2 (all cases)
Job overall	6.2	5.6
Amount of work	5.1	5.2
Promotion prospects	4.1	4.1
Job security	5.7	5.9
Pattern of hours	4.8	5.2
Pay	4.2	4.7
Relationship with line manager	5.3	5.7
Relationship with colleagues	6.2	6.4
Chance to use initiative	5.1	5.4
Actual work	5.4	5.6
Opportunity to use skills	4.9	5.2
Training available	5.0	5.2

Note: Respondents scored each aspect from 1 (very dissatisfied) to 7 (highly satisfied).

Table A.15 Changes in reading habits over the study period, and the differences between voluntary and non-voluntary course participants (numbers of respondents)

	Voluntary	*Non-voluntary*	*Total*
Newspapers			
Read less	24	2	26
Read the same	87	26	113
Read more	60	4	64
Total	171	32	203
Magazines			
Read less	29	2	31
Read the same	95	29	124
Read more	47	1	48
Total	171	32	203
Books			
Read less	30	2	32
Read the same	92	23	115
Read more	49	7	56
Total	171	32	203
Manuals			
Read less	14	0	14
Read the same	125	28	153
Read more	32	4	36
Total	171	32	203

On an overall measure (whether report any form of increased reading) the difference between voluntary and non-voluntary learners is significant at the 1% level (1-tail test).

Table A.16 Proportions expecting a given outcome from the course

	%
Increase skills	39
Prepare for future job	22
Develop new skills	59
Increase skills used at home	12
Other reasons	35

Table A.17 Learners' reported outcomes of course (item by item basis)

	%
Increased confidence at work	66
Developed new skills	61
Increased confidence outside work	59
Met new people	58
Affected how current job is done*	45
Helped with use of computers outside work	33
Helped with use of computers at work	27
Made work more interesting	25
Increased chances for promotion	11
Increased chances of a better job	10
Helped earn more money	2

* 40% elaborated: all reported positive impact

Note: Whether or not a course increased confidence at work was highly (and positively) related to whether a learner also thought it had helped them to do their current job better/had affected how they did the job.

National qualifications

Table A.18 Levels of attainment: adult basic skills

Entry level 1	
Entry level 2	
Entry level 3	
Level 1	Equivalent to GCSE D–F
Level 2	Equivalent to GCSE A–C

Table A.19 National qualifications framework during the period of the research

Level	Examples
Entry	Entry Level Certificate in Adult Literacy
1	GCSEs grades D–G Level 1 NVQ in Bakery
2	GCSEs grades A*–C Level 2 Diploma for Beauty Specialists
3	A Levels Level 3 NVQ in Aeronautical Engineering
4	Level 4 Certificate in Early Years Level 4 BTEC Higher National Diploma in 3D Design
5	Level 5 NVQ in Construction Management Level 5 Diploma in Translation

Source: Qualifications and Curriculum Authority 2000.

Notes

Introduction

1 UK National Inquiry 2010; OECD; ASEM.
2 We originally proposed a three year tracking period, but the length of time taken in completing the initial sample precluded this. Some of the most recently recruited learners had their final interview after two rather than two and a half years. While this was done because of research grant constraints, it also meant that, fortuitously, data collection was complete before the current recession.
3 For specific analyses, missing data may take the total number of cases below this.
4 There was, fortunately, no relationship between initial reading level and likelihood of dropping out.

1 Literacy learning at work

1 The best-known system of this type exists in the USA, where adults – typically in their twenties – can take their 'GED' – i.e. the General Educational Development tests which are formally equivalent to an American or Canadian high school diploma. However, comparable systems exist in a good number of other countries (e.g. Hong Kong, Sweden).
2 The best known are the PISA studies which compare performance of young people aged 15.
3 In one case – France – there was so much surprise about the population's apparently poor skills that the results were withheld at the government's insistence: the published reports covered seven countries in 1995 and a further five in 1997. A later review of the IALS methodology confirmed the existence of some serious methodological and analysis problems; but the general finding – that in many rich countries, large numbers of people had very poor literacy skills – is robust. See Carey (ed.) 2000.
4 Moser 1999: 9.

2 Perspectives and key concepts

1 Pallas 2002 researches a broader array of experiences, drawing on the adult education component of the 1995 wave of the National Household Education Survey (US) that provides a nationally representative sample of 19,700 interviews.

2 In the latter, Whitley (2000) has shown how work systems in different countries contrast in the ways they structure and control how work is allocated and performed and rewarded: 'these systems are linked to the nature of firms, interest groups, and dominant governance principles or 'rules of the game' in different societies, which in turn stem from different patterns of industrialization' (2000: 88).

3 The effects of literacy development in the workplace: The dearth of evidence

1 See especially Rainbird et al. (eds) 2004, Evans et al. (eds) 2002, Billett 2001.
2 For the purposes of the analyses reported here, Dearden et al. have equated the IALS results to the NCDS ones, and through these, to the current national levels in the UK. This was done in a purely practical way by the researchers: that is, they have set out to preserve the same basic distribution of attainment levels in the population. Levels here therefore refer to the five current national ones in the UK: Entry 1–3, Level 1 and Level 2. As an indication of the standards these refer to, Level 1 in literacy and numeracy corresponds to the reading and mathematics level expected from 11-year-olds in the school national curriculum; for full details see QCA (2000).
3 The population is partitioned differently for these two comparisons, since only about a fifth of the population, based on NCDS estimates, has literacy skills below Level 1, compared with about a half for numeracy.
4 For NCDS, controls were family background (i.e. parents' educational level, social class, financial difficulties in family when child aged 7) plus various childhood variables (school type, parental interest in education) and ability at age 7. For IALS data, a more limited set of background variables was available/used.
5 Encompassing agricultural training, medical training, teacher training, legal training, science training, government/public admin training and various other kinds of training.
6 These were part of a monthly employee recognition programme in which supervisors, co-workers or customers nominated workers who had performed exceptionally well. Introduction of controls (years of education, tenure, age) reduced the size of the coefficients markedly.
7 It should be noted that adults' own evaluations of their skills also vary markedly according to how the question is asked. National surveys that ask whether people have any general difficulties with reading or writing indicate that only a small proportion feel they do (averaging around 5 per cent); but this rises to 19 per cent when a specific question is asked about correct spelling (Bynner and Parsons 2006).

4 The challenges of implementing literacy learning in the workplace

1 For an account of recontextualization in workplace learning, see Evans et al. (2010).

2 Data collection from the three sites occurred over a 14-month period. Participant observations were conducted for each of the sites using an observation checklist developed in an earlier study (Taylor *et al.* 2003). Interviews were held with three tutors who also completed a Teaching Perspectives Inventory, 19 learners were observed and 11 were interviewed individually and in groups. The focus groups took place at the start of the lesson and focused on the question: what is collaborative learning? Lesson plans, schemes of work, teaching materials and student writing were also collected.

6 Literacy learning, workplace practices and lives beyond work

1 Although Gorard et al. acknowledge the lack of weight accorded to individual agency, and have sought to address such a weakness through their work on 'learner identities' (e.g. Gorard et al. 2001), they still cling to an overarching theoretical model in which individual choices fall within structural determinants that are predictable from the individual's early life.
2 These findings are also consistent with Evans and Heinz's findings on young adults' transitions, which showed that while trajectories and behaviours had structural foundations in gender and social class, young people could move out of their 'predicted' trajectory and this was dependent upon the interplay of transition behaviours with organizational structures and environmental influences.
3 i.e. were in the first quartile of learners in terms of improvement between Time 1 and Time 2 literacy assessments.
4 English for speakers of other languages.

7 The organizational impact of literacy learning at work

1 This very large public sector organization had stopped applying for public funding for its long-standing learning centre because of the bureaucracy involved.
2 It is the one occupational area in which ETPs were able to enrol a substantial number of small employers (Hillage et al. 2006).
3 Four very large public sector employers, one company with a Learndirect centre and one hospital trust.
4 The degree to which funding is 'output related', with full payment only on completion of the qualification, varies; but is especially high under Train-to-Gain funded contracts. See Learning and Skills Council 2008, Linford 2008.
5 There is not and never has been a central register or source of information on how many workplace schemes existed, or how many workplace learners were recruited; as the government confirmed in a written answer to a parliamentary question (David Lammy in reply to Boris Johnson, June 18 2007) no relevant data exist.

6 Speech by the Deputy Director of the Adult Basic Skills Strategy Unit (ABSSU), DfES, Workplace Basic Skills Network International Conference 13–14 November 2002.
7 This figure is an average based on the cost profiles used by a number of higher education institutions when calculating per-hour costs for audited external contracts.

8 The interplay of 'formal' and 'informal' learning at work

1 The learning centre at Coopers was undergoing a period of uncertainty in 2007 following an extremely scathing Ofsted report in the summer of 2007 which classified the Learndirect sector as 'inadequate' in all aspects (Effectiveness of provision, Capacity to improve, Achievement and standards, Quality of provision, Leadership and management) apart from 'equality of opportunity'. The weaknesses highlighted in the report included 'low success rates on ICT courses', 'inadequate coaching and training' and an 'insufficient number of qualified staff'. The report nonetheless recognized under the category of 'equality of opportunity' the strengths of the centre in providing a positive physical environment that was accessible to company employees and the community at large.
2 This ULR received national acclaim for his role in developing learning opportunities at Thorpton, winning a runner-up award in a national competition.

9 The findings in international context: continuities and emerging themes

1 An international seminar at Woods Hole in 2006 set up bilateral collaborations, leading to the published collection edited by Reder and Bynner (2009).
2 Latent growth curve models, event history models, and modelling techniques from economics and programme evaluation (treatment effects models; propensity score matching) have been used to make quasi experimental comparisons of participants and non-participants in adult education programmes).
3 Research covered 'LLN' – literacy language and numeracy – we focus on literacy here.
4 Furthermore, the challenges of scale highlighted in the US, UK and New Zealand research – for small groups, SMEs and distributed locations – point to the need, articulated in the New Zealand context for travelling subsidies, mobile advisors and tutors, as well as facilities like the 'learning bus' and mobile libraries and computers.
5 Nelson's survey (Nelson 2004) asked how many workplaces continue to fund programs that were initiated with public funds, and found higher levels of sustainability than we report in Chapter 7.
6 Work is being carried out by Ed Waite within the LLAKES Centre's research programme examining the feasibility of 'whole organization' approaches.

10 Improving literacy learning in and through work

1 Train to Gain is dominated by private training providers, and in 2007, the chief executives of the two largest companies gave evidence to the House of Commons Select Committee on Education and Skills explaining how the programme works. There are 14 forms required when they take on a learner, which take about two hours to complete. Hence 'we lose a number of people because they just cannot be bothered to go through the process, even though we hold the pen for them ... To put it into perspective, I have got something like 50 people who are employed full time on processing bits of paper, which is inordinate waste' (House of Commons Education and Skills Select Committee 2007: Q273, Q274, supplementary memorandum from Dan Wright).

Bibliography

Abramovsky, L., Battistin, E., Fitzsimons, E., Goodman, A., and Simpson, H. (2005) *The Impact of the Employer Training Pilots on the Take-up of Training among Employers and Employees*, Research Report RR694, London: Institute for Fiscal Studies/DfES and Adult Learning Inspectorate.

ALBSU (1993) *The Cost to Industry: basic skills and the UK workforce*, London: Adult Literacy and Basic Skills Unit.

Ananiadou, K., Jenkins, A. and Wolf, A. (2003) *The Benefits to Employers of Raising Workforce Basic Skills Levels: a review of the literature*, London: National Research and Development Centre for Adult Literacy and Numeracy.

Ananiadou, K., Jenkins, A. and Wolf, A. (2004) 'Basic skills and workplace learning: what do we actually know about their benefits?', *Studies in Continuing Education*, 26 (2): 289–308.

Ananiadou, K., Emslie-Henry, R., Evans, K. and Wolf, A. (2004) *Identifying Effective Workplace Basic Skills Strategies for Enhancing Employee Productivity and Development*, London: National Research and Development Centre for Adult Literacy and Numeracy.

Appleby, Y. and Barton, D. (2008) *Responding to People's Lives*, London: National Research and Development Centre for Adult Literacy and Numeracy.

Arulampalam, W., Booth, A. and Elias, P. (1997) 'Work-related training and earnings growth for young men in Britain', *Research in Labor Economics*, 16: 119–147.

Aspin, L. (2004) 'Social capital and productivity'. Unpublished paper. Available at http://www.tlrp.org/dspace/handle/123456789/186 (accessed 8 April 2010).

Asplund, R. (2004) *The Provision and Effects of Company Training. A brief review of the literature*, Discussion Paper 907, Helsinki: The Research Institute of the Finnish Economy.

Barber, M. (2007) *Instruction to Deliver Tony Blair. Public services and the Challenge of Achieving Targets*, London: Politico's Publishing.

Barnett, C. (1986) *The Audit of War: the illusion and reality of Britain as a great nation*, London: Macmillan.

Baron, R.A. and Byrne, D. (2004) *Social Psychology*, Boston: Pearson.

Bartel, A. (1995) 'Training, wage growth and job performance: evidence from a company database', *Journal of Labor Economics*, 13: 401–425.

Barton, D., Hamilton, M. and Ivanic, R. (2000) *Situated Literacies*, London: Routledge.

Basic Skills Agency (2000) *Basic Skills Are Union Business*, London: Basic Skills Agency.

Bassi, L.J. (1994) 'Workplace education for hourly workers', *Journal of Policy Analysis and Management*, 13 (1): 55–75.

Beck, U. (1992) *Risk Society: towards a new modernity*, London: Sage Publications.

Becker, G.S. (1964, 1993, 3rd ed.) *Human Capital: a theoretical and empirical analysis, with special reference to education*, Chicago: University of Chicago Press.

Benseman, J., Alkema, A., Wright, C. and Irving, E. (2010) 'I feel like a genius – in my own way. I can do things I couldn't do before', Interim report on the Upskilling Partnership Programme, New Zealand: Department of Labour.

Biesta, G. and Tedder, M. (2007) 'Agency and learning in the lifecourse: towards an ecological perspective', *Studies in the Education of Adults*, 39 (2): 132–149.

Billett, S. (2001) *Learning in the Workplace. Strategies for effective practice*, London: Allen & Unwin.

Billett, S. (2002) 'Toward a workplace pedagogy: guidance, participation and engagement', *Adult Education Quarterly*, 53 (1): 27–43.

Billett, S. (2004) 'Co-participation at work: learning through work and throughout working lives', *Studies in the Education of Adults*, 36 (2): 190–205.

Bloom, Michael, Burrows, M., Lafleur, B. and Squires, R. (1997) *The Economic Benefits of Improving Literacy Skills in the Workplace*, Ottawa: The Conference Board of Canada.

Blundell, R., Dearden, L. and Meghir, C. (1996) *The Determinants and Effects of Work Related Training in Britain*, London: Institute for Fiscal Studies.

Blundell, R., Dearden, L., Meghir, C. and Sianesi, B. (1999) 'Human capital investment: the returns from education and training to the individual, the firm and the economy', *Fiscal Studies*, 20 (1): 1–23.

Booth, A. and Satchell, S. (1994) 'Apprenticeships and job tenure', *Oxford Economic Papers*, 46: 474–495.

Brooks, G., Davies, R., Duckett, L., Hutchison, D., Kendall, S. and Wilkin, A. (2001) *Progress in Adult Literacy: do learners learn?* London: Basic Skills Agency.

Bynner, J. and Parsons, S. (1997) *It Doesn't Get Any Better*. London: Basic Skills Agency.

Bynner, J. and Parsons, S. (2006) *New Light on Literacy and Numeracy*, London: National Research and Development Centre for Adult Literacy and Numeracy.

Bynner, J. and Parsons, S. (2009) 'Insights into basic skills from a UK longitudinal study (2009)', in S. Reder and J. Bynner (eds) *Tracking Adult Literacy and Numeracy Skills: findings from longitudinal research*, New York and London: Routledge.

Bynner, J., McIntosh, S., Vignoles, A., Dearden, L., Reed, H. and Van Reenen, J. (2001) *Improving Adult Basic Skills: benefits to the individual and to society,* Research Report 251, London: DfEE.

Cappelli, P. (2002) 'Why do employers pay for college?', NBER Working Paper 9225, Cambridge MA: National Bureau of Educational Research.

Carey, S. (ed.) (2000) *Measuring Adult Literacy: The International Adult Literacy Survey (IALS) in the European Context,* London: Office for National Statistics.

Carr-Hill, R., Passingham, S. and Wolf, A. with Kent, N. (1996) *Lost Opportunities. The language skills of linguistic minorities in England and Wales,* London: Basic Skills Agency.

Chevalier, A. (2000) *Graduate Over-education in the UK,* Discussion Paper 7, London: Centre for the Economics of Education.

Chisholm, L. (2008) 'Re-contextualising learning in second modernity', *Research in Post-Compulsory Education*, 13 (2): 139–147.

Chisholm, L., Fennes, H. and Spanning, R. (eds) (2007) *Competence Development as Workplace Learning,* Report of the Asia-Europe-Meeting Research and Education Hub on Lifelong Learning, Innsbruck: University of Innsbruck Press,

Coffield, F. (2002) 'Britain's continuing failure to train: the birth pangs of a new policy', *Journal of Education Policy,* 17 (4): 483–498.

Coffield, F. (2004) 'Alternative routes out of the low skills equilibrium: a rejoinder to Lloyd and Payne', *Journal of Education Policy,* 19 (6): 733–740.

Coffield, F., Steer, R., Hodgson, A. Spours, K., Edward, S. and Finlay, I. (2005) 'A new learning and skills landscape? The central role of the Learning and Skills Council', *Journal of Education Policy*, 20 (5): 631–656.

Coffield, F., Edward, S., Finlay, I., Hodgson, A., Spours, K. and Steer, R. (2008) *Improving Learning, Skills and Inclusion: the impact of policy on post-compulsory education,* London: Routledge.

Coleman, J.S. (1990) *Foundations of Social Theory*, Cambridge, MA: Harvard University Press.

Comings, J. (2004) 'The process and content of adult education in family literacy programs', in B. Wasik (ed.) *Handbook of Family Literacy,* Englewood Cliffs, NJ: Lawrence Erlbaum Associates.

Comings, J.P. (2009) 'Student persistence in adult literacy and numeracy programmes', in S. Reder and J. Bynner (eds) *Tracking Adult Literacy and Numeracy Skills,* New York and London: Routledge.

Cooper, H., Nye, B., Charlton, K., Linday, J. and Greathouse, S. (1996) 'The effect of summer variation on test scores: a narrative and meta-analytic review', *Review of Educational Research,* 66: 227–268.

Cooper, J. (2007) *Cognitive Dissonance: 50 years of a classic theory,* London: Sage.

Deakin Crick, R., Broadfoot, P. and Claxton, G. (2004) Developing an effective lifelong learning inventory: the ELLI Project. *Assessment in Education*, 11: 247–273.

Dearden, L., Machin, S., Reed, H., and Wilkinson, D. (1997) *Labour Turnover and Work-Related Training*, London: Institute for Fiscal Studies.

Dearden, L., Reed, H. and van Reenan, J. (2000) 'Estimates of the impact of improvements in basic skills on aggregate wages, employment, taxes and benefits', in J. Bynner (ed.) *The Social Benefits of Basic Skills*, London: Centre for the Wider Benefits of Learning.

Dearden, L., McIntosh, S., Myck, M. and Vignoles, A. (2002) 'The returns to academic, vocational and basic skills in Britain', *Bulletin of Economic Research*, 5: 249–274.

Dearden, L., McGranahan, L. and Sianesi, B. (2004) *Returns to Education for the Marginal Learner: Evidence from the BCS70*, CEE Discussion Papers 0045, London: Centre for the Economics of Education.

Dearden, L., Reed, H. and Van Reenen, J. (2005) *The Impact of Training on Productivity and Wages: evidence from British panel data*, CEP Discussion Paper 0674, London: Centre for Economic Performance, LSE.

de Coulon, A., Marcenaro-Gutiérrez, O. and Vignoles, A. (2007) *The Value of Basic Skills in the UK Labour Market*, Discussion paper 0077, London: Centre for the Economics of Education.

Department for Education and Employment (1999) *A Fresh Start. The Moser Report*, London: DfEE.

Department for Education and Employment (2001) *Skills for Life: the national strategy for improving adult literacy and numeracy skills*, London: DfEE.

Department for Education and Skills (2003a) *Adult Literacy, Numeracy and ESOL: a guide to Learning and Skills Council Funding 2003/4*, London: DfES.

Department for Education and Skills (2003b) *Employer Toolkit to Improve Literacy and Numeracy at Work*, London: DfES.

DfES, First Statistical Release Post-16 Learner Participation 2007–2008, http://www.dcsf.gov.uk/rsgateway/DB/SFR/s000855/index.shtml

Downey, D.B., van Hippel, P.T. and Book, B.A. (2004) 'Are schools the great equalizer? Cognitive inequality during the summer months and the school year', *American Sociological Review*, 69: 613–635.

Edwards, N. (2003) 'Doctors and managers: poor relationships may be damaging patients – what can be done?' *Quality and Safety in Health Care*, 12 (Suppl 1): i21–i24.

Edwards, R. (1998) 'Flexibility, reflexivity and reflection in the contemporary workplace', *International Journal of Lifelong Education* 17 (6): 377–388.

Ekström, E. (2003) *Earnings Effects of Adult Secondary Education in Sweden*, Working Paper 2003:16. Stockholm: IFAU.

Elias, P. (1994) 'Job related training, trade union membership and labour mobility: a longitudinal study', *Oxford Economic Papers*, 46: 563–578.

Eraut, M. (2004) Informal learning in the workplace. *Studies in Continuing Education*, 26, (2), 247–273.

Ernst & Young (1993) *Literacy, Education and Training: their impact on the UK economy*, London: Ernst & Young.

Evans, K. (2002) 'The challenges of making learning visible', in K. Evans, P. Hodkinson, and L. Unwin (eds) *Working to Learn: transforming learning in the Workplace*, London: Kogan Page.

Evans, K. (2009) *Learning, Work and Social Responsibility*, Dordrecht: Springer.

Evans, K. and Heinz, W. (1993) 'Studying forms of transition: methodological innovation in a cross-national study of labour market entry in England and Germany', *Comparative Education*, 49: 145–158.

Evans, K. and Heinz, W.R. (1994). *Becoming Adults in England and Germany*, London: Anglo German Foundation.

Evans, K. and Rainbird, H. (2002) 'The significance of workplace learning for a learning society', in K. Evans, P. Hodkinson and L. Unwin (eds), *Working to Learn: transforming learning in the workplace*, London: Kogan Page.

Evans, K. and Kersh, N. (2006) 'Adults learning in, for and through the workplace: the significance of biography and experience', Paper presented at British Educational Research Association Annual Conference, University of Warwick, 7-10 September.

Evans, K. and Waite, E. (2008) *Adult Workers' Engagement in Informal and Formal Learning: insights from four UK organisations*, Ottawa: Canadian Literacy Secretariat.

Evans, K. and Waite, E. (2010) 'Stimulating the innovation potential of "routine" workers through workplace learning' The European Review of Labour and Research, 16(2): 243–258.

Evans, K., Guile, D. and Harris, J. (2010) *Rethinking Work-Based Learning. The Sage Handbook of Workplace Learning*, London: Sage.

Evans, K., Hodkinson, P. and Unwin, L. (eds) (2002) *Working to Learn: Transforming learning in the workplace*, London: Kogan Page.

Evans, K., Kersh, N. and Kontiainen, S. (2004) 'Recognition of tacit skills: sustaining learning outcomes in adult learning and work re-entry', *International Journal of Training and Development*, 8 (1): 54–72.

Evans, K., Hodkinson, P., Rainbird, H. and Unwin, L. (2006) *Improving Workplace Learning*, Abingdon: Routledge.

Evans, K., Harris, J. and Guile, D. (2007) 'Putting knowledge to work', Symposium paper presented at 5th International Conference on Researching Work and Learning, Cape Town, December 2007.

Evans, K., Guile, D., Harris, J. and Allan, J. (2010) 'Putting knowledge to work: a new approach', *Nurse Education Today*, 30 (3): 245–251.

Ferri, E., Bynner, J. and Wadsworth, M. (eds) (2003) *Changing Britain, Changing Lives. Three generations at the turn of century*, London: Institute of Education.

Finegold, D. and Soskice, D. (1988) 'The failure of training in Britain: analysis and prescription', *Oxford Review of Economic Policy*, 4 (3): 21–51.

Finlay, I., Hodgson, A. and Steer, R. (2007) 'Flowers in the desert: the impact of policy on basic skills provision in the workplace', *Journal of Vocational Education and Training*, 59 (2): 231–248.

Fuller, A. and Unwin, L. (2004) 'Expansive learning environments: integrating organizational and personal developments', in H. Rainbird, A. Fuller and A. Munro (eds) *Workplace Learning in Context*, London and New York: Routledge.

Fuller, A. and Unwin, L. (2006) 'Expansive and restrictive learning environments', in K. Evans, P. Hodkinson, H. Rainbird, and L. Unwin (eds.) *Improving Workplace Learning*, London: Routledge.

Geary, J. (1995) 'Work practices: the structure of work', in P. Edwards (ed.) *Industrial Relations: Theory and Practice in Britain*, Oxford: Blackwell.

Giddens, A. (1990) *The Consequences of Modernity*, Cambridge: Polity Press.

Gorard, S. and Rees, G. (2002) *Creating a Learning Society? Learning careers and policies for lifelong learning*, Bristol: The Policy Press.

Gorard S., Rees G. and Fevre, R. (1999) 'Learning trajectories: analysing the determinants of workplace learning', paper presented at the ESRC Seminar Series Working to Learn, University of Surrey, 24 June.

Gorard, S., Gareth, R., Fevre, R. and Furlong, J. (1998) 'Learning trajectories: travelling towards a learning society?', *International Journal of Lifelong Education*, 17 (6): 400–410.

Gorard, S, Gareth, R., Fevre, R. and Welland, T. (2001) 'Lifelong learning trajectories: some voices of those "in transit"', *International Journal of Lifelong Education*, 20 (3): 169–187.

Green, A., Wolf, A. and Leney, T. (2000) *Convergence and Divergence in European Education and Training Systems*, London: Institute of Education.

Green, F. (1997) *Review of Information on the Benefits of Training for Employers*, Research Report 7, London: DfEE.

Green, F. (2009) *Employee Involvement, Technology and Job Tasks*, NIESR Discussion Paper 326, London: NIESR.

Greenhalgh, C. (2002) 'Does an employer training levy work? The incidence of and returns to adult vocational training in France and Britain', *Fiscal Studies*, 23 (2): 223–263.

Groot, W. (1995) 'Type specific returns to enterprise-related training', *Economics of Education Review*, 14 (4): 323–333.

Grubb, W.N. and Lazerson, M. (2004) *The Education Gospel: the economic value of schooling*, Cambridge MA: Harvard University Press.

Heidegger, G. (2004) 'Suggestions for improving the framework conditions for re-enter initiatives. European policy recommendations', in K. Evans and B. Niemeyer (eds) *Reconnection: Countering Social Exclusion Through Situated Learning*, Dordrecht: Springer.

Hillage, J. and Mitchell, H. (2004) *Employer Training Pilots: first year evaluation report*, London: DfES and HM Treasury.

Hillage, J., Loukas, G., Newton, B. and Tamkin, P. (2006) *Employer Training Pilots: final evaluation report*, Research Report 774 (London, DfES).

Hodkinson, P., Hodkinson, H., Evans, K., Kersh, N., Fuller, A., Unwin, L. and Senker, P. (2004) 'The significance of individual biography in workplace learning', *Studies in the Education of Adults*, 36 (1), 6–24.

Hollenbeck, K. and Timmeney, B. (2008) 'Lessons learned from a workplace literacy initiative', *Upjohn Institute Employment Research*, 15 (2): 4–6.

Hood, C. (2007) 'The numbers game', *Ethos*, 9:1–2. Available HTTP: <http://www.ethosjournal.com/frontline-focus/item/49-the-numbers-game> (accessed 19 March 2010).

House of Commons Education and Skills Committee (2007) *Post-16 Skills*, London: The Stationery Office.

House of Commons Public Accounts Committee (2009) *Skills for Life: progress in improving adult literacy and numeracy*, London: The Stationery Office.

House of Commons Standing Committee on Human Resources Development and the Status of Persons with Disabilities (2003) *Raising Adult Literacy Skills: the need for a Pan-Canadian response,* Ottawa: Communications Canada Publishing.

Hughes, J., Jewson, N. and Unwin, L. (eds) (2007) *Communities of Practice,* London: Routledge.

Hyman, R. and Streeck, W. (1988) *New Technology and Industrial Relations,* Oxford: Basil Blackwell.

Jarvis, P., Holford, J., Griffin, C. and Dubelaar, J. (1997) *Towards the Learning City. An evaluation of the Corporation of London's adult education voucher scheme,* London: Corporation of London Education Department.

Jenkins, A. and Wolf, A. (in submission) 'Basic skills courses in the workplace: learners' progress and outcomes'.

Jenkins, A., Greenwood, C. and Vignoles, A. (2007) *The Returns to Qualifications in England: updating the evidence base on Level 2 and Level 3 Vocational Qualifications,* London: Centre for The Economics of Education.

Jenkins, A., Vignoles, A., Wolf, A. and Galindo-Rueda, F. (2003) 'The determinants and labour market effects of lifelong learning', *Applied Economics,* 35: 1711–1721.

Keep, E. (1999) 'Britain's VET policy and the "Third Way" – following a high skills trajectory or running up a dead end street?', *Journal of Education and Work,* 12 (3): 323–346.

Keep, E. and Mayhew, K. (1999) 'The assessment: knowledge, skills and competitiveness',? *Oxford Review of Economic Policy,* 15 (1): 1–15.

Keep, E., Mayhew, K. and Payne, J. (2006) 'From skills revolution to productivity miracle – not as easy as it sounds?', *Oxford Review of Economic Policy,* 22 (4): 539–559.

Kell, C. (2009) *In-house Literacy, Language and Numeracy (LLN) Initiatives in New Zealand Workplaces: a report produced for the Department of Labour* (RFT 143), Auckland: Auckland University of Technology.

Koepp, R. (2002) *Clusters of Creativity,* Chichester: John Wiley & Sons.

Krueger, A. and Rouse, C. (1994) 'New evidence on workplace education'. Unpublished working paper, Princeton University.

Krueger, A. and Rouse, C. (1998) 'The effect of workplace education on earnings, turnover, and job performance', *Journal of Labor Economics,* 16: 61–94.

Lammy, D. (2007) Written reply to parliamentary question 3 Sep 2007, Hansard column 1781W.

Lammy, D. (2008) Keynote speech to 2008 Skills for Life Workplace Conference, 8 July 2008. Available HTTP: <http:// www.davidlammy.co.uk/da/89786> (accessed 10 March 2010).

Lave, J. and Wenger, E. (1991) *Situated Learning. Legitimate peripheral participation,* Cambridge: Cambridge University Press.

Learning and Skills Council (2006) *National Employers Skills Survey 2005: main report,* Coventry: LSC.

Learning and Skills Council learner statistics (2007) http://webarchive.nationalarchives.gov.uk/20090104235956/http://www.lsc.gov.uk/providers/Data/statistics/

Learning and Skills Council (2008) *Funding Guidance 2008–9,* Coventry, LSC.

Lee, A (2007) Editorial, *Literacy and Numeracy Studies,* 15 (2): 2.

Lerman, R.I., McKernan, S-M. and Riegg, S. (2004) The scope of employer-provided training in the United States, in C.J. O'Leary, R.A. Straits & S.A. Wandner (eds) *Job Training Policy in the United States,* Kalamazoo, MI: W.E. Upjohn Institute for Employment Research.

Lessof, C., Miller, M., Phillips, M., Pickering, K., Purdon, S. and Hales, J. (2003) *New Deal for Lone Parents Evaluation: findings from the quantitative survey,* WAE Report 147, London: Department for Work and Pensions.

Lillard, L. and Tan, H. (1992) 'Private sector training: who gets it and what are its effects', *Research in Labor Economics,* 13: 1–62.

Linford, N. (2008) *The Hands-on Guide to Post-16 Funding for School Sixth Forms, Training Providers and Further Education Colleges,* London: Edexcel Ltd.

Livingstone, D.W. (1999) 'Lifelong learning and underemployment in the knowledge society: a North American perspective', *Comparative Education,* 35 (2): 162–186.

Lonsdale, M. and McCurry, D. (2004) *Literacy in the New Millennium,* Adelaide: NCVER.

McConnell, S. and Glazerman, S.M. (2001) *National Job Corps Study: the benefits and costs of Job Corps,* Washington, DC: Mathematica Policy Research, Inc.

Machin, S. and Vignoles, A. (eds) (2005) *What's the Good of Education,* Princeton, NJ: Princeton University Press.

Machin, S., McIntosh, S., Vignoles, A. and Viitanen, T. (2001) *Basic Skills, Soft Skills and Labour Market Outcomes: secondary analysis of the National Child Development Study* (RR250), London: DfEE.

Meadows, P. and Metcalf, H. (2005) *Evaluation of the Impact of Skills for Life Learning Report on Sweep 2,* Research Report RR701, London: Department for Education and Skills.

Metcalf, H. and Meadows, P. (2004) *Evaluation of the Impact of Basic Skills Learning: Report on wave 1,* London: NIESR.

Metcalf, H. and Meadows, P. (2009) Outcomes for basic skills learners: a four-year longitudinal study, in S. Reder and J. Bynner (eds), *Tracking Adult Basic Skills: findings from longitudinal research,* New York and London: Routledge.

Metcalf, H., Meadows, P., Rolfe, H., Dhudwar, A., Coleman, N., Wapshott, J. and Carpenter, H. (2009) *Evaluation of the Impact of Skills for Life Learning: Longitudinal Survey of Adult Learners on College-based Literacy and Numeracy Courses, Final Report,* London: Department for Innovation, Universities and Skills.

Minister of State for Human Resources Development (2005) *Towards a Fully Literate Canada,* Ottawa: Advisory Committee on Literacy and Essential Skills.

Moser, C. (1999) *A Fresh Start. The Moser Report,* London: DfEE.

National Audit Office (2004) *Skills for Life: improving adult literacy and numeracy,* Report by the Comptroller and Auditor General, London: NAO.

National Audit Office (2008) *Skills for Life: progress in improving adult literacy and numeracy,* Report by the Comptroller and Auditor General, London: NAO.

National Centre for Social Research (2003) *Evaluation of Employment Zones: Report on a cohort survey of long term unemployed people in the zones and a matched set of comparison areas,* London: Department for Work and Pensions.

National Research and Development Centre for adult literacy and numeracy (2004) *Go!* magazine and tests, London: NRDC.

Nelson, C. (2004) 'After the grant is over. Do workplaces continue to fund programs that were initiated with public funds?' *Focus on Basics,* 7 (B): 1–6.

OECD (1997) *Literacy Skills for the Knowledge Society,* Paris: OECD.

OECD (2002) *Education at a Glance,* Paris: OECD.

OECD (2004a) *Education at a Glance,* Paris: OECD.

OECD (2004b) *Policy Brief: lifelong learning,* Paris: OECD.

Pallas, A. (2002) 'Educational transitions, trajectories, and pathways', in J.T. Mortimer and M.J. Shanahan (eds), *Handbook of the Life Course,* New York: Springer US.

Papen, U. (2005) *Adult Literacy as Social Practice: More than skills,* London: Routledge.

Pearson, G. (1996) *More Than Money Can Say: The impact of ESL and literacy training in the Australian workplace. Volume 1: The executive summary, the findings and the case studies,* Canberra: Commonwealth of Australia.

Performance and Innovation Unit (2001) *In Demand – adult skills in the 21st century,* London: Cabinet Office.

Prais, S.J. (1995) *Productivity, Education and Training. An International Perspective,* Cambridge: Cambridge University Press.

Qualifications and Curriculum Authority (2000) *National Standards for Adult Literacy and Numeracy,* London: QCA.

Rainbird, H., Full, A. and Munro, A. (eds) (2004) *Workplace Learning in Context,* Routledge: London and New York.

Rainbird, H., Sutherland, J., Edwards, P., Holly, L. and Munro, L. (2003) *Employee voice and its influence over training precision,* London: Department of Trade and Industry.

Reder, S. (1994) 'Practice engagement theory: a sociocultural approach to literacy across language and cultures', in B. Ferdman, R. Weber and A. Ramirez (eds), *Literacy across languages and cultures,* New York: State University of New York Press.

Reder, S. (2009) 'The development of literacy and numeracy in adult life', in S. Reder and J. Bynner (eds) *Tracking Adult Literacy and Numeracy Skills: findings from longitudinal research,* New York and London: Routledge.

Reder, S. and Bynner, J. (eds) (2009) *Tracking Adult Literacy and Numeracy Skills: findings from longitudinal research,* New York and London: Routledge.

Rhys Warner, J., Vorhaus, J., Appleby, Y., Bathmaker, A-M., Brooks, G., Cole, P., Pilling, M. and Pearce, L. (2008) The Learner Study: the impact of the Skills for Life strategy on adult literacy, language and numeracy learners, London: National Research and Development Centre for Adult Literacy and Numeracy.

Rismark, M. and Sitter, S. (2003) 'Workplaces as learning environments: interaction between newcomer and work community', *Scandinavian Journal of Educational Research*, 47 (5): 495–510.

Roberts, P. and Gowan, R. (2007) *Canadian Literature Review and Bibliography*, Ottawa: Canadian Council on Social Development.

Robinson, P. (1997) *Literacy and Numeracy and Economic Performance*, Working Paper No. 888, London: Centre for Economic Performance, London School of Economics.

Rogoff, B. (1995) 'Sociocultural activity on three planes', in J.V. Wertsch, P. del Rio and A. Alvarez (eds), *Sociocultural Studies of Mind*. New York: Cambridge University Press.

Ross, B.H. (ed.) (2006) *The Psychology of Learning and Motivation*, London: Academic Press.

Sanderson, M. (1999) *Education and Economic Decline in Britain, 1870 to the 1990s*, Cambridge: Cambridge University Press.

Sargant, N. (2000), *The Learning Divide Revisited: A Report on the Findings of a UK-wide Survey on Adult Participation in Education and Learning*, Leicester: NIACE.

Scheeres, H. (2004) 'The textualised workplace', *Reflect*, 1: 22.

Schuller, T. and Watson, D. (2009) *Learning Through Life: inquiry into the future for lifelong learning (IFLL)*, Leicester: NIACE.

Simon, S. (2009) Written answer to Parliamentary Question, 1 June 2009: Hansard Column 206W.

Solomon, N., Boud, D. and Rooney, D. (2006) 'The in-between: exposing everyday learning at work', *International Journal of Lifelong Education*, 25 (1): 3–13.

Speckesser, S. and Bewley, H. (2006) *The Longer Term Outcome of Work Based Learning for Adults*, Research Report 390, London: Department of Work and Pensions.

Spilsbury, D. (2002) *Learning and Training at Work 2001*, London: Department for Education and Skills.

Statistics Canada (2005) *Adult Literacy and Life Skills Survey: learning a living*, Ottawa: Statistics Canada.

Steel, N. (2001) 'Knowledge acquisition in the field of practice', in M. Taylor (ed.) *Adult Literacy Now*, Toronto: Irwin Publishing.

Sticht, T. and Mikulecky, L. (1984) *Job-related Basic Skills: Cases and conclusions*, Ohio: National Center for Research in Vocational Education.

Street, B.V. (1995) *Social Literacies: critical approaches to literacy in development, ethnography and education*, Harlow: Longman.

Taylor, M. and Evans, K. (2009) 'The formal and informal training of workers with low skills: an international dialogue between Canada and the United Kingdom', *Journal of Adult and Continuing Education*, 15 (1): 37–54.

Taylor, M., Evans, K. and Abasi, A. (2007a) 'Understanding teaching and learning in adult literacy training: practices in Canada and the United Kingdom', *Literacy and Numeracy Studies: International Journal in the Education and Training of Adults*, 15 (2): 57–72.

Taylor, M., Evans, K. and Mohamed, A. (2007b) 'The interplay between formal and informal training for basic-level workers: comparing experiences in Canada and the United Kingdom', Proceedings of the 26th Annual Conference of the Canadian Association for the Study of Adult Education, Halifax, NS: CASAE, pp. 589–594.

Taylor, M., Abasi, A., Pinsent-Johnson, C. and Evans, K. (2007c) 'Collaborative learning in communities of literacy practice', *Adult Basic Education and Literacy Journal,* 1 (1): 4–11.

Taylor, M., King, J., Pinsent-Johnson, C. and Lothian, T. (2003) 'Collaborative practices in adult literacy programs', *Adult Basic Education: An Interdisciplinary Journal for Literacy Educators,* 13 (2): 81–99.

Thomas, S. and Goldstein, H. (eds) (2008) *Assessment in Education,* 15 (3). Special edition, International Comparative Studies in Achievement.

Torgerson, C., Brooks, G., Porthouse, J., Burton, M., Robinson, A., Wright, K. and Watt, I. (2004) *Adult Literacy and Numeracy: interventions and outcomes: a review of controlled trials,* London: NRDC.

Torres, C. (2009) *Globalizations and Education,* New York: Teachers College Press, Columbia University.

Unwin, L. and Fuller, A. (2003) *Expanding Learning in the Workplace: making more of individual and organisational potential,* A NIACE policy discussion paper, London: NIACE.

Weaver-Hightower, M.B. (2008) 'An ecology metaphor for educational policy analysis: a call to complexity', *Educational Researcher,* 37 (3): 153–167.

Whitley, R. (2000) *Divergent Capitalisms: the social structuring and change of business systems,* Oxford: Oxford University Press.

Wolf, A. (1994) *Basic Skills Research: bibliography of research in adult literacy and basic skills 1972–1992,* London: Adult Literacy and Basic Skills Unit.

Wolf, A. (2002) *Does Education Matter? Myths about education and economic growth,* London: Penguin.

Wolf, A. (2004) 'Education and Economic Performance: simplistic theories and their policy consequences', *Oxford Review of Economic Policy,* 20 (2): 315–333.

Wolf, A. (2009) *An Adult Approach to Further Education,* London: Institute of Economic Affairs.

Wolf, A. (2010) *How to Shift Power to Learners,* London: LSN Centre of Innovation in Learning.

Wolf, A. and Evans, K. (2009) *Enhancing Skills for Life: adult basic skills and workplace learning,* Final report to ESRC, Swindon: ESRC.

Wolf, A., Jenkins, A. and Vignoles, A. (2006) 'Certifying the workforce: economic imperative or failed social policy?', *Journal of Education Policy,* 21 (5): 535–566.

Wolf, A., Aspin, L., Ananiadou, K. and Waite, E. (2010 in press) 'The rise and fall of workplace basic skills programmes: lessons for policy and practice', *Oxford Review of Education,* 36 (4): 385–405.

Index

changes in, 87–8
concept of, 92, 93
perspectives, analytic, 19, *20,* 20–3
policy on basic skills provision
    changes in, 11–12
    implication of research for, 161–3
policy studies in education, 29–30
post-modernity, 92
productivity, assumed impact of low
    literacy on, 18
profit, lack of for providers, 125,
    127–30
programmes, basic skills. *See* training
promotion of courses, 55–8
provision of basic skills. *See* basic
    skills provision

qualifications
    impact of, 40–1, 42
    of learners in sample, 76
    output-related funding, 125–7
    targets in, 13
questionnaires
    learners, 170–4
    managers', 174–6

Rainbird, H., 29, 164
reading habits, changes in, 88–9
reading levels, impact on, *81,* 81–2,
    83, *84*
recruitment process, 128–9
Reder, S., 21, 72, 153
Rees, G., 24–5
reflexivity, 92
relationships outside the classroom,
    71–2
research study
    attrition, 75, 187
    benchmarking of learners, 25,
        26–7
    data collection, 74
    design of, 3–6, **4, 5,** 74
    in-depth interviews, 25, 28
    mixed methods, 19–20, 28
    objectives, 1–2
    policy implications of, 161–3
    timescale, 187
    See also learner sample;
        methodology
Roberts, P., 152
Rouse, C., 44–5

sample of learners. *See* learner
    sample
Satchell, S., 43
satisfaction
    with courses, 85, 87, 163
    employers' feedback, 119–22
    job, 147
Scottish Adult Literacy and
    Numeracy Strategy, 116
second language learners. *See* ESOL
    learners
sectors involved in research, 167,
    168
self-esteem, 62
setting up courses, 55–8
situated learning theory, 22–3
skills, economic purpose of, 12–13
Skills for Life strategy
    assumptions behind, 17–18
    rationale behind, 15
    See also basic skills provision;
        training
social capital as outcome, 122–3,
    124
social ecology of learning, 28, 29–32,
    163
social organization of learning
    literacy as human capital, *20,* 21
    literacy as social practice, *20,*
        22–3
social practice, literacy as, *20,* 21–3
Speckesser, S., 50
stability of basic skills provision, 162
standardization of assessment, 17–18
subsidies for training in basic skills,
    44
Sweden, 39

Tan, H., 42
target culture, 13
teaching, evidence on effectiveness
    of, 2
Teaching Perspectives Inventory,
    157–8, 169–70
technology, introduction of, 110
T2G, 115, 126, 160, 190
theoretical lenses, 19, *20,* 20–3
Thorpton Local Authority, 144–6
titles of courses, 56–7
top-down approach, limitations of,
    90